THE
BRITISH ARMY
GUIDE

Editor – Charles Heyman

Copyright © R & F (Defence Publications) 2005

ISBN 1 84415 280 4

Price £5.99

Pen & Sword Books Ltd
47 Church Street
Barnsley S70 2AS

Telephone: 01226-734222   Fax: 01226-734438
www.pen-and-sword.co.uk

The Information in this publication has been gathered from unclassified sources.

Front Cover: Soldiers from the Royal Welch Fusiliers are recovered by helicopter following a patrol in Iraq. (Crown Copyright)

Rear Cover: During their deployment in Iraq, soldiers from the Black Watch prepare to move north. (Crown Copyright)

Contents List

CHAPTER 6 – ARTILLERY

CHAPTER 7 – ARMY AVIATION

CHAPTER 8 - ENGINEERS

CHAPTER 1 – OVERVIEW

General Information

Populations – European Union – Top Five Nations (2005 estimates)

Germany	82.4 million
France	59.7 million
Italy	57.6 million
United Kingdom	59.3 million
Spain	41.0 million

Finance – European Union – Top Five Nations (2004 figures)

	GDP	Per Capita Income
Germany	US$2,400 bn	US$29,300
United Kingdom	US$1,950 bn	US$30,100
France	US$1,570 bn	US$29,400
Italy	US$1,420 bn	US$25,900
Spain	US$760 bn	US$21,200

UK Population

England	49.6 million
Wales	2.9 million
Scotland	5.06 million
Northern Ireland	1.68 million
Total	59.3 million

Figures are from the 2001 UK Government census. The population split in Northern Ireland is approximately 56% Protestant and 41% Roman Catholic with the remaining 3% not falling into either classification.

UK Population Breakdown – Military Service Groups (2004 estimates)

Age Group	Total	Males	Females
15–19	3.6 million	1.8 million	1.7 million
20–24	3.5 million	1.7 million	1.7 million
25–29	3.8 million	1.8 million	1.9 million
30–34	4.4 million	2.1 million	2.3 million
35–39	4.6 million	2.2 million	2.3 million
40–44	4.1 million	2.0 million	2.0 million
45–49	3.7 million	1.8 million	1.8 million

UK Area (in square kilometres)

England	130,423
Wales	20,766
Scotland	77,167
Northern Ireland	14,121
Total	242,477

Government

The executive government of the United Kingdom is vested nominally in the Crown, but for practical purposes in a committee of Ministers that is known as the Cabinet. The head of the ministry and leader of the Cabinet is the Prime Minister and for the implementation of policy, the Cabinet is dependent upon the support of a majority of the Members of Parliament in the House of Commons. Within the Cabinet, defence matters are the responsibility of the Secretary of State for Defence. The Secretary of State for Defence has three principal deputies; the Minister for the Armed Forces; Minister for Defence Procurement and the Minister for Veterans.

The Missions of the Armed Forces

The MoD mission statement for the armed forces reads as follows "Defence policy requires the provision of forces with a high degree of military effectiveness, at sufficient readiness and with a clear sense of purpose, for conflict prevention, crisis management and combat operations. Their demonstrable capability, conventional and nuclear, is intended to act as an effective deterrent to a potential aggressor, both in peacetime and during a crisis. They must be able to undertake a range of Military Tasks to fulfil the missions set out below, matched to changing strategic circumstances." These missions are not listed in any order of priority:

A: Peacetime Security: To provide forces needed in peacetime to ensure the protection and security of the United Kingdom, to assist as required with the evacuation of British nationals overseas, to afford Military Aid to the Civil Authorities in the United Kingdom, including Military Aid to the Civil Power, Military Aid to Other Government Departments and Military Aid to the Civil Community.

B: Security of the Overseas Territories: To provide forces to meet any challenges to the external security of a British Overseas Territory (including overseas possession and the Sovereign Base Areas) or to assist the civil authorities in meeting a challenge to internal security.

C: Defence Diplomacy: To provide forces to meet the varied activities undertaken by the Ministry of Defence to dispel hostility, build and maintain trust, and assist in the development of democratically accountable armed forces (thereby making a significant contribution to conflict prevention and resolution).

D: Support to Wider British Interests: To provide forces to conduct activities to promote British interests, influence and standing abroad.

E: Peace Support and Humanitarian Operations: To contribute forces to operations other than war in support of British interests and international order and humanitarian principles, the latter most likely under UN auspices.

F: Regional Conflict Outside the NATO Area: To contribute forces for a regional conflict (but on an attack on NATO or one of its members) which, if unchecked, could adversely affect European security, or which could pose a serious threat to British interests elsewhere, or to international security. Operations are usually under UN or Organisation for Security Co-operation in Europe auspices.

G: Regional Conflict Inside the NATO Area: To provide forces needed to respond to a regional crisis or conflict involving a NATO ally who calls for assistance under Article 5 of the Washington Treaty.

H: Strategic Attack on NATO: To provide, within the expected warning and readiness preparation times, the forces required to counter a strategic attack against NATO.

This mission statement is further sub-divided into a number of Military Tasks (MT) which accurately define the way in which these missions are actually accomplished.

Total British Armed Forces (as at 1 January 2005)
Regular: 202,350: Regular Reserves 201,370; Volunteer Reserves 38,850; Cadet Forces 155,590; MoD Civilians 118,200.

Regular Army 109,850 (trained and untrained but excluding 3,540 Gurkhas); Royal Navy 40,160 (including 5,500 Royal Marines); Royal Air Force 52,340.

Strategic Forces: $4 \times$ Vanguard Class submarines each with up to $16 \times$ Trident (D5) Submarine Launched Ballistic Missiles (SLBM) deploying with $48 \times$ warheads per submarine. If necessary a D5 missile could deploy with 12 MIRV (multiple independently targetable re-entry vehicles). Future plans appear to be for a stockpile of 200 operationally available warheads and 58 missile bodies. Strategic Forces are provided by the Royal Navy.

Royal Navy: 40,160: $4 \times$ SSBN; $11 \times$ Tactical Submarines; $3 \times$ Aircraft Carriers (1 in refit); $11 \times$ Destroyers; $20 \times$ Frigates; $6 \times$ Amphibious Warfare Vessels; $22 \times$ Mine Counter Measures Vessels; $5 \times$ Offshore Patrol Craft; $18 \times$ Inshore Patrol Craft; $1 \times$ Ice Patrol Ship; $4 \times$ Survey Vessels; $3 \times$ Harrier Squadrons (includes $2 \times$ squadrons assigned to Joint Force Harrier); $9 \times$ Helicopter Squadrons (includes $4 \times$ squadrons assigned to Joint Helicopter Command); $3 \times$ Royal Marines Commando Groups; Royal Fleet Auxiliary $3 \times$ Fleet Tankers; $4 \times$ Support Tankers; $6 \times$ Fleet Replenishment Ships; $1 \times$ Aviation Training Ship; $4 \times$ Landing Ships; $1 \times$ Forward Repair Ship; $6 \times$ Roll On-Roll Off Vessel.

Merchant Navy: Merchant Naval Vessels Registered in the UK, Crown Dependencies and Overseas Territories: $163 \times$ Large Tankers; $236 \times$ General Cargo Ships; $62 \times$ Refrigerated Cargo Ships; $152 \times$ Cellular Container Ships; $58 \times$ Ro-Ro Ships; $25 \times$ Passenger (Cruise) Ships; $8 \times$ Large Tugs.

Note: This listing refers to vessels of 500 gross tons and over.

Air Force: 52,340: $5 \times$ Strike/Attack Squadrons with $60 \times$ Tornado GR1/4; $5 \times$ Offensive Support Squadrons (includes $2 \times$ squadrons in the Joint Force Harrier) with $43 \times$ Harrier GR7/T10 and $22 \times$ Jaguar GR1A/3/3A; $4 \times$ Air Defence Squadrons with $70 \times$ Tornado F3; 3

× Maritime Patrol Squadrons with 20 × Nimrod MR2; 5 × Reconnaissance Squadrons with 24 × Tornado GR1A/4A, 12 × Jaguar GRGR1A/3/3A, 3 × Nimrod R1 and 4 × Canberra; 2 × Airborne Early Warning Squadrons with 6 × AEW Sentry; 15 × Transport and Tanker Squadrons with 18 × VC10, 8 × Tristar, 51 × Hercules; 6 × Support Helicopter Squadrons; 31 × Chinook, 37 × Puma and 18 × Merlin; 2 × Search and Rescue Helicopter Squadrons with 18 × Sea King HAR3/3A. 5 × RAF Regiment Surface to Air Missile Squadrons; 8 × RAF Regiment Ground Defence Squadrons; 4 × RAF Regiment STO Squadrons.

Army: 109,850 (excluding 3,540 Gurkhas); 1 × Corps Headquarters in Germany (ARRC); 1 × Armoured Divisional HQ in Germany; 1 × Mechanised Divisional HQ in UK; 4 × Divisional/District HQs in UK and 1 in Germany; 3 × Deployable Brigade Headquarters in Germany and 4 in the UK; 13 × Regional/Non-deployable Brigade HQs in the UK (includes 2 × Infantry Brigade HQs in Northern Ireland).

Joint Forces: 1 × Permanent Joint HQ; 1 × Joint Force HQ; Under Command Director Special Forces – 3 × SAS Regiments (including 2 × TA); 4 × Special Boat Squadrons; 1 × Joint NBC Regiment; **Joint Helicopter Command:** 1 × Air Assault Brigade HQ; 4 × Royal Navy Helicopter Squadrons with 33 × Sea King HC4, 6 × Lynx AH7 and 8 × Gazelle; 6 × Army Air Corps Regiments (including 1 TA) with 116 Lynx, 113 Gazelle and 5 × Islanders (67 × Longbow Apache being delivered); 6 × RAF Helicopter Squadrons with 31 × Chinook HC1/2; 37 Puma and 18 × Merlin; **Joint Force Harrier:** 2 × Royal Navy Squadrons with 17 × Sea Harrier F/A2 and 4 × T4/T8; 3 × RAF Squadrons with 40 × Harrier GR7 and 3 × Harrier T10.

British Army Equipment Summary
Armour: 386 × Challenger 2; (48 × Challenger 1 for disposal); 136 × Sabre; 54 × Striker (with Swingfire ATGW); 320 × Scimitar; 1,467 × Fv 432/430 family ; 667 × MCV 80 Warrior; 637 × Spartan; 605 × Saxon; 11 × Fuchs (NBC).

Artillery and Mortars: 450 × 81 mm mortar (including 110 × self-propelled); 2093 × 51 mm Light Mortar; 178 × AS 90; 63 × 227 mm MLRS; 112 × 105 mm Light Gun.

Air Defence: 57 × Rapier C Fire Units (including 24 × SP); 145 × Starstreak (LML); 135 × HVM (SP).

Army Aviation: 116 × Lynx ; 113 Gazelle; 5 × BN2; 67 × WAH-64D Apache on order (20 in service during early 2005)

Ministry of Defence (MoD)
In 1963 the three independent service ministries were merged to form the present Ministry of Defence (MoD). This large organisation which directly affects the lives of about half a million servicemen, reservists and MoD employed civilians, is controlled by The Secretary of State for Defence who is assisted by three ministers. These are the Minister of State for the Armed Forces, the Minister for Defence Procurement and the Minister for Veterans' Affairs.

The Secretary of State for Defence chairs The Defence Council. This Defence Council is the body where policy decisions are made that ensure the UK Armed Forces are run efficiently, and in accordance with the wishes of the government of the day.

Defence Council

The composition of The Defence Council is as follows:

◆ The Secretary of State for Defence
◆ Minister for the Armed Forces
◆ Minister for Defence Procurement
◆ Parliamentary Under Secretary of State for Defence
◆ Chief of the Defence Staff
◆ Vice Chief of the Defence Staff
◆ Chief of the Naval Staff and First Sea Lord
◆ Chief of the Air Staff
◆ Chief of the General Staff
◆ Permanent Under-Secretary of State
◆ Chief of Defence Procurement
◆ Chief Scientific Adviser
◆ Second Permanent Under-Secretary of State

General Sir Michael Walker.

Chief of The Defence Staff

The Chief of the Defence Staff (CDS) is the officer responsible to the Secretary of State for Defence for the co-ordinated effort of all three fighting services. He has his own Central Staff Organisation and a Vice Chief of the Defence Staff who ranks as number four in the services hierarchy, following the three single service commanders. Until May 2006 the Chief of the Defence Staff will continue to be:

General Sir Michael Walker KCB CMG CBE ADC Gen

General Sir Michael Walker was born on 7 July 1944 in Salisbury, Southern Rhodesia. He was educated partly in Rhodesia and partly in Yorkshire. On leaving school he taught at a preparatory school for 18 months before attending the Royal Military Academy, Sandhurst. He was commissioned into the Royal Anglian Regiment in 1966 and served with the 1st Battalion as a platoon commander in Celle and Catterick. In 1969 he was posted to Cyprus as an ADC to the GOC Near East Land Forces. He returned to his battalion in 1971 and during the course of the next five years served in Northern Ireland, Cyprus and Tidworth variously as Operations Officer, Regimental Signals Officer and Adjutant. In 1975 he was posted to the Ministry of Defence as a Staff Officer.

He attended the Army Staff Course at Shrivenham and Camberley, returning to his battalion in Tidworth as a Company Commander. At the end of 1979 he was posted back to the Ministry of Defence to the Directorate of Military Operations. On promotion to Lieutenant Colonel he was appointed Military Assistant to the CGS from 1982 to 1985. He then commanded his battalion in Londonderry and Gibraltar. He commanded 20 Armoured Brigade in Detmold from December 1987 and after three years in command was appointed Chief of Staff 1 (British Corps) in Bielefeld (Germany). General Walker assumed the appointment of GOC North East District and Command 2 Infantry Division on 30 September 1991 and then GOC Eastern District on 1 April 1992. In December 1992 he returned to the Ministry of Defence as Assistant Chief of the General Staff.

In December 1994, as a Lieutenant General, he assumed command of the ARRC in Rheindahlen, Germany, and deployed with HQ ARRC to Bosnia Herzegovina from December 1995 to November 1996 to command the multinational land component of IFOR. On relinquishing command of the ARRC he became the Commander-in-Chief Land Command, based at Wilton in Wiltshire and became Chief of the General Staff on 14 April 2000. In April 2003 he became the Chief of the Defence Staff following the retirement of Admiral Sir Michael Boyce.

From May 2006 General Sir Michael Walker will retire and his successor as Chief of the Defence Staff will be Air Chief Marshal Sir Jock Stirrup KCB AFC ADC FRAeS FCMI RAF.

Air Chief Marshal Sir Jock Stirrup KCB AFC ADC FRAeS FCMI RAF

Air Chief Marshal Stirrup was educated at Merchant Taylors' School, Northwood and the Royal Air Force College Cranwell, and was commissioned in 1970.

After a tour as a Qualified Flying Instructor he served on loan with the Sultan of Oman's Air Force, operating Strikemasters in the Dhofar War. Returning to the United Kingdom in 1975 he was posted to No 41(F) Squadron, flying Jaguars in the Fighter Reconnaissance role, before taking up an exchange appointment on RF-4C Phantoms in the United States. He then spent two years at RAF Lossiemouth as a flight commander on the Jaguar Operational Conversion Unit, and subsequently attended the Joint Service Defence College in 1984. He commanded No II(AC) Squadron, flying Fighter Reconnaissance Jaguars from Royal Air Force Laarbruch, until 1987 when he took up the post of Personal Staff Officer to the Chief of the Air Staff.

He assumed command of Royal Air Force Marham in 1990, just in time for Operation GRANBY, and then attended the 1993 Course at the Royal College of Defence Studies. He completed No 7 Higher Command and Staff Course at Camberley prior to becoming the Director of Air Force Plans and Programmes in 1994. He became Air Officer Commanding No 1 Group in April 1997 and was appointed Assistant Chief of the Air Staff in August 1998. He took up the appointment of Deputy Commander-in-Chief Strike Command in 2000. At the same time he assumed the additional roles of Commander of NATO's Combined Air Operations Centre 9 and Director of the European Air Group. He spent the last few months of his tour, from September 2001 to January 2002, as UK National Contingent Commander and Senior British Military Advisor to CINCUSCENTCOM for Operation VERITAS, the UK's contribution to the United States led Operation ENDURING FREEDOM in Afghanistan.

Air Chief Marshal Stirrup was appointed KCB in the New Year Honours List 2002 and became Deputy Chief of the Defence Staff (Equipment Capability) in March 2002. He was appointed Chief of the Air Staff, on promotion, on 1 August 2003 and in March 2005 was named as the Chief of the Defence Staff (Designate)as from May 2006.

Air Chief Marshal Stirrup is married with one son and enjoys golf, music, theatre and history.

Air Chief Marshal Sir Jock Stirrup

Chain of Command

The Chief of the Defence Staff (CDS) commands and co-ordinates the activities of the three services through the following chain-of-command:

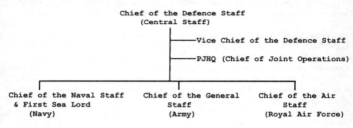

The three single service commanders exercise command of their single services through their respective headquarters. However, the complex inter-service nature of the majority of modern military operations, where military, air and naval support must be co-ordinated has led to the recent establishment of a permanent tri-service Joint Headquarters.

Permanent Joint Headquarters (PJHQ)

The UK MoD established a Permanent Joint Headquarters (PJHQ) at Northwood in Middlesex for joint military operations on 1 April 1996. This headquarters brought together on a permanent basis, intelligence, planning, operational and logistics staffs. It contains elements of a rapidly deployable in-theatre Joint Force Headquarters that has the capability of commanding rapid deployment front line forces.

The UK MoD Defence Costs Study of January 1994 identified a number of shortcomings with the command and control of UK military operations overseas. The establishment of PJHQ was an attempt to provide a truly joint force headquarters that would remedy the problems of disruption, duplication and the somewhat 'ad hoc' way in which previous operations had been organised

MoD officials have described the primary role of PJHQ as 'Working proactively to anticipate crises and monitoring developments in areas of interest to the UK'. The establishment of PJHQ has set in place a proper, clear and unambiguous connection between policy and the strategic direction and conduct of operations. Because it exists on a permanent basis rather than being established for a particular operation, PJHQ is involved from the very start of planning for possible operations. Where necessary, PJHQ then takes responsibility for the subsequent execution of these plans.

PJHQ, commanded by the Chief of Joint Operations (CJO), (currently a three star officer) occupies existing accommodation above and below ground at Northwood in Middlesex. PJHQ is responsible for planning all UK-led joint, potentially joint, combined and multinational operations and works in close partnership with MoD Head Office in the planning of operations and policy formulation, thus ensuring PJHQ is well placed to implement policy. Having planned the operation, and contributed advice to Ministers, PJHQ will then conduct such operations. The most recent example of PJHQ operational planning is the UK involvement in coalition operations in Iraq since 2003 and the the UK's continuing involvement with the International Security Assistance Force (ISAF) in Afghanistan. When another nation is in the lead, PJHQ exercises operational command of UK forces deployed on the operation.

Being a permanent joint Headquarters, PJHQ provides continuity of experience from the planning phase to the execution of the operation, and on to post-operation evaluation and learning of lessons.

Principal Additional Tasks of PJHQ Include:
♦ Monitoring designated areas of operational interest
♦ Preparing contingency plans
♦ Contributions to the UK MoD's decision making process
♦ Exercise of operational control of overseas commands (Falklands, Cyprus and Gibraltar)
♦ Managing its own budget
♦ Formulation of joint warfare doctrine at operational and tactical levels
♦ Conducting joint force exercises
♦ Focus for Joint Rapid Reaction Force planning and exercising.

Overview Of International Operations
From 1 Aug 1996 PJHQ assumed responsibility for current operations in the Middle East and the Former Yugoslavia. Non-core functions, such as the day-to-day management of the Overseas Commands in Cyprus, Falkland Islands, and Gibraltar, are also delegated by MoD Head Office to the PJHQ. This allows MoD Head Office to concentrate in particular on policy formulation and strategic direction. As of January 2005 PJHQ has been involved with UK commitments in the following areas:

Afghanistan, Albania, Algeria, Angola, Bosnia, Burundi, East Timor, Eritrea, Honduras, Iraq (including operations during 2003/04/05), Kosovo, Montenegro, Montserrat, Mozambique, Sierra Leone, East Zaire, West Zaire (Democratic Republic of the Congo).

Headquarters Structure
PJHQ, brings together at Northwood some 400 civilian, specialist and tri-service military staff from across the MoD. The headquarters structure resembles the normal Divisional organisation, but staff operate within multidisciplinary groups which draw from across the headquarters. The headquarters must have the capability of supporting a number of operations simultaneously on behalf of the UK MoD.

PJHQ in the MoD Chain of Command

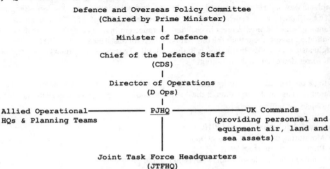

```
              Defence and Overseas Policy Committee
                 (Chaired by Prime Minister)
                              |
                     Minister of Defence
                              |
                 Chief of the Defence Staff
                           (CDS)
                              |
                    Director of Operations
                         (D Ops)
                              |
Allied Operational———————————PJHQ———————————UK Commands
HQs & Planning Teams                    (providing personnel and
                                         equipment air, land and
                                         sea assets)
                              |
                 Joint Task Force Headquarters
                         (JTFHQ)
```

PJHQ Headquarters Structure

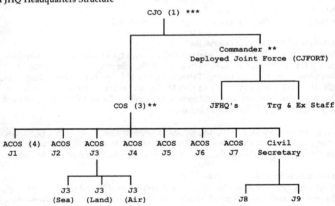

```
                              CJO (1) ***
            _____|_____
           |                                         |
           |                              Commander **
           |                      Deployed Joint Force (CJFORT)
           |                          _____|_____
           |                         |                |        |
        COS (3) **               JFHQ's      Trg & Ex Staff
   _____|_____
  |     |     |     |     |     |     |           |
ACOS  ACOS  ACOS  ACOS  ACOS  ACOS  ACOS        Civil
(4)    J2    J3    J4    J5    J6    J7        Secretary
 J1                                          _____|_____
         _____|_____                    |           |
        |       |       |                   J8          J9
        J3      J3      J3
      (Sea)  (Land)   (Air)
```

Notes:
(1) CJO – Chief of Joint Operations; (2) *** Denotes the rank of the incumbent (3) COS - Chief of Staff; (4) ACOS - Assistant Chief of Staff.

J1 Personnel and Admin	J6 Communication and Information Systems
J2 Intelligence	J7 Doctrine and Training
J3 Operations	J8 Plans
J4 Logistics	J9 Finance
J5 Policy	

The overall annual PJHQ budget is in the region of £480 million (for 2004/2005). Our estimate for the annual running costs of the Headquarters during 2004/2005 is approximately £45 million.

Included in the overall PJHQ budget are the costs of the UK forces in the Falkland Islands, Cyprus and Gibraltar. Major operations such as the 1999 Kosovo commitment, Afghanistan and the 2003 operation in Iraq are funded separately by way of a supplementary budget, and in almost all cases this requires government level approval. Small operations and the cost of reconnaissance parties are funded from the standard PJHQ budget.

Joint Rapid Reaction Force (JRRF)

The JRRF is essentially the fighting force that PJHQ has immediately available. The JRRF provides a force for rapid deployment operations using a core operational group of the Army's 16th Air Assault Brigade and the Royal Navy's 3rd Commando Brigade, supported by a wide range of air and maritime assets including the Joint Force Harrier and the Joint Helicopter Command.

The force uses what the MoD has described as a 'golfbag' approach with a wide range of units available for specific operations. For example, if the operational situation demands assets such as heavy armour, long range artillery and attack helicopters, these assets can easily be assigned to the force. This approach means that the JRRF can be tailored for specific operations, ranging from support for a humanitarian crisis to missions including high intensity operations.

The 'reach' of the JRRF will be enhanced by the Royal Navy's new amphibious vessels HMS Albion and HMS Bulwark, currently entering service. Both of these ships will be able to carry 650 troops plus a range of armoured vehicles including main battle tanks. A flight deck will allow ship-to-shore helicopter operations.

Responsibility for providing units to the JRRF remains with the single service commands who ensure that units assigned are at an extremely high state of readiness. JRRF units remain committed to NATO and a JRRF-assigned battalion group provides the UK commitment to the Allied Command **Europe Mobile Force (Land)**

The force commander is the CJRRFO (Chief of the Joint Rapid Reaction Force) who is responsible to the Chief of Joint Operations (CJO) at PJHQ. CJRRFO is supported by the Joint Force Operations Staff at PJHQ who provide a fully resourced Joint Task Force Headquarters (JTFHQ) at 48 hours notice to move anywhere in the world.

Joint Force Logistics Component

The Joint Force Logistics Component (JFLogC) provides a joint logistic headquarters with force logistics under the command of PJHQ. It delivers co-ordinated logistic support to the deployed Joint Force in accordance with the commander's priorities. The composition of the JFLogC will be determined by PJHQ during the mission planning stage. Two logistic brigades have been assigned to JFLogC, one of these brigades was operational from March 2001 and the second should be available from March 2003.

Defence Logistics Organisation (DLO)

Following the establishment of PJHQ at Northwood it became important to combine the separate logistics functions of the three Armed Forces. As a result, in 2000 the three distinct separate service logistic functions were fused into one and the DLO was formed.

With its mission 'to sustain UK capability, current and future', the DLO spends approximately £8 billion a year to support front line operations. The DLO is responsible for keeping the services fully equipped and ready to act at any time, in war or peace as the main logistics provider to the UK Armed Forces the DLO's responsibilities include:

- Logistics planning, resource management, contractual support and policy
- Global fleet management of land-based equipment
- Support of the naval fleet and all naval systems
- Communication and Information Systems
- Transport and movements
- Food and ration packs
- Ammunition
- Fuel, Oil and Lubricants
- Postal services
- Clothing and tentage
- Storage for all equipment and material.

With approximately 28,000 personnel, the DLO is one of the largest organisations within the MoD. At the core of the DLO are its Integrated Project Teams (IPT's) which concentrate on supplying and supporting the armed forces. These teams fall into the five business units of Equipment Support (Land), Equipment Support (Air), The Warship Support Agency, the Defence Communication Services Agency and the Defence Supply Chain. While each of these divisions is charged with a distinct task, together they keep the UK Armed Forces moving. The sixth unit that makes up the DLO is the Deputy Chief of Defence Logistics (DCDL). This area includes the DLO HQ, charged with setting policy and guidance for the DLO as a whole.

The DLO needs to keep on track to achieve its Strategic Goal (to reduce output costs by 20% before March 2006), whilst maintaining a first-class service to the personnel and units engaged in training and operations.

During late 2004 and early 2005 the DLO is undergoing a major restructuring programme that will remove the previous Business Units and manage the IPTs within a new structure. The new structure will be introduced gradually and the MoD claims that the DLO will become more effective.

The United Kingdom Defence Budget

> "You need three things to win a war,
> Money, money and more money".
> Trivulzio (1441–1518).

In general terms defence is related to money. Estimates for the world's top five defence budgets for 2005 (in billions of US$ and the latest year for which accurate figures are available) are as follows:

United States	US$ 429 billion
United Kingdom	US$ 50 billion
Japan	US$ 47 billion
France	US$ 42 billion
Germany	US$ 32 billion

For 2005 the Russian Defence Budget estimate is US$15 billion and the Chinese defence budget is estimated at being in the region of US$27 billion. The figures in the above table are figures derived from £ Sterling, Euro and Yen exchange rates in early 2005.

In the 2004-2005 Financial Year (FY) the UK Government allocated £29.86 billion on defence. Expenditure in FY 2004-2005 represented about 2.4% of GDP. In 1985 UK defence expenditure represented 5.2% of GDP.

The most recent defence expenditure figures are as follows:

2004/2005	£26.590 billion (near cash figure)
2005/2006	£26.917 billion (near cash figure)

In 2003/2004, Defence accounted for 2.5% of gross domestic product (GDP). This compares with about 13.7% for the Social Protection budget, about 6.8% for Health and 5.3% for Education.

Under the early 1990s 'New Management Strategy' the UK defence budget was allocated to a series of 'Top Level Budget Holders' each of whom were allocated a budget with which to run their departments. The money allocated to these Top Level Budgets (TLBs) constitutes the building bricks upon which the whole of the defence budget is based.

Top Level Budgets 2004-2005 (Departmental Expenditure Limits)

Naval Operational Areas (C-in-C Fleet)	£3,739 million
Army Operational Areas (C-in-C Land Command)	£5,5620 million
General Officer Commanding (Northern Ireland)	£650 million
Air Force Operational Areas (AOC RAF Strike Command)	£4,148 million
Chief of Joint Operations	£480 million
Chief of Defence Logistics	£7,834 million
Second Sea Lord/Naval Home Command	£673 million

Adjutant General (Army) Personnel & Training Command	£1,740 million
RAF Personnel & Training Command	£976 million
Central	£2,954 million
Defence Procurement Agency	£2,293 million
Corporate Science and Technology	£491 million

The high unit costs of individual items of equipment illustrate the problems faced by defence planners when working out their annual budgets. At 2005 prices the following items cost:

Kinetic Energy Round for Challenger	£3,000 each
155 mm High Explosive Round	£900 each
Individual Weapon (IW)	£800 each (estimate)
5.56 mm round for IW	£1
One Rapier Missile	£60,000
One Challenger 2 MBT	£4.5 million (approx)
Combat High Boot	£95 per pair
Starstreak Missile	£100,000 each
Attack Helicopter	£42 million (region)
Eurofighter	£60 million (estimate)
Merlin Support Helicopter	£34 million

Costs of Military Operations in Iraq

| Costs during FY 2002-2003 | £848 million |
| Costs during FY 2003- 2004 | £1,311 million |

We believe it is likely that costs for FY 2004–2005 will be in excess of £500 million.

Costs of Military Operations in Afghanistan

Costs during FY 2001–2002	£222 million
Costs during FY 2002–2003	£311 million
Costs during FY 2003–2004	£36 million

We would expect the expenditure figure for FY 2004–2005 to be in line with that of FY 2003–2004.

Defence Budgets – NATO Comparison (2004 Figures)

The nations of the North Atlantic Treaty Organisation (NATO), spent some US$631 billion on defence during 2004. For ease of conversions from national currencies, amounts are shown in US$.

Country	2004 Budget (billions of US$)	Country	2004 Budget (billions of US$)
Belgium	3.3	Luxembourg	0.25
Bulgaria	0.5	Netherlands	7.6
Canada	11.1	Norway	4.2
Czech Republic	1.9	Poland	4.4
Denmark	2.9	Portugal	2.1
Estonia	0.2	Romania	1.5
France	40.0	Spain	8.0
Germany	29.7	Slovakia	0.71
Greece	3.7	Turkey	8.5
Hungary	1.8	United Kingdom	47.0
Italy	17.5	United States	434.0
Latvia	0.22	**Total**	**631.7**
Lithuania	0.31		

Note: Iceland has no military expenditure although it remains a member of NATO.

It is probably worth noting that European members of NATO spent approximately US$185 billion, while the US spent some US$434 billion. Collectively, the European members of NATO spent 42% of the US total.

An interesting comparison is made by the total national defence budget divided by the total number of full time personnel in all three services. 2004 figures for the top five world defence spending nations are as follows:

Nation	2004 Defence Budget (US$)	Total Service Personnel	Cost per Serviceman
United States	434 billion	1,433,600	302,734
United Kingdom	47 billion	202,350	232,270
Japan	45 billion	239,900	187,578
France	40 billion	259,050	154,410
Germany	29 billion	284,500	101,933

BRITISH ARMY STATISTICS

British Army Major Units (Early 2005)

Regular Army

Armoured Regiments	10
Infantry Battalions	40
Home Service Battalions	4 (1)
Army Air Corps Aviation Regiments	5
Artillery Regiments	14
Engineer Regiments	11
Signals Regiments	1
Equipment Support Battalions	7
Logistic Regiments	21

Medical Regiments/Field Hospitals	8
Regular Special Air Service Regiment	1

Note: (1) Includes the Royal Gibraltar Regiment.

Territorial Army (TA)

TA Yeomanry Regiments	4
TA Infantry Battalions	15
TA Aviation Regiments	1
TA Artillery Regiments	7 (1)
TA Engineer Regiments	5
TA Signals Regiments	11
TA Equipment Support Battalions	4
TA Logistic Regiments	17
TA Medical Regiments/Units	15
TA Special Air Service Regiments	2

In general these Battalions/Regiments (both Regular and TA) are commanded by Lieutenant Colonels and have a strength of between 500 and 800 personnel.

Note: (1) Includes Honourable Artillery Company (HAC).

Deployment of The Regular Army (As at 1 April 2004)

Land Command	Officers	Soldiers
Field Army	4,600	48,400
Joint Helicopter Command	1,400	11,300
Commander Regional Forces	1,200	9,100
Land Support	300	100
Northern Ireland	700	6,600 (1)
	8,200	**75,500**

(1) Excludes Royal Irish Regiment (HS)

Adjutant General (Personnel & Training Command)

Army Personnel Centre	100	100
Army Programme	900	2,000
Army Trainees	1,200	13,000
Chief of Staff	300	500
Recruitment & Training Agency	1,100	5,200
General Staff	600	500
	4,200	**21,300**

Defence Logistics Organisation

Equipment Support (Land)	100	200

Troops Deployed/Stationed outside the UK mainland (September 2004)

Germany	21,250
Northern Ireland	11,180 (including Royal Irish Regiment)
Bosnia-Herzegovina	720
Macedonia	10
Sierra Leone	20
Iraq and the Gulf	9,070
Gibraltar	490
Belize	30
Kenya	10
Canada	210
Falkland Islands	1,270
Afghanistan	650
Cyprus	3,510
Brunei	800

Manning Figures (Including personnel under training)

Regular Army (As at 1 April 2004)

	2004	1995	1990
Trained Officers	13,500	13,100	16,200
Trained Soldiers	85,900	91,500	121,000
Untrained Officers	1,200	900	1,200
Untrained Soldiers	12,100	6,300	14,400
	112,700	**111,800**	**152,800**

Note: Previous years figures are given for comparison purposes. These figure do not include the Home Service element of the Royal Irish Regiment.

Regular Army Reserves (As at 1 April 2004)

Army Reserves	31,200
Individuals liable to recall	110,700
Territorial Army	38,300

Recruitment – Regular Army (During Financial Year 2003/2004)

	(2003/04)	(1980/81)
Officers	740	1,489
Soldiers	12,760	27,382
	13,500	**28,871**

Note: 1980/81 figures are given for comparison.

Outflow – Regular Army (During Financial Year 2003/2004)

	(2003/04)	(1990/91)	(1980/81)
Officers (Trained)	950(1)	1,860	1,497
Soldiers	13,640(2)	20,964	20,422
	14,590	**22,824**	**21,919**

(1) Includes 170 untrained officers
(2) Includes 4,850 untrained soldiers

Army Cadet Force

	(1 Apr 2004)	(1 Apr 1980)
Total Army Cadets	71,300	74,600

The Army Cadets are run and administered by the MoD. The total budget provided to the Army Cadets in FY 2003-2004 was £50 million.

Service personnel overseas during Christmas 2004

	Deployed on operations	Numbers serving overseas but not on operations	Percentage of trained strength
Royal Navy	1,200	450	4.5%
Army	7,850	19,200	26%
Royal Air Force	1,750	3,200	10%

UK Army Establishment Figures during June 2004 (Trained Personnel)

	Requirement	Strength
Household Cavalry/Royal Armoured Corps	5,975	5,835
Royal Artillery	8,330	7,795
Royal Engineers	9,160	8,850
Royal Signals	8,630	8,580(1)
Infantry	26,185	25,840
Army Air Corps	2,105	1,860
Royal Logistic Corps	16,205	15,450
Royal Army Medical Corps	2,920	2,665
Royal Electrical and Mechanical Engineers	10,370	9,705
Adjutant General's Corps (Provost)	2,075	2,040
Adjutant General's Corps (Staff Personnel)	4,036	441(2)
Adjutant General's Corps (Army Legal Service)	–	88(2)
Adjutant General's Corps (Education))	–	315(2)
Royal Army Veterinary Corps	190	175
Small Arms School Corps	122	30(2)
Royal Army Dental Corps	420	395
Intelligence Corps	1,410	1,345
Army Physical Training Corps	455	435

Corps of Army Music	1,155	1,025
Queen Alexandra's Royal Army Nursing Corps	1,035	805
RAChD	165	140
Gurkhas	3,445	3,394

(1) September 2004 figure
(2) Early 2002 figures

UK Army (Officer) Establishment Figures at 1 January 2005

	Establishment	Strength
Staff	830	820
Household Cavalry/Royal Armoured Corps	800	860
Royal Artillery	1,020	1,060
Royal Engineers	1,290	1,200
Royal Signals	960	1,000
Infantry	2,500	2,950
Army Air Corps	510	480
Royal Logistic Corps	1,670	1,640
Royal Army Medical Corps	980	860
Royal Electrical and Mechanical Engineers	800	850
Adjutant General's Corps (Provost)	230	210
Adjutant General's Corps (Staff Personnel)	480	470
Adjutant General's Corps (Army Legal Service)	120	90
Adjutant General's Corps (Education))	330	330
Royal Army Veterinary Corps	20	20
Small Arms School Corps	30	30
Royal Army Dental Corps	170	150
Intelligence Corps	330	280
Army Physical Training Corps	50	40
Corps of Army Music	30	40
Queen Alexandra's Royal Army Nursing Corps	400	260
RAChD	160	130
Total	**13,720**	**13,760**

Note: UK Regular Army includes nursing services and excludes Full Time Reserve Service personnel, Gurkhas, the Home Service battalions of the Royal Irish Regiment and mobilised reservists. All figures have been rounded to the nearest 10.

100 Years Ago – Strength of the British Army at 1 Jan 1905

Regular Army	195,000
Colonial Troops or Native Indian Corps	14,000
Army Reserve	80,000
Militia	132,000
Yeomanry (Cavalry)	28,000

Note: Regular forces in India totalled 74,500

Three years previously Regular Army totals by Corps were:

Household Cavalry	1,390
Cavalry of the Line	20,200
Horse Artillery	3,483
Field Artillery	15,509
Mountain Artillery	1,200
Garrison Artillery	18,400
Royal Engineers	7,130
Foot Guards	5,873
Infantry of the Line	132,332
Colonial Corps	5,217
Army Service Corps	3,555
Ordnance Staff	920
Armourers	352
Medical Services	2,993
	218,554

The force reduction in 1905 was due to the drawdown following the end of the war in South Africa.

CHAPTER 2 – ARMY ORGANISATIONS

The routine management of the Army is the responsibility of The Army Board the composition of which is shown in the next listing.

The Army Board
The Secretary of State for Defence
Minister of State (Armed Forces)
Minister of State (Defence Procurement)
Parliamentary Under-Secretary of State for Defence
Chief of the General Staff
Second Permanent Under-Secretary of State
Adjutant General
Quartermaster General
Master General of the Ordnance
Commander in Chief (Land Command)
Commander UK Support Command
Assistant Chief of the General Staff

Decisions made by the Army Board are acted upon by the military staff at the various headquarters worldwide. The Chief of the General Staff is the officer responsible for the Army's contribution to the national defence effort and he maintains control through the commander and the staff branches of each of these headquarters. Each military headquarters is organised along exactly the same lines with identical branches at each level in the chain of command.

Chief of The General Staff

General Sir Mike Jackson MBE CBE CB KCB DSO ADC Gen
General Jackson was born in 1944, and was educated at Stamford School, The Royal Military Academy Sandhurst and Birmingham University. Commissioned from Sandhurst into the Intelligence Corps in December 1963, he studied for an in-service degree in Russian Studies from 1964 to 1967. After graduating, he spent two years on secondment to the Parachute Regiment and subsequently transferred from the Intelligence Corps in 1970. During the early 70s he served in Northern Ireland, and with the TA in Scotland.

He attended the Staff College in 1976, after which he spent two years as the Chief of Staff of the Berlin Infantry Brigade. He then commanded a parachute company for two years, once more in Northern Ireland.

After a six month course at the National Defence College at Latimer in 1981, he joined the Directing Staff at the Staff College. His two and a half year tour at Camberley included a ten week attachment to the Ministry of Defence during the Falklands conflict.

He commanded 1st Battalion The Parachute Regiment from March 1984 to September 1986. Throughout his period of command the Battalion was part of the NATO Allied Command Europe Mobile Force (Land), a role which included three winters spent in

Norway on arctic training. For just over two years, until the end of 1988, he was the Senior Directing Staff (Army) at the Joint Service Defence College, Greenwich.

Following the Higher Command and Staff Course at Camberley in early 1989, he spent six months on a Service Fellowship at Cambridge writing a paper on the future of the British Army. In 1989, he moved back to Northern Ireland to command 39 Infantry Brigade. The years 1992 and 1993 were spent in the Ministry of Defence as Director General Personnel Services (Army). He commanded the 3rd (UK) Division from March 1994 to July 1996. In August 1995 he was selected to assume command of UNPROFOR in Bosnia at the end of that year; in the event, after the success of the Dayton talks, he spent the first half of 1996 in Bosnia commanding IFOR's Multinational Division South West.

He assumed the appointment of Commander ACE Rapid Reaction Corps in the rank of Lieutenant General in February 1997, following a brief assignment as Director General Development and Doctrine. He deployed with ARRC HQ, as Commander Kosovo Force, to Macedonia in March 1999 and subsequently commanded Kosovo Force in Pristina from June to October 1999. He assumed the appointment of Commander in Chief Land Command on 1 March 2000 and became Chief of the General Staff in early 2003.

General Sir Mike Jackson was awarded the MBE in 1979, the CBE in 1992, the CB in 1996, the KCB in 1998, the DSO in 1999 and ADC Gen in 2001. He is married to Sarah, and has two sons, a daughter and three grandchildren. His interests include music, reading, travel, skiing and tennis.

General Sir Mike Jackson.

Chain-of-Command

The Army is commanded from the MoD via two subsidiary headquarters and a number of smaller headquarters worldwide. The Joint Headquarters (JHQ) at Northwood in Middlesex has an important input into this chain-of-command and it is almost certain that any operation with which the army is involved will be under the overall command of PJHQ. The following diagram illustrates this chain-of-command.

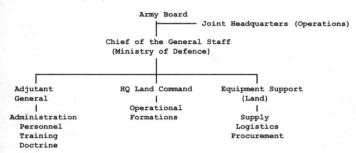

Staff Branches

The Staff Branches that you would expect to find at every military headquarters from the Ministry of Defence (MoD) down to Brigade level are as follows:

Commander –	Usually a General (or Brigadier) who commands the formation.
Chief of Staff –	The officer who runs the headquarters on a day-to-day basis and who often acts as a second-in-command. Generally known as the COS.
G1 Branch –	Responsible for personnel matters including manning, discipline and personal services.
G2 Branch –	Responsible for intelligence and security
G3 Branch –	Responsible for operations including staff duties, exercise planning, training, operational requirements, combat development and tactical doctrine.
G4 Branch –	Logistics and quartering.
G5 Branch –	Civil and military cooperation

HQ Land Command

Following the MoD's 'Front Line First' study, plans were drawn up to reorganise HQ United Kingdom Land Forces (HQ UKLF) in a new formation designated HQ Land Command that became operational on 1 April 1995. HQ Land Command is located at Erskine Barracks, Wilton near Salisbury and controls about 75% of the troops in the British Isles and almost 100% of its fighting capability.

Land Commands's role is to deliver and sustain the Army's operational capability, whenever required throughout the world, and the Command comprises all operational troops in Great Britain, Germany, Nepal and Brunei, together with the Army Training Teams in Canada, Belize and Kenya.

Land Command has almost 75,000 trained Army personnel – the largest single Top Level Budget in Defence, with a budget of just over £5.5 billion. It contains all the Army's fighting equipment, including attack helicopters, Challenger 2 tanks, Warrior Infantry Fighting Vehicles, AS90 and the Multi-Launched Rocket System (MLRS).

Land Command is one of the three central commands in the British Army, the other two being the Adjutant General (with responsibility for administration, personnel and training) and Equipment Support (Land) responsible for supply and logistics. The Command is responsible for providing all the Army's fighting troops throughout the World. These are organised into eight formations and are commanded by Major Generals.

Ready Divisions
There are two 'Ready' Divisions: the 1st (UK) Armoured Division, based in Germany, and the 3rd (UK) Division in the United Kingdom. Both of these divisions are earmarked to form part of the Allied Command Europe Rapid Reaction Corps (ARRC), NATO's premier strategic formation; but they also have the flexibility to be employed on rapid reaction tasks or in support of other Defence Roles.

In addition to their operational roles, they also command the Army units in specified geographic areas: in the case of the 1st Division, this area is made up of the garrisons in Germany where the Division's units are based; and in the case of the 3rd Division the South West of England.

Regenerative Divisions
There are three Regenerative Divisions, based on old Districts in the United Kingdom. These are the 2nd Division with its Headquarters at Edinburgh, the 4th Division with its Headquarters at Aldershot, and the 5th Division with its Headquarters at Shrewsbury. These Regenerative divisions are responsible for all non-deployable Army units within their boundaries, and could provide the core for three new divisions, should the Army be required to expand to meet a major international threat.

Districts
Two Districts remain: London District (although subordinated to 4th Division for budgetary purposes), and the United Kingdom Support Command (Germany). London District is responsible for all Army units within the M25 boundary. The United Kingdom Support Command (Germany) with its Headquarters at Rheindahlen has similar responsibilities, but also provides essential support functions for 1 (UK) Armoured Division and the Headquarters of the ARRC.

These divisional and district areas are further sub-divided into brigades and garrisons, which also have a varying mix of operational and infrastructure support responsibilities. As a result of the Defence Costs Studies, some brigade headquarters, which previously had purely operational functions, have been amalgamated with garrison headquarters to achieve savings and greater efficiency.

The Structure of Land Command

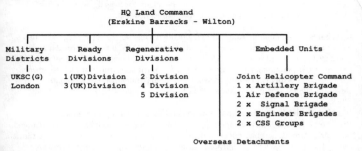

```
                    HQ Land Command
                (Erskine Barracks - Wilton)

Military      Ready       Regenerative                Embedded Units
Districts   Divisions      Divisions
   |           |              |
UKSC(G)    1(UK)Division   2 Division      Joint Helicopter Command
London     3(UK)Division   4 Division      1 x Artillery Brigade
                           5 Division      1 Air Defence Brigade
                                           2 x  Signal Brigade
                                           2 x Engineer Brigades
                                           2 x CSS Groups

                                       Overseas Detachments
```

Note: Overseas Detachments include Belize, Canada, Brunei, Nepal and Kenya. Garrisons in Northern Ireland, Cyprus and the Falkland Islands are commanded from the MoD via PJHQ. Operations in Afghanistan, Bosnia, Iraq, Kosovo and Sierra Leone are also commanded by PJHQ.

The overseas detachments in Canada, Belize, Brunei and Nepal are commanded directly from Headquarters Land Command at Wilton.

Embedded units include:

1 Artillery Brigade consists of two artillery regiments, equipped with the multiple launch rocket system, and a surveillance and target acquisition regiment, equipped with the Phoenix remotely piloted vehicle, radar and sound ranging equipment. For operations, the brigade may have assigned to it a Territorial Army artillery regiment, equipped with the multiple launch rocket system, and a Territorial Army observation post regiment.

7 Air Defence Brigade consists of two air defence artillery regiments equipped with Rapier surface to air missile systems. For operations, the brigade may have three Territorial Army air defence artillery regiments assigned to it, each equipped with Javelin close air defence systems.

1 Signal Brigade consists of two signal regiments and the Allied Command Europe Rapid Reaction Corps support battalion.

11 Signal Brigade consists of a strategic communications signal regiment and a trunk communications signal regiment. For operations, the brigade may have five Territorial Army signal regiments assigned to it.

29 (Corps support) Engineer Brigade may have two Territorial Army engineer regiments assigned to it.

12 (Air Support) Engineer Brigade could consist of an air support engineer regiment and two independent air support squadrons. For operations, the brigade may have two Territorial Army air support engineer regiments assigned to it.

Combat Service Support Group (United Kingdom) consists of a supply regiment, two transport regiments, a general support medical regiment which has both regular and territorial army squadrons, three field hospitals, and a field medical equipment depot. For operations, the group may have assigned to it two Territorial Army transport regiments, five Territorial Army field hospitals, and a Territorial Army Royal Electrical and Mechanical Engineers maintenance battalion.

Combat Service Support Group (Germany) may consist of a supply regiment; two transport regiments, and a general support medical regiment which has both Regular and Territorial Army squadrons. For operations, the group may have assigned to it a Territorial Army transport regiment, six Territorial Army field hospitals, a Territorial Army field medical equipment depot, and a Territorial Army Royal Electrical and Mechanical Engineers maintenance battalion.

Although Land Command is not responsible for running operations in Northern Ireland, the Former Yugoslavia, Afghanistan, Sierra Leone, Cyprus, the Falkland Islands and Iraq (a responsibility of PJHQ), it will provide the operational troops for these areas. Some 7,000 troops are involved in Northern Ireland at present, either deployed in the Province or training for deployment; and a further 15,000 are deployed in Afghanistan, Cyprus, the Former Yugoslavia, Sierra Leone the Falkland Islands and Iraq.

Some 500 troops are involved at any one time in MoD-sponsored equipment trials, demonstrations and exhibitions. Public Duties in London take up two/three battalions at any one time. All troops not otherwise operationally committed are also available to provide Military Aid to the Civil Authorities in the United Kingdom.

LAND COMMAND DIVISIONAL/DISTRICT SUMMARIES

1 (UK) Armoured Division and British Forces Germany (BFG)
The 1st Armoured Division was formed in 1940. Since the Second World War the Division has been retitled three times and became the 1st (United Kingdom) Armoured Division in 1993, having successfully fought in the Gulf War of 1991. The Division has its headquarters at Herford in Germany and commands three Armoured Brigades situated throughout North West Germany and is the major component of British Forces Germany.

British Forces Germany (BFG) is the composite name given to the British Army, Royal Air Force and supporting civil elements stationed in Germany.

The terms British Army of the Rhine (BAOR) and Royal Air Force Germany (RAFG), until recently were the traditional names used to describe the two Service elements of the British Forces stationed in Germany.

For many years following World War II, and as a result of the confrontation between NATO and the former Warsaw Treaty Organisation, the UK Government had stationed four Army divisions and a considerable part of its Air Force at five airbases in the Federal Republic of Germany. On the whole this level of commitment was maintained until 1992 and although these forces appeared to be solely national, they were in fact closely integrated with the NATO Northern Army Group (NORTHAG) and the 2nd Allied Tactical Air Force (2 ATAF).

As a result of political changes in Europe and the UK Government's 'Options for Change' programme, the British Army's presence in Germany has been reduced to three armoured brigades and a divisional headquarters with logistical support. The majority of the RAF presence has been withdrawn.

Composition of 1(UK) Armoured Division

1 (UK) Armoured Division has its headquarters at Herford in Germany (about 50 kms from Hanover) and the three Armoured Brigades under command are located at Osnabruck, Bergen-Hohne and Paderborn.

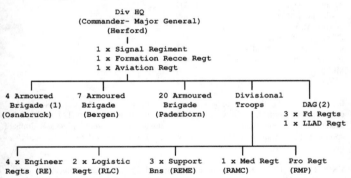

Note: (1) Under Future Army Structure (FAS) proposals 4 Armoured Brigade will re-role to become a mechanised brigade. Restructuring should be complete by 2008. (2) DAG (Divisional Artillery Group) This DAG could be reinforced by Rapier Air Defence and MLRS units from the UK as necessary. (3) Personnel total in Germany is approximately 21,000 with about 17,000 in 1 (UK) Armoured Division. During early 2005 this Division could provide the Headquarters (HQs) for up to nine Battlegroups.

Non-UK brigades

For non-national operations such as NATO military tasks in support of the Allied Rapid Reaction Corps (ARRC), 1 (UK) Armoured Division could have two extra brigades available for deployment. These two brigade would be the Danish Reaction Brigade and 4 (Czech) Reaction Brigade.

102 Logistics Brigade

This brigade provides third line combat service support wherever this is required army wide but is the first 'port of call' for combat service support to 1 (UK) Armoured Division. The Brigade Headquarters is at Gutersloh in West Germany, reasonably close to the Headquarters of 1 (UK) Armoured Division in Herford.

102 Logistics Brigade has the following major/minor units under command:

262 Signal Squadron (Gutersloh)
6 Supply Regiment RLC (Gutersloh and Dulmen)
7 Transport Regiment RLC (Bielefeld and Fallingbostel)
8 Transport Regiment RLC (Catterick – Yorkshire)
5 Regiment RMP (Edinburgh – Scotland)
34 Field Hospital RAMC (Edinburgh – Scotland)
102 Military Working Dog Support Unit RAVC (Sennelager)

Estimate of Force Levels in 1 (UK) Armoured Division (1 Jan 2005)

Army Personnel	17,000
Challenger 2 MBT	150
Warrior AIFV	450
Other Tracked Vehicles	1,100
Helicopters (Army Aviation)	24
Artillery Guns	66
MLRS	0
AVLB	18

It is probable that in the event of hostilities (as was the case in recent operations in Iraq) considerable numbers of officers and soldiers from the Territorial Army (TA) would be used to reinforce this division. These reinforcements would consist of individuals, drafts of specialists, or by properly formed TA units varying in size from Mobile Bath Units of 20 men, to Major Units over 500 strong.

UKSC(G) – The United Kingdom support Command (Germany) has responsibility for British Army Troops on the Continent of Europe that are not part of 1st (United Kingdom) Armoured Division. Its headquarters replaces that of the British Army of the Rhine, whose sign it has adopted. The headquarters of UKSC(G) is located at Rheindahlen and has about 600 personnel under command.

2nd Division

The 2nd Division has responsibility for the whole of England north of the Humber, and Scotland. The division was first formed in 1809 to fight in the Peninsular War and one of its most famous engagements was during the Burma Campaign in 1944 when, at the battle for Kohima, the tide finally turned against the Japanese Army. The Divisional Headquarters is in Edinburgh.

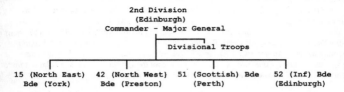

52(Inf) Brigade is a light infantry brigade with light role battalions at Edinburgh, Chester and Preston under command.

3 (UK) Division

The 3rd (United Kingdom) Division is the only operational (Ready) Division in the UK. The Division has a mix of capabilities encompassing armoured and wheeled elements in its three mechanised brigades. The Division which was first formed during the Napoleonic Wars now also has responsibility for South-West England. The 'Iron-Triangle' insignia was chosen for it in the early part of World War II by its commander the then, Major General B L Montgomery.

HQ 3 (UK) Division

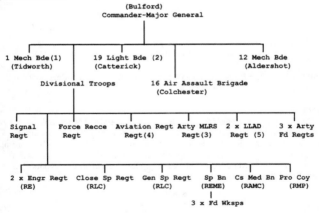

We have shown 16 Air Assault Brigade in this diagram as an example of how this formation might be deployed. 16 Air Assault Brigade is under the command of the Joint Helicopter Command (JHC). However, the JHC is not an Operational Headquarters and for operations, 16 Air Assault Brigade will probably be detached to under command of HQ Allied Rapid Reaction Corps, PJHQ, HQ 1 (UK) Division or HQ 3 (UK) Division.

Note: (1) 1 Mechanised Brigade; (2) 19 Brigade will re-role to become a light brigade as from January 2005. It should be ready for deployment in 2006 when it will serve as the contingent NATO response force. (3) Artillery Regiment with Multi Launch Rocket System (if allocated); (4) Army Air Corps Regiment with Lynx & Gazelle (from Joint Helicopter Command as required); (5) Air Defence Regiments with Rapier and HVM air defence systems; (6) The composition of this division allows the UK MoD to retain a balanced force for out of NATO area operations should that become necessary.

3 Commando Brigade (a Royal Naval formation) is available to support 3(UK) Div if necessary. Details of the organisation of 3 Cdo Bde are given in the Miscellaneous Chapter.

4th Division

The 4th Division has military responsibility for South East England, including Bedfordshire, Essex and Hertfordshire and its headquarters is in Aldershot. The division now has three brigades under command, 2 Infantry Brigade based in Shorncliffe, 145 Home Counties Brigade in Aldershot and 49 Eastern Brigade based in Chilwell The divisional symbol is the Tiger.

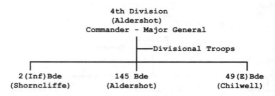

2 (Inf) Bde is a light infantry brigade with infantry battalions based at Chepstow, North Luffenham and Tern Hill under command.

5th Division

The 5th Division has responsibility for military units and establishments in Wales, the West Midlands and the North West of England and the Headquarters is in Shrewsbury. The Division emblem, inherited from Wales and Western District, depicts the Welsh Dragon, the cross of St Chad (7th Century Bishop of Mercia), and the Red Rose of Lancaster. The 5th Division fought at Waterloo and played a significant part in the endeavours of the BEF in both World Wars.

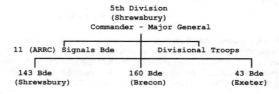

London District

London District is responsible for all Army units within the M25 boundary. The activity for which the Headquarters and the District is most well known is State Ceremonial and Public Duties in the Capital. The district insignia shows the Sword of St Paul representing the City of London and the Mural Crown representing the County of London. The District has its Headquarters in Horse Guards.

Between 500 and 600 troops are involved at any one time in MoD-sponsored equipment trials, demonstrations and exhibitions. Public Duties in London also take up two/three battalions at any one time. All troops not otherwise operationally committed are also available to provide Military Aid to the Civil Authorities in the United Kingdom.

United Kingdom Support Command (Germany)

The United Kingdom Support Command (Germany) with its Headquarters at Rheindahlen has similar responsibilities, but also provides essential support functions for the 1st Division and the Headquarters of the ARRC.

These divisional and district areas are further sub-divided into brigades and garrisons, which also have a varying mix of operational and infrastructure support responsibilities. As a result of the Defence Costs Studies, some brigade headquarters, which previously had purely operational functions, have been amalgamated with garrison headquarters to achieve savings and greater efficiency.

Army Brigades

Under the Future Army Structure (FAS) proposals the UK Armed Forces will have the following operational brigades available for deployment once restructuring is complete:

Light Brigades: 16 Air Assault Brigade; 19 Light Brigade; 3 Commando Brigade

Mechanised Brigades: 1 Mechanised Brigade; 4 Mechanised Brigade; 12 Mechanised Brigade

Armoured Brigades: 7 Armoured Brigade; 20 Armoured Brigade

Armoured Brigade Organisation

The following diagram illustrates the possible composition of an Armoured Brigade in 1(UK) Armd Div on operations.

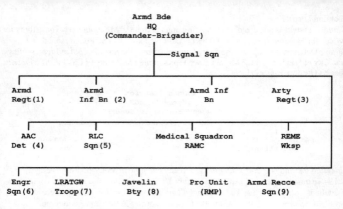

Totals: 58 × Challenger MBT (Possibly)
145 × Warrior AIFV
340 × AFV 432/Spartan Armoured Vehicles
24 × AS 90 SP Gun
Approx 5,000 personnel

Notes: (1) Armoured Regiment with approx 58 × Challenger MBT; (2) Armoured Inf Battalion with approx 52 × Warrior (with rifle coys) and approx 40 × FV432; (3) Artillery Regiment with 24 × AS90 SP Guns; (4) Army Air Corps Detachment (possibly 9 × Lynx & 4 × Gazelle); (5) Transport Squadron RLC with approximately 60–70 trucks; (6) Engineer Squadron with 68 vehicles but depending upon the task could involve a complete engineer battalion; (7) Long Range Anti-Tank Guided Weapon Troop (Swingfire) but due to be replaced in the longer term; (8) RA Bty with possibly 36 × HVM AD missiles; (9) Armoured Recce Squadron.

This Brigade could provide the HQs for three Battlegroups.

Mechanised Brigade Organisation

The following is an example of the possible Mechanised Brigade organisation.

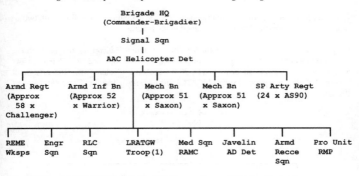

Note: (1) Long Range AntiTank Guided Weapons – Currently Striker/Swingfire.

16 Air Assault Brigade

Nearly 10,000 personnel form the personnel component of 16 Air Assault Brigade. Using everything from the latest Apache helicopter to air-mobile artillery equipment and high velocity air defence missiles, this Brigade has marked a considerable leap forward in Britain's defence capability.

The Brigade capitalises on the combat capabilities of the former 24 Airmobile Brigade and 5 Airborne Brigade, including two parachute battalions with an increase in combat service support. The introduction of the Apache Attack Helicopter, due in operational service within the next two years, will provide a new generation of weapons systems bringing major improvements in military capability. This brigade is under the command of the JHC (Joint Helicopter Command) and would be detached to other formations for operations.

Under the Future Army Restructuring plans 1 Para will re-role as a 'Ranger' type or Special Forces Support Group available for operations from 2008.

It is believed that the Special Forces Support Group will be located at St Athlan, in South Wales, close to the SAS headquarters in Hereford. The force will be composed of around 450 Parachute Regiment soldiers and 200 personnel from both the Royal Marines and the RAF Regiment.

Soldiers wishing to become part of the Special Forces Support Group will need to be able to offer more than the average infantryman but the entrance requirements will be different from those of the SAS.

The other two Parachute Regiment battalions will remain with 16 Air Assault Brigade and continue to provide the lead airborne battlegroup in rotation.

It would appear that 16 Air Assault Brigade will retain 4 × infantry battalions with two non Parachute Regiments battalions assigned to the Brigade.

Support helicopters are provided by the RAF (from the Joint Helicopter Command) and the Brigade would normally expect to operate with 18 × Chinook and 18 × Puma. An air assault infantry battalion can be moved by 20 × Chinook equivalents lifts. Each air assault infantry battalion is equipped with 42 × ATGW firing posts – a total of 84 within the Brigade.

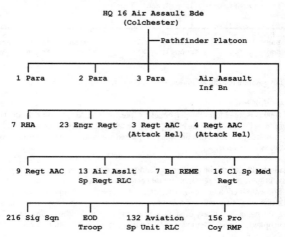

Light Brigade

Although details of the new Light Brigade structure have not yet been announced (April 2005), our projection for a possible structure during 'out of area' operations might resemble the following:

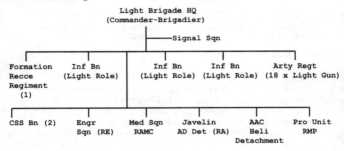

Note: (1) If required LRATGW (up to 12 × Swingfire/Spartan) will be held in the Formation Recce Regiment – other ATGW will be held by individual Light Role Infantry Battalions; (2) This Combat Service Support Battalion will have a mix of RLC and REME elements.

The Battlegroup

A division usually consists of three brigades. These brigades are further sub-divided into smaller formations known as battlegroups. The battlegroup is the basic building brick of the fighting formations.

A battlegroup is commanded by a Lieutenant Colonel and the infantry battalion or armoured regiment that he commands, provides the command and staff element of the formation. The battlegroup is then structured according to task, with the correct mix of infantry, armour and supporting arms.

The battlegroup organisation is very flexible and the units assigned can be quickly regrouped to cope with a change in the threat. A typical battlegroup fighting a defensive battle on the FEBA (Forward Edge of the Battle Area), and based upon an organisation of one armoured squadron and two mechanised companies, could contain about 600 men, 16 tanks and about 80 armoured personnel carriers.

The number of battlegroups in a division and a brigade could vary according to the task the formation has been given. As a general rule you could expect a division to have as many as 12 battlegroups and a brigade to have up to three or four. The following diagram shows a possible organisation for an armoured battlegroup in either 1(UK) Armd Div or 3(UK) Div.

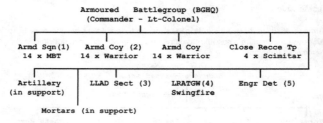

Company Groups/Task Group

Each battlegroup will operate with smaller organisations called task groups or company groups. These groups which are commanded by a Major, can be allocated tanks, armoured personnel carriers and supporting elements depending upon the aim of the formation. Supporting elements such as air defence, anti-tank missiles, fire support and engineer expertise ensure that the combat team is a balanced all arms grouping, tailored specifically for the task. In general a battlegroup similar to the one in the previous diagram could be expected to form three company groups.

A possible Company Group/Task Group organisation could resemble the following diagram:

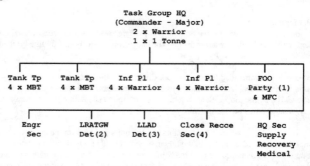

Notes: (1) Forward Observation Officer (FOO – usually a Captain) with his party from the Royal Artillery. This FOO will be in direct communication with a battery of eight guns and the Artillery Fire Direction Centre. The MFC is usually a sergeant from an infantry battalion mortar platoon who may have up to six mortar tubes on call. In most Combat Teams both the FOO and MFC will travel in close proximity to the Combat Team Commander; (2) Possibly 2 × Striker with Swingfire; (3) Possibly 2 × Spartan with HVM; (4) Possibly 2 × Scimitar.

Allied Command Europe Mobile Force Land AMF(L) Contingent

The UK's pool of Joint Rapid Reaction Forces cover all of the military tasks for which there is a requirement to provide forces at short notice. This includes the UK's commitment to NATO's Allied Command Europe (ACE) through the UK contribution to the ACE Rapid Reaction Corps and the ACE Mobile Force (Land) or AMF(L). The first echelon is always held at very high readiness for 'early entry operations' – for example to secure a landing point and possibly to provide an initial military capability. Its second echelon will provide follow-up forces normally held at slightly longer readiness.

The first echelon land element would be able to provide lead battlegroups of land and amphibious forces (including if required an armoured battlegroup), and a special forces component. A fully equipped, rapidly deployable Joint Task Force HQ exists to command these initial forces and be able to expand to command a larger force if required.

For AMF(L) land operations the second echelon force could consist of a brigade-sized force. This could range from a light, commando or airmobile brigade or if required an armoured brigade.

During a recent AMF(L)exercise in Norway the UK contribution included
1 × Infantry Bn, 1 × Armoured Sqn, 1 Locating Bty, 1 × Artillery Bty,
1 × Signals Sqn, 1 × Engineer Field Troop, 1 × Army Air Corps Flight,
1 × Transport Sqn, 1 × Ordnance Company, REME Workshop, Field Ambulance (Medical Squadron) detachment and an Intelligence section. The overall personnel total was probably in the region of 1450 personnel.

Northern Ireland

The military presence in support of the civilian authorities in Northern Ireland is controlled by HQ Northern Ireland (HQNI) which is located at Lisburn, just outside Belfast.

The number of armed forces personnel (Army, Navy and RAF), under the command of the General Officer Commanding Northern Ireland (GOC NI), stationed in Northern Ireland at 30 November 2004 was 11,000. This figure would appear to include about 30 personnel from the Royal Navy/Royal Marines and approximately 900 Royal Air Force personnel.

The GOC NI also has under his command troops that are rear based in Great Britain that can be called forward to the Province as and when required. In addition other troops can be made available to the GOC NI from HQ Land Command if required. As a Top Level Budget Holder (TLB) the GOC NI was allocated £650 million during the financial year 2004/2005.

HQNI is responsible for military operations in support of the Police Service of Northern Ireland (PSNI). For command purposes Northern Ireland is subdivided into two brigade areas:

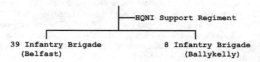

```
                    HQ Northern Ireland
                         (Lisburn)



                              ──HQNI Support Regiment

      ┌──────────────────────────────┐
  39 Infantry Brigade           8 Infantry Brigade
      (Belfast)                    (Ballykelly)
```

39 Brigade area corresponds with the PSNI Urban Region and includes Belfast City, the province's two main airports and the seaport of Belfast. In addition 39 Brigade is responsible for half of Lough Neagh, the largest body of inland water in the UK.

8 Brigade area corresponds with the PSNI's Rural Region and includes Londonderry (the second largest city in the Province). The Brigade area includes areas of Antrim, Fermanagh, South Armagh, County Londonderry, mid-Tyrone and Strangford Lough.

Under the operational command of these brigades (during early 2005) were:

Army: 4 × Resident Infantry Battalions on roughly two year tours
      2 × Infantry Battalions on short six month tours
      1 × Engineer Regiment
      1 × Royal Signals Regiment
      1 × Army Air Corps Regiment
      3 × Home Service Battalions of the Royal Irish Regiment
      1 × RLC Logistic Support Regiment
      1 × REME Workshop
      1 × RMP Regiment

RAF: 1 × Puma Squadron
     1 × RAF Regiment Field Squadron

Navy: 1 × Support and Liaison Detachment

There are three home service battalions of the Royal Irish Regiment with a total strength of 3,400 (included in the previous total of 11,000). This figure of 3,400 is made up of about 2,100 full time personnel and 1,300 part time personnel.

Battalion headquarters locations are as follows:

2nd Battalion The Royal Irish Regiment – Holywood
3rd Battalion The Royal Irish Regiment – Armagh
4th Battalion The Royal Irish Regiment – Omagh

Ulster Statistics

The last year for which comprehensive statistics are available was 2000.

44

	2000	1980
Deaths (Regular Army)	0	8
Deaths (Royal Irish)	0	8
Injuries	27	77
Bombs neutralised	77	120
Explosives neutralised	417 kg	2,905 kg
Used in explosions	324(estimate)	4,108 kg
Explosives found	311 kg	821 kg
Weapons found	142	203
Ammunition found	10,721 rounds	28,078 rounds

The worst year for terrorist violence was in 1972 when 131 service personnel were killed and 578 injured. At one stage in 1972 there were over 30,000 service personnel in the Province.

Background to the Future Army Structure (FAS)
During December 2004 the UK MoD made the following announcement regarding FAS.

"The current structure of the Army is based on the most demanding tasks it has to be able to conduct, namely large-scale war-fighting. Experience in the way that the Field Army has been structured in the last seven years has shown that this does not suit the pattern of concurrent medium and small-scale operations that it has been routinely exposed to, particularly for key enablers. FAS will ensure that the Army is structured for the most likely tasks with a true war-fighting capability at its core, whilst retaining the ability to generate for the most demanding tasks.

The requirement to mount expeditionary operations at medium and small scale more rapidly requires a re-balancing from heavy forces to a lighter, more deployable structure. The three mechanised brigades will take on a rapid intervention medium weight role, although it is recognised that they will not achieve the full level of deployability required until the introduction of new air-portable platforms, particularly the Future Rapid Effect System (FRES).

In addition to FRES, the Army's contribution to effects-based warfare will be enhanced by the introduction of the APACHE attack helicopter as well as long range precision attack munitions from 155 mm guns and rockets and improved Intelligence, Surveillance, Target Acquisition and Reconnaissance (ISTAR) capabilities. These are in addition to digitised communications (BOWMAN and FALCON), under the umbrella of Networked Enabled Capability (NEC), which aim to link more closely sensors, decision-makers and weapons systems.

Greater emphasis on expeditionary capability will mean that combat service support units will form robust brigade logistic groups and ensure more force elements are closely matched in readiness and training terms to the combat elements that they are supporting.

Operations TELIC and VERITAS have marked the emergence of the TA as the reserve of first choice to support our land forces on operations. Greater integration into the restructured FAS Army will make the TA even more useable and deployable. TA personnel will continue to contribute to enduring commitments on a voluntary basis as they have been doing so effectively over the last few years.

Timetable

FAS Implementation will not happen overnight. FAS has been in the planning stages for several months and a detailed implementation plan has been endorsed by the Army Board and its timetable is as follows:

a. Phase 1. Now until end of 2008. Structural changes. 4 Armoured Brigade will re-role to a mechanised brigade and 19 Mechanised Brigade will re-role to a light brigade via an interim structure.

b. Phase 2. 2008–2012. Infrastructure adjustments in place. FRES experimentation carried out.

c. Phase 3. Beyond 2012. FRES and full range of ISTAR, NEC, deep target attack and Air Manoeuvre capabilities delivered.

Summary

FAS aims to produce a war-fighting Army, geared for expeditionary operations, structured for the most likely tasks at brigade level but able to generate forces for less frequent but larger deployments. It will be balanced in combat capability, able to deploy, support and maintain forces on operations, with integrated reserves and more predictable tour intervals.

FAS will produce an agile, balanced, intervention capability consisting of medium and light forces underpinned by effective, capable heavy forces able to conduct operations across the full spectrum of conflict.

Details of how FAS will affect the Household Cavalry and the Royal Armoured Corps, Infantry, Artillery, Army Air Corps, Engineers, Communications and Combat Service Support are included within the relevant chapters.

CHAPTER 3 – INTERNATIONAL COMMITMENTS

NATO Command Structure
The United Kingdom is a member of NATO (North Atlantic Treaty Organisation) and the majority of military operations are conducted in concert with the forces of NATO allies. In 1993, NATO was reorganised from three into two major Commands with a further re-organisation of these two commands in 2003. The first is ACO (Allied Command Operations), with its headquarters at Mons in Belgium and the second is ACT (Allied Command Transformation) with headquarters at Norfolk, Virginia (USA).

NATO operations in which the United Kingdom was a participant would almost certainly be as part of a NATO force under the command and control of Allied Command Operations (ACO). The current Supreme Allied Commander is General James L Jones.

SACEUR – General James L Jones
General Jones is the Supreme Allied Commander, Europe (SACEUR) and the Commander of the United States European Command (COMUSEUCOM). From the Supreme Headquarters Allied Powers Europe, Mons, Belgium, General Jones leads Allied Command Europe (ACE), comprising NATO's military forces in Europe. The mission of ACE is to preserve the peace, security, and territorial integrity of the NATO member nations in Europe. As COMUSEUCOM, General Jones commands five US components: US Army, Europe; US Navy, Europe; US Air Forces in Europe, US Marine forces in Europe and Special Operations Command, Europe. The European Command's mission is to support and achieve US interests and objectives throughout 93 countries in Central and Eastern Europe, Africa and portions of the Middle East. The command performs a variety of functions including planning for and conducting contingency operations such as noncombatant evacuations and humanitarian relief operations; providing combat-ready forces to both Allied Command Europe and other US unified commands; and conducting intelligence activities and security assistance.

General Jones spent his formative years in France, returning to the United States to attend the Georgetown University School of Foreign Service, from which he earned a Bachelor of Science degree in 1966. He was commissioned a Second Lieutenant in the Marine Corps in January 1967. Upon completion of The Basic School, Quantico, Virginia, in October 1967, he was ordered to the Republic of Vietnam, where he served as a Platoon and Company Commander with Company G, 2nd Battalion, 3rd Marines. While overseas, he was promoted to First Lieutenant in June 1968.

Returning to the United States in December 1968, General Jones was assigned to Camp Pendleton, California, where he served as a Company Commander until May 1970. He then received orders to Marine Barracks, Washington, DC, for duties as a Company Commander, serving in this assignment until July 1973. He was promoted to Captain in December 1970. From July 1973 until June 1974, he was a student at the Amphibious Warfare School, Quantico, Virginia.

In November 1974, he received orders to report to the 3rd Marine Division on Okinawa, where he served as the Company Commander of Company H, 2nd Battalion, 9th Marines, until December 1975. From January 1976 to August 1979, General Jones served in the Officer Assignments Section at Headquarters Marine Corps, Washington, DC. During this assignment, he was promoted to Major in July 1977. Remaining in Washington, his next assignment was as the Marine Corps Liaison Officer to the United States Senate, where he served until July 1984. He was promoted to Lieutenant Colonel in September 1982.

He was then selected to attend the National War College in Washington, DC. Following graduation in June 1985, he was assigned to command the 3rd Battalion, 9th Marines, 1st Marine Division, Camp Pendleton, California, from July 1985 to July 1987.

In August 1987, General Jones returned to Headquarters Marine Corps, where he served as Senior Aide to the Commandant of the Marine Corps. He was promoted to Colonel in April 1988, and became the Military Secretary to the Commandant of the Marine Corps in February 1989. During August 1990, General Jones was assigned as the Commanding Officer, 24th Marine Expeditionary Unit at Camp Lejeune, North Carolina. During his tour with the 24th MEU, he participated in Operation Provide Comfort in Northern Iraq and Turkey. He was advanced to Brigadier General on April 23, 1992. General Jones was assigned to duties as Deputy Director, J-3, US European Command, Stuttgart, Germany, on July 15, 1992. During this tour of duty, he was reassigned as Chief of Staff, Joint Task Force Provide Promise, for operations in Bosnia-Herzegovina and Macedonia.

Returning to the United States, he was advanced to the rank of Major General in July 1994, and was assigned as Commanding General, 2nd Marine Division, Marine Forces Atlantic, Camp Lejeune, North Carolina. General Jones next served as Director, Expeditionary Warfare Division (N85), Office of the Chief of Naval Operations, during 1996, then as the Deputy Chief of Staff for Plans, Policies and Operations, Headquarters Marine Corps, Washington, DC. He was advanced to Lieutenant General on July 18, 1996.

His next assignment was as the Military Assistant to the Secretary of Defence. He was promoted to General on June 30, 1999, and became the 32nd Commandant of the United States Marine Corps on July 1, 1999. General Jones assumed duties as the Commander of US European Command on 16 January 2003 and Supreme Allied Commander Europe on 17 January 2003.

General Jones' personal decorations include: the Defense Distinguished Service Medal with two oak leaf clusters, Silver Star Medal, Legion of Merit with four gold stars, Bronze Star Medal with Combat "V", and the Combat Action Ribbon.

General James L Jones.

Allied Command Operations (ACO)
Allied Command Operations, with its headquarters, SHAPE, near Mons, Belgium, will be responsible for all Alliance operations. The levels beneath SHAPE will be significantly streamlined, with a reduction in the number of headquarters. The operational level will consist of two standing Joint Force Commands (JFCs) one in Brunssum, the Netherlands, and one in Naples, Italy – which can conduct operations from their static locations or provide a land-based Combined Joint Task Force (CJTF) headquarters and a robust but more limited standing Joint Headquarters (JHQ), in Lisbon, Portugal, from which a deployable sea-based CJTF HQ capability can be drawn.

The current organisation of Allied Command Operations is as follows:

```
                         SHAPE
          (Supreme Headquarters Allied Powers Europe)
                     Mons - Belgium
            (Supreme Allied Commander Europe)

ACE Rapid                                    NATO Airborne Early
Reaction Forces                              Warning Force
Forces (ARRF)                                (NAEW-F)

       JFC Brunssum      JFC Naples      JHQ Lisbon
                                     (Deployable Maritime HQ)
```

Component Headquarters at the tactical level

The component or tactical level will consist of six Joint Force Component Commands (JFCCs), which will provide service-specific – land, maritime, or air – expertise to the operational level. Although these component commands will be available for use in any operation, they will be subordinated to one of the Joint Force Commanders.

Joint Forces Command – Brunssum

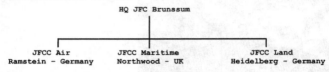

Joint Forces Command – Naples

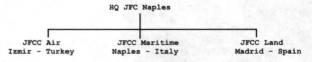

Static Air Operations Centres (CAOC)

In addition to the above component commands there will be four static Combined Air Operations Centres with two more deployable as follows:

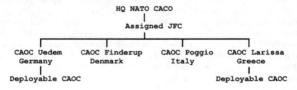

As the deployable CAOCs will need to exercise their capability to mobilise and deploy, the current facilities at Torrejon Air Base in Spain will probably be the primary site for training and exercising in that region. A small NATO air facility support staff would be stationed at Torrejon to support this capability.

Allied Command Transformation (ACT)

Allied Command Transformation, with its headquarters in Norfolk, US, is overseeing the transformation of NATO's military capabilities. In doing so, it is to enhance training, improve capabilities, test and develop doctrines and conduct experiments to assess new concepts. It will also facilitate the dissemination and introduction of new concepts and promote interoperability. There will be an ACT Staff Element in Belgium primarily for resource and defence planning issues.

ACT will command the Joint Warfare Centre in Norway, a new Joint Force Training Centre in Poland and the Joint Analysis and Lessons Learned Centre in Portugal. ACT Headquarters will also supervise the Undersea Research Centre in La Spezia, Italy. There will be direct linkages between ACT, Alliance schools and NATO agencies, as well as the US Joint Forces Command. A NATO Maritime Interdiction Operational Training Centre in Greece, associated with ACT, is also envisaged. In addition, a number of nationally- or multinationally-sponsored Centres of Excellence focused on transformation in specific military fields will support the command.

The (2003) NATO concept

Under the 2003 concept, NATO forces should be able to rapidly deploy to crisis areas and remain sustainable, be it within or outside NATO's territory, in support of both Article 5 and Non-Article 5 operations. The successful deployments of the Allied Command Europe Rapid Reaction Corps (ARRC) to two NATO-led Balkan operations (the Implementation Force (IFOR) to Bosnia Herzegovina in 1995 and Kosovo Force (KFOR) to Kosovo in 1999) are early examples of non-Article 5 crisis response operations outside NATO territory.

The new concept will have its largest impact on land forces. Maritime and air forces are by nature already highly mobile and deployable and often have a high state of readiness. Most of NATO's land based assets, however, have been rather static and have had limited (strategic) mobility. In the new structure, land forces should also become highly deployable and should have tactical and strategic mobility. The mobility requirements will have great impact on the Alliance's transport and logistic resources (sea, land and air based). The need for quick reaction requires a certain amount of highly trained forces that are readily available. Further, interoperability (the possibility of forces to co-operate together with other units) and sustainability (the possibility to continue an operation for an extended period of time) are essential in the new force structure.

Multinationality

To express the Alliance's solidarity and its political cohesiveness and to enhance flexibility, there is also a need for multinationality, not only with regard to member countries, but further still. In the case of NATO-led crisis response operations there should be room for the participation of Partner countries or other non-NATO countries. Last but not least, adequate co-ordination mechanisms with international organisations must be ensured in these operations.

High Readiness Forces and Forces of Lower Readiness

There will be forces of two different kinds of readiness posture. First, forces with a higher state of readiness and availability, the so-called High Readiness Forces (HRF) to react on short notice. Second, forces with a lower state of readiness (FLR) to reinforce and sustain. Graduated Readiness Headquarters will be developed to provide these forces with command and control facilities.

◆ **Land forces:** Their deployable headquarters will be able to command and control assigned forces up to the corps-size level. Also a wide range of options will be available to command and control land forces at the brigade and division size to operate as stand-alone formation or subordinated to a higher HQ.

◆ **Maritime forces:** Their deployable headquarters will be able to command and control assigned forces up to the NATO Task Force Level. Also a wide range of options will be available to command and control maritime forces at NATO Task Unit level to operate as stand-alone formation or subordinated to a higher HQ.

◆ **Air forces:** The air forces will use the air command and control facilities of the present NATO Command Structure.

Implementation

At the level of the NATO Supreme Commanders programmes are underway to evaluate and certify the candidate HQ's according to the new standards and requirements. The High Readiness Forces (Land) Headquarters have already been certified and the Headquarters of Forces with Lower Readiness (Land) will follow in the coming years. The certification of the High Readiness Forces (Maritime) Headquarters will be finalised in 2004.

High Readiness Forces (Land) Headquarters candidates:

The Allied Command Europe Rapid Reaction Corps (ARRC) HQ in Rheindalen (Germany) with the United Kingdom as framework nation;

The Rapid Deployable German-Netherlands Corps HQ, based on the 1st German-Netherlands Corps HQ in Munster (Germany);

The Rapid Deployable Italian Corps HQ based on the Italian Rapid Reaction Corps HQ in Solbiate Olona close to Milan (Italy);

The Rapid Deployable Spanish Corps HQ based on the Spanish Corps HQ in Valencia (Spain);

The Rapid Deployable Turkish Corps HQ based on the 3rd Turkish Corps HQ near Istanbul (Turkey);

The EUROCORPS HQ in Strasbourg (France) sponsored by Belgium, France, Germany, Luxembourg and Spain.

Note: The EUROCORPS Headquarters which has a different international military status based on the Strasbourg Treaty, has signed a technical arrangement with SACEUR and can also be committed to NATO missions.

Forces of Lower Readiness (Land) Headquarters candidates:

The Multinational Corps HQ North-East in Szczecin (Poland) sponsored by Denmark, Germany and Poland;

The Greece "C" Corps HQ near Thessaloniki (Greece).

High Readiness Forces (Maritime) Headquarters:
Headquarters Commander Italian Maritime Forces on board of Italy's GARIBALDI;

Headquarters Commander Spanish Maritime Forces (HQ COMSPMARFOR) on board of LPD CASTILLA;

Headquarters Commander United Kingdom Maritime Forces (HQ COMUKMARFOR) on board a UK carrier.

The Allied Rapid Reaction Corps (ARRC)
The concept of the Allied Rapid Reaction Corps was initiated by the NATO Defence Planning Committee in May 1991 and confirmed during November 1991. The concept called for the creation of Rapid Reaction Forces to meet the requirements of future challenges within the alliance. The ARRC provides the Supreme Allied Commander Europe with a multinational corps sized grouping in which forward elements can be ready to deploy within 14 days (lead elements and recce parties at very short notice).

As stated by SHAPE the mission of the ARRC is: "HQ ARRC, as a High Readiness Force (Land) HQ, is prepared to deploy under NATO, EU or coalition auspices to a designated area, to undertake combined and joint operations across the operational spectrum as:

◆ a Corps HQ
◆ a Land Component HQ
◆ a Land Component HQ in command of the NATO Response Force
◆ a Joint Task Force HQ for Land-centric operations

in order to support crisis management options or the sustainment of ongoing operations."

As NATO's first and most experienced High Readiness Force (Land) Headquarters the ARRC is actively engaged in the NATO Response Force (NRF) transformation initiative.

Currently the ARRC trains for missions across the spectrum of operations from deterrence and crisis management to regional conflict.

Headquarters ARRC is located in Rheindahlen, Germany with a peace-time establishment of 400 personnel. It comprises staff from all the contributing nations. A French liaison officer is officially accredited to the Headquarters. As the Framework Nation, the UK provides the infrastructure, administrative support, communications and 60% of the staff.

The Commander (COMARRC) and Chief of Staff are UK 3 Star and 2 Star generals and the Deputy Commander is an Italian 2 Star general. The other appointments, as with the training and exercise costs, are shared among the contributing nations.

During early 1996, HQ ARRC deployed to Sarajevo in the Former Yugoslavia to command the NATO Implementation Force (IFOR). In 1999 HQ ARRC was responsible for operations in Kosovo.

High Readiness Force (Land) Operations

HQ ARRC procedures for the deployment and employment of multinational forces, particularly in light of technological developments, are constantly reviewed, updated, tested and validated to ensure that in any scenario, the combat effectiveness of the corps is greater than the sum of its parts.

Command Posts and Deployment: Due to the need to be able to respond flexibly to the whole range of potential operations, HQ ARRC has been developing the capability for rapidly deployable and modular HQs. Deployment will begin with the despatch of a Forward Liaison and Reconnaissance Group (FLRG) within 48 hours of the order being given which can then be quickly followed up.

Within four days the key enablers from 1 (UK) Signal Bde would be within theatre and three days later HQ ARRC Forward and HQ Rear Support Command (RSC) Forward – as required – could be established. While there is a standard 'default' setting for personnel numbers, the actual staff composition is 'tailored' to the task and can vary from approximately 50 to 150 staff, depending on the requirement. The 'in-theatre' task would then be supported by the remainder of the staff, using sophisticated 'Reachback' techniques and equipment.

The Early Entry HQs are capable of sustained independent operations if required but can also be used as enablers if it is decided to deploy the full HQ ARRC. This deployment concept has been tested and evaluated on several exercises and has proven its worth. In parallel, HQ ARRC is continuously looking to make all of its HQs lighter and more survivable.

Outline Composition of the ARRC (ACE Rapid Reaction Corps

For operations the ARRC might have some of the following formations under command:

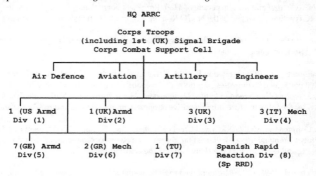

Notes: (1) United States; (2) Resident in Germany (3) Resident in the UK (4) IT – Italy (5) GE Germany (6) GR Greece (7) TU – Turkish.

The operational organisation, composition and size of the ARRC would depend on the type of crisis, area of crisis, its political significance, and the capabilities and availability of lift assets, the distances to be covered and the infrastructure capabilities of the nation receiving assistance. It is considered that a four-division ARRC would be the maximum employment structure.

The main British contribution to the ARRC is 1 (UK) Armoured Division that is stationed in Germany and there is also a considerable number of British personnel in both the ARRC Corps HQ and Corps Troops. In addition, in times of tension 3(UK) Mechanised Division and 16 Air Assault Brigade will move to the operational area to take their place in the ARRC's order of battle. In total, we believe that if the need arose some 40,000 British soldiers could be assigned to the ARRC together with substantial numbers of Regular Army Reservists and formed TA Units.

Iraq

British Forces are serving in Iraq as part of the Coalition Force authorised under United Nations Security Council Resolution 1546. This mandate will expire upon the completion of the political process or if requested by the Government of Iraq.

The UK Government has stated that it is committed to Iraq for as long as the Iraqi Government judge that the coalition is required to provide security and assist in the development of the Iraqi Security Forces.

On 1 January 2005, some 9,150 UK armed forces personnel were deployed on Operation Telic. Of this number approximately 8,000 were serving within Iraq. The majority of United Kingdom troops deployed to Iraq deploy for six-month tours and are in units commanded by the Multinational Division (South-East).

Multinational Division (South East)MND(SE)

The Headquarters of the MND(SE) is located at Basrah International Airport in Southern Iraq. This is a composite multinational headquarters with the majority of the personnel and infrastructure being provided by the UK.

MND(SE) covers four provinces in Iraq with subsidiary headquarters at: Shaibah (UK National Support Element) Maysan, Al Muthanna, Talil Airbase, As Samawah and Dhi Qar.

The primary activities of MND(SE) are:

a.) Supporting the ongoing political process in Iraq
b.) Security Sector Reform – Training the new Iraqi security Forces with partnership operations where MND(SE) forces back-up, assist and monitor these Iraqi Security Forces.
c.) Normalisation – Helping to get society on its feet again by assisting in the restoration of water, power, health, education, judiciary, oil industry and heritage and encouraging commercial markets and the economy.

At the end of January 2005 the following UK major units were under the command of the MND (SE):

4 Armoured Brigade Headquarters and Signal Squadron
The Queen's Dragoon Guards
The Royal Dragoon Guards
4th Regiment Royal Artillery
1st Battalion Scots Guards
1st Battalion Welsh Guards
1st Battalion The Duke of Wellington's Regiment
2nd Battalion the Princess of Wales' Royal Regiment
21 Engineer Regiment.

A very high readiness reserve battalion (VHRR) is held in the UK at 10 days' readiness to deploy to Iraq.

In addition to the UK personnel, in early 2005 MND(SE) had approximately 5,000 troops from countries that include: Australia, Czech Republic, Denmark, Italy, Japan, South Korea, Lithuania, Netherlands, Norway, Portugal, and Romania.

Costs: Total additional costs of the operations in Iraq for FY2002–03 were £848 million, and for FY2003–04 £1,311 million, a total of £2,159 million.

The projected costs for Iraq during FY2004-05 are £975 million.

Reservists: During the course of 2004 some 2,350 reservists were called out and accepted into service to support operations in Iraq. The majority of these reservists completed six-month tours.

NATO Support: At the ministerial meeting in Brussels on 9 December 2004, Foreign Ministers of the 26 NATO countries agreed to move ahead with expanding NATO's role in Iraq. 23 NATO countries have agreed to provide support to the NATO Training Mission-Iraq by providing personnel and equipment to train the Iraqi Security Forces in and outside of Iraq. Of these 23 countries, fifteen have agreed to deploy forces within Iraq. These are Bulgaria, Canada, Denmark, Hungary, Italy, Latvia, Lithuania, the Netherlands, Norway, Poland, Portugal, Romania, Turkey, the United Kingdom and the United States.

Iraqi National Guard: The mission of the Iraqi national guard is to conduct internal security operations, including support to Ministry of Interior forces and constabulary duties.

The training process comprises three weeks' basic training for the individual, followed by four weeks' collective training. Currently (February 2005), more than 36,500 personnel are trained, equipped and operational in the Iraqi national guard. HQ Multi-National Force Iraq assesses that the future strength of the Iraqi national guard will be more than 56,000 personnel.

During early 2005 there would appear to be approximately 115,000 Iraqi Security Force personnel available (36,000 National Guard and approximately 79,000 police associated personnel).

Afghanistan

As of early 2005 the UK had approximately 650 armed forces personnel serving with the International Security Assistance Force (ISAF) in Afghanistan.

However, it is believed that the UK contribution in Afghanistan may number as many as 5,000 troops when the UK assumes command of the NATO peace support operation in the country in 2006. The predominantly British HQ of the Allied Rapid Reaction Force (HQ ARRC). Some commentators expect British soldiers to replace American troops in the two southern provinces of Kandahar and Helmand. This region is the heartland of Afghanistan's Pashtuns, many of whom still support the Taliban.

UK operations in Afghanistan were costed at £35.9 million in FY2003-04. Estimates for FY2004-05 are in the region of £53 million.

During early 2005 some 8,000 armed forces personnel from 36 nations were supporting ISAF. Nations supporting the ISAF mission are:

Albania; Austria; Azerbaijan; Belgium; Bulgaria; Canada; Croatia; Czech Republic; Denmark; Estonia; Finland; France; FYROM; Germany; Greece; Hungary; Iceland; Ireland; Italy; Latvia; Lithuania; Luxembourg; Netherlands; New Zealand; Norway; Poland; Portugal; Romania; Slovakia; Slovenia; Spain; Sweden; Switzerland; Turkey; United Kingdom and the United States of America.

European Union – Helsinki Headline Goal 2010

The European Union (EU) has adopted the following illustrative scenarios which form the basis for force planning to meet the EU Helsinki Headline Goal 2010:

◆ Stabilisation, reconstruction and military advice to third countries
  Conflict Prevention
◆ Evacuation Operation in a non-permissive environment
  Separation of Parties by Force
◆ Assistance to Humanitarian Operations.

To this end the EU has established an EU planning cell at SHAPE and a new civil-military cell within the EU Military Staff. At EU Military Staff level the civil-military cell will improve coherence between the EU's civilian and military responses, develop expertise in managing the civilian-military interface, and undertake advance strategic planning for joint civil-military operations. This will also provide the capacity to generate an ad hoc Operations Centre for an operation, in particular where a joint civil-military response is required, where no national headquarters is identified, and if agreed unanimously by EU member states.

The European Council agreed that these cells should be established by the end of 2004, with the ability to set up an Operations Centre available by 1 January 2006.

UK Commitment to the European Helsinki Goal 2010

In early 2005 the UK MoD confirmed a declaration of up to 12,500 troops towards the Helsinki Headline Goal on a voluntary case-by-case basis. Of this figure about 35% are infantry troops.

The UK currently offers three brigades which allows the UK to provide either an Armoured Brigade (based on Warrior Armoured Fighting Vehicles and Challenger 2 Main Battle Tanks), a Mechanised Brigade (based on Saxon Infantry Fighting Vehicles and Challenger 2 Main Battle Tanks) or an Air Assault Brigade consisting of lightly equipped infantry in the Air Manoeuvre role. An amphibious brigade (3 Commando Brigade) from the Royal Navy may also be available. Up to 18 UK warships and 72 UK combat aircraft are also available for EU operations.

However, these national forces are made available for EU operations on a voluntary, case-by-case basis, as for NATO or UN operations. UK contributions to such operations are provided from within existing forces.

As yet (early 2005) there is no standing European Rapid Reaction Force nor any EU agreement to create one. What has sometimes been referred to as a 'European Rapid Reaction Force' is, in fact, a catalogue of forces which member states could make available to the EU should they choose to participate in a particular EU-led operation. Any contribution to a particular EU-led operation would depend on the operation's requirements, the availability of forces at the time and the willingness of EU members to participate.

EU Military Agreements

The following table sets out the main multilateral military structures outside NATO which include European Union members. A number of these also include non-EU countries. In addition, there are many other bilateral military agreements between individual EU member states.

The UK is a party to military agreements in respect of four of the structures listed in the following table. Military agreements between other EU members are a matter for those member states' governments.

Structure	EU participants
EAG – European Air Group	Belgium, France, Germany, Italy, Spain, UK
European Airlift Centre	Belgium, France, Germany, Italy, Netherlands, Spain, UK
Sealift Co-ordination Centre (Eindhoven)	Netherlands, UK
European Amphibious Initiative (including the UK/Netherlands Amphibious Force)	France, Italy, Netherlands, Spain, UK

SHIRBRIG – Stand-by High Readiness Brigade	Austria, Denmark, Finland, Ireland, Italy, Lithuania, Netherlands, Norway, Poland, Portugal, Slovenia, Spain, Sweden. (Observers: Czech Republic, Hungary)
SEEBRIG – South-Eastern Europe Brigade	Greece, Italy, Slovenia
NORDCAPS – Nordic Co-ordinated Arrangement for Military Peace Support	Finland, Sweden, Denmark Germany, Belgium, Spain, France,
EUROCORPS	Luxembourg, France, Germany, Spain, Belgium
EUROFOR	France, Italy, Portugal, Spain
EUROMARFOR	France, Italy, Portugal, Spain

For information the EU consists of:

Austria; Belgium; Cyprus (Greek part); Czech Republic; Denmark; Estonia; Finland; France; Germany; Greece; Hungary; Ireland; Italy; Latvia; Lithuania; Luxembourg; Malta; Netherlands; Poland; Portugal; Slovakia; Slovenia; Spain; Sweden; United Kingdom.

The Future
One of the probable reasons why peacekeeping/peacemaking or peace support operations will almost certainly continue to be necessary:

> "There are five Great National Delusions. The first is that there are solutions to all the problems. The second is that only a strong centre can solve the problems. The third is that the strong centre must embody one's own views exclusively. The fourth Great Delusion is that heroic surgery is required, and the fifth, that the heroic surgeons must be oneself, and one's cronies armed with scalpels as big as machettes."
> *Louis de Bernieres – The Troublesome Offspring of Cardinal Guzman.*

CHAPTER 4 – THE HOUSEHOLD CAVALRY AND THE ROYAL ARMOURED CORPS

The Household Cavalry (HCav) and The Royal Armoured Corps (RAC) have traditionally provided the tank force and armoured (formation) reconnaissance component of the British Army. More recently they have also become responsible for providing the Army element of the Joint NBC Regiment.

Armour has provided battle winning shock action and firepower since the earliest tanks helped to break the stalemate of the Western Front during the First World War. In the same way, formation reconnaissance, with the ability to penetrate the enemy's forward defences and gain information by using stealth and firepower, has shaped the way in which armour has been used to its best advantage.

Defence represents the best use of ground features in conjunction with engineering and concealed firepower. The ability of armour to overwhelm all but the heaviest defences and deliver a group of highly capable armoured fighting platforms into the combat area remains a battle winning capability embraced by all major armies.

The modern main battle tank weighs between 50 and 70 tonnes, can move at up to 60 kph and can virtually always guarantee a first round hit with its main armament out to 2000 m. Last tested in combat in the Gulf War of 2003, UK armoured forces demonstrated the advantages of armour in a desert landscape. Amongst these were the ability to cover rough terrain quickly and by the use of superior concentrated firepower, create operational level, rather than simple local tactical, advantage. These tanks used the most up to date information systems and state of the art imaging and sighting systems to locate, close with and destroy the enemy. The 2003 Gulf War experience underlined the need for all elements of manoeuvre forces to be able to move swiftly and securely with protection and firepower to maintain a high 'operational tempo'. This includes infantry, artillery and of course the massive logistic supply required.

However, since the earliest discovery of the power of the tank, military planners and scientists have sought ways of negating its power and defeating its protection to reduce its advantage. To counter these enhancements, in turn the tank has repeatedly been adapted and improved to maintain its advantage. Thermal imaging sights enable the tank to acquire a target and identify it by day or by night and in conditions of much reduced visibility. The tank's organic armour protection can be supplemented with explosive reactive armour packs that detonate on contact with an incoming round, disrupting its destructive power. More sophisticated anti-tank weapons, mines, missiles and indeed helicopters, have created a new battlefield environment of sensing and counter-sensing while trying to manoeuvre to exercise firepower advantage.

The UK's Armoured regiments are equipped with 'Challenger 2 ' built by Vickers whereas the Formation Reconnaissance regiments are equipped with the 'Scimitar' tracked reconnaissance vehicles built by Alvis. The planned replacement of these systems is integrated into future UK defence planning. The replacement for Scimitar will be the new reconnaissance vehicle which will be provided by one of the variants of the Future Rapid

Effect System (FRES) which will be introduced around the turn of the decade. Challenger 2, which was fully fielded into service in January 2002, will not be due for replacement until around 2030. Future enhancements to Challenger 2 are likely to be those that enhance its protection in the face of more capable and accurate detectors and weapons, while maintaining its ability to strike at the enemy. The replacement reconnaissance vehicle will embody as many interim capability enhancements as possible and experience in this field might to some extent shape the ultimate replacement for the tank itself.

While the future design of the MBT may be affected by new technologies such as surveillance from space, Unmanned Aerial Vehicles and attack from complex unseen helicopter mounted or seeker weapons, the military will continue to require a mechanism to verify and occupy territory. This force, however small or specialised will require personnel who will need the protection, lethality and mobility which we have come to look upon as the role of the cavalry in both attack and reconnaissance. This assumption until history proves it wrong, suggests that the spirit and elan we have come to expect of the Armoured Corps will still have a major role in the Army of the 21st Century

In the less predictable post Cold War security climate, many countries of concern have biological or chemical weapons capabilities. It is possible that such weapons may also be used by terrorist non-state actors. NBC defence is thus an essential element of Force Protection. It is necessary for a force to prepare and conduct a comprehensive series of measures to ensure that it can not only survive attack by NBC weapons, or from the effects of other toxic hazards in the environment, but also to continue to operate, and fight, thereafter. This requirement is not only important to the accomplishment of armoured and armoured reconnaissance missions, but also to those conducted by any element of the Army deployed in conditions where there is a NBC threat. Director Royal Armoured Corps (DRAC) advises and assists the Army in preparing for this eventuality.

Organisation

The RAC is composed of 12 regular regiments (including the two regiments of the Household Cavalry, discussed below) and four reserve Yeomanry regiments in the TA. Apart from the Royal Tank Regiment, which was formed in the First World War with the specific task of fighting in armoured vehicles, the regular element of the RAC is provided by those regiments which formed the mounted units of the pre-mechanised era. The Yeomanry regiments are tasked with providing contingent component increments for operations to the regular regiments in each of the roles of Armour, Reconnaissance, NBC and Armour Replacement.

Although very much part of the RAC as an 'Arm', the Household Cavalry (HCav) is a discrete corps consisting of two regiments. The Household Cavalry Mounted Regiment (HCMR), which is permanently stationed in London, has the task of providing mounted troops for state ceremonial functions. The Household Cavalry Regiment (HCR) is stationed in Windsor. It is a Formation Reconnaissance (FR) Regiment that plays a full role in operational and training activity within the Field Army. Officers and soldiers from the

Household Cavalry are posted between the two regiments as needs dictate. (For general purposes, including this publication, the term RAC includes the HCav.)

Under the Future Army Structure (FAS) proposals the following changes will affect the RAC.

a.) One Challenger 2 Regiment will re-role to become a Formation Reconnaissance Regiment.
b.) Three Challenger 2 squadrons will be converted to become three Interim Medium Armour Squadrons.
c.) A Command and Support Squadron will be established for each Formation Reconnaissance regiment.

Following FAS changes we believe that the 11 regular field force units of the RAC will be deployed as follows:

a.) *In Germany.* Three Armoured Regiments and two FR Regiments stationed in:

- Fallingbostel   (Armd Regt)
- Munster   (Armd Regt)
- Sennelager   (Armd Regt)
- Hohne   (FR Regt)
- Osnabruck   (FR Regt)

b.) *In the UK.* One Armoured Regiment, four FR Regiments and the Joint NBC Regiment stationed in:

- Catterick (FR Regiment)
- Tidworth (Armoured Regiment)
- Windsor (FR Regiment – HCR)
- Swanton Morley (FR Regiment)
- RAF Honington (Jt NBC Regiment)

Note: The Household Cavalry Mounted Regiment is permanently stationed in London.

1 RTR have become the first Army element of a new Joint NBC Regiment. This role requires two NBC Defence squadrons, whilst the third remains as an armoured squadron with the Land Warfare Training Centre Battlegroup at Warminster in Wiltshire. The Joint NBC Regiment supports all existing plans for NBC defence throughout any future joint force actions, as well as for the British Army. In peace this regiment could be used to support action following radiological accidents and chemical spills. The core element of this new regiment is the 11 × NBC Fuchs reconnaissance vehicles that were supplied to the British Army during the 1990 Gulf War. These specialist vehicles are divided into reconnaissance and detection troops across three small squadrons and are equipped with the joint US/UK Interim Biological Detection System (IBDS), the British version of which was developed at the Chemical Defence Establishment at Porton Down in Wiltshire.

The Future

The argument that 'the days of the tank are over' has been around for many years, and certainly since the appearance of the man-portable guided missile in large numbers such as during the Yom Kippur war. The advent of the highly capable Attack Helicopter and long-range, smart top-attack precision munitions have only added to this debate. However, tanks remain in the world in large numbers – at least 100,000 by current estimates – and in a surprisingly large number of countries. Whilst the supremacy of armour on the modern battlefield will continue to be challenged by ever more sophisticated anti-tank systems, the requirement for highly mobile, protected direct firepower that can operate in all conditions and climates will remain an enduring requirement to support the infantry. It is this 'endurance' characteristic and the ability to operate in all circumstances which is unique and is not shared by helicopters and aircraft.

What is certain to change is the shape and size of future tanks. The key is that new technology will allow protection to be delivered in quite different ways. Traditionally, protection has been provided through ballistic armour which, because of its weight, has to be optimised over a relatively narrow frontal arc, with reduced protection on the sides, top rear and belly. Thus full protection is only possible on a small proportion of the total surface area. In the future a more holistic approach is likely to incorporate a wide range of 'survivability' characteristics in view of the three-dimensional and all round threat. These measures include: signature reduction in all aspects – acoustic, visual, thermal, radar cross-section etc; suites of active and passive defensive aids and electro-optic countermeasures; and inherent redundancy in vehicle design and crew i.e. the ability to sustain considerable damage yet be able to continue fighting. The concept is based on a theory of *'don't be detected – if detected, don't be acquired – if acquired, don't be hit – if hit, don't be penetrated – if penetrated, don't be killed'*. Such an approach is likely to see future tanks of much smaller design and of significantly lesser weight. In turn, reduced weight and size will improve mobility and enable armour to be deployed more rapidly, strategically if necessary, whilst also reducing the very considerable mobility and logistic support that the heavy 60–70 tonne MBTs tanks of today require.

In terms of firepower, smart, extended range munitions such as fire and forget Gun Launched Anti-tank Guided Missiles, pre-programmable ammunition and other novel natures are all likely to increase the potency of armour. In coming to a balanced view on the future of the tank, the heavy modern tank of today has as much in common with the Mark V tank of 1916 as it will have with it's successor in 2030.

Digitisation of the future battlefield has been identified as essential, but base architecture programmes essential for the target data transmission through battlefield management systems is currently running some ten to fifteen years behind schedule. This time lag may enable the tank in its present form to survive for much longer than many analysts had previously predicted.

As we enter the 21st Century, we see the major defence orientated countries of the world undergoing a major doctrinal and conceptual rethink based on the information age, embracing new IT and digital technology capabilities. The future, however, always has its roots in the present and while the large fleets of tanks we now have may be more visible from space, and more difficult to protect from remotely fired missiles and guns, the armies who have them will continue to explore and exploit armoured 'stretch' technologies to ensure their armoured capability is credible until successor technologies appear in service.

In terms of NBC defence, there will be an increasing requirement to provide a detection capability, coupled with the rapid passage of NBC hazard information. Such assets should be capable of matching the performance of other reconnaissance troops. Whilst detection may remain a core reconnaissance skill, in depth identification and analysis will be required, provided by a range of vehicles across the joint battlespace. The need to conduct rapid and efficient decontamination will remain. These capabilities must be supported by a robust suite of other NBC defensive measures designed to minimise casualties whilst maximising operational efficiency.

Formation Reconnaissance Regiment

Following the FAS, Formation Reconnaissance will be re-organised to provide five regular regiments. Formation Reconnaissance regiments are usually under the direct command of a divisional headquarters but may be under its command of a brigade headquarters. Their more usual task in a defensive scenario is to identify the direction and strength of the enemy thrusts, impose maximum delay and damage to the enemy's reconnaissance forces while allowing main forces to manoeuvre to combat the threat. They would be assisted in such a task by using their own organic long range anti-tank guided weapons (the Swingfire missile on CVR(T) Striker) and other assets that might be attached such as anti-tank helicopters (Lynx with TOW and perhaps Apache Longbow (WAH64D) in the future). In support would be the indirect fire guns (AS90) and Multiple Launch Rocket System (MLRS) of the divisional artillery, and an air defended area (ADA) maintained by Rapier and Stormer HVM air defence missiles.

The basic task of Formation Reconnaissance is to obtain accurate information about the enemy and develop an intelligence picture in their areas of responsibility for their superior commanders in the chain-of- command, as quickly as possible.

Organisation Charts

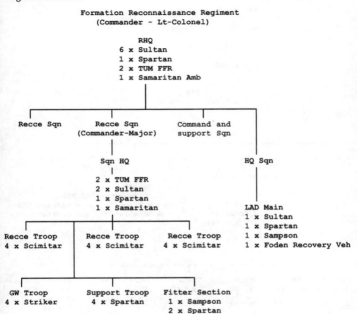

```
            Formation Reconnaissance Regiment
               (Commander - Lt-Colonel)

                         RHQ
                     6 x Sultan
                     1 x Spartan
                     2 x TUM FFR
                     1 x Samaritan Amb


   Recce Sqn      Recce Sqn         Command and
                (Commander-Major)   support Sqn

                    Sqn HQ                       HQ Sqn
                 2 x TUM FFR
                 2 x Sultan
                 1 x Spartan
                 1 x Samaritan                LAD Main
                                            1 x Sultan
                                            1 x Spartan
                                            1 x Sampson
                                            1 x Foden Recovery Veh

 Recce Troop    Recce Troop    Recce Troop
 4 x Scimitar   4 x Scimitar   4 x Scimitar


 GW Troop       Support Troop   Fitter Section
 4 x Striker    4 x Spartan     1 x Sampson
                                2 x Spartan
```

Notes:

(1) Full wartime establishment is approximately 600 all ranks.

(2) Under the 2004 FAS proposals a Command and Support Squadron (to include a Ground Surveillance Troop) will be established for each Formation Reconnaissance regiment. Expect this squadron to have a TACF/FAC party; Surveillance troop and an NBC troop.

Armoured Regiment Organisation Chart

The following diagram shows the current structure of an Armoured Regiment equipped with Challenger 2. Regiments equipped with Challenger 2 (CR2) have four 'sabre' squadrons with an all up total of 58 tanks in each regiment when deployed for war.

Armoured Regiment

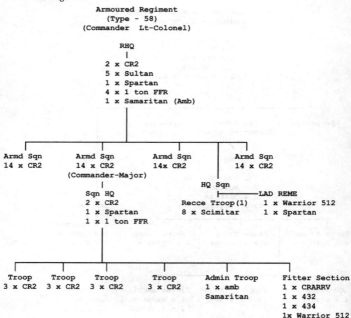

Notes:

(1) Recce Troop under direct command of CO in the field.

(2) Tank Troop commanded by 2Lt/Lt with Troop Sergeant as 2ic in own tank. The third tank is commanded by a Corporal.

(3) Totals: 58 × CR2, 8 × SCIMITAR, 4 × CRARV. Total strength for war is approx 550.

(4) A Challenger 2 has a crew of 4 – Commander, Driver, Gunner and Loader/Operator.

(5) Under FAS proposals the fourth Armoured Regiment CR2 Squadron will be replaced by an Interim Medium Armour Squadron based on a similar structure to a CR2 Squadron but equipped with CVR(T) Scimitar.

Joint Nuclear, Biological and Chemical Regiment (Jt NBC Regt)

Following the Strategic Defence Review, the Jt NBC Regt was created and is based at RAF Honington, Suffolk. The Regiment is composed of two squadrons from 1 RTR and 27 Sqn RAF Regiment plus supporting staff from other army units. The Jt NBC Regt fields specialist NBC defence equipment, specifically the Fuchs nuclear and chemical reconnaissance and survey vehicle, the Prototype Biological Detection System (PBDS) and the Multi-Purpose Decontamination System (MPDS). The PBDS is due to be replaced by greater numbers of a new and more capable Integrated Biological Detection System (IBDS) within the next few years. The Regiment will be an essential element of any joint force operation where there is an NBC threat, enhancing the integral NBC defence capabilities of the remainder of the force. Not only will the Regiment support Army formations but also other vital assets such as air bases, logistic areas and key lines of communication.

In peace the Army may be asked to provide Military Assistance to the Civil Authorities. In these circumstances, the Joint NBC Regiment may be called on to deal with radiological, biological or chemical hazards. The Joint NBC Regiment offers a new and challenging role to the Armoured Corps, requiring new skills, innovative ideas and a significant intellectual challenge. The Regiment provides a firm basis on which to develop the Joint NBC defence capability in the future.

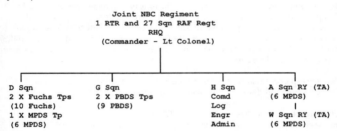

```
                    Joint NBC Regiment
                 1 RTR and 27 Sqn RAF Regt
                            RHQ
                 (Commander - Lt Colonel)



  D Sqn              G Sqn           H Sqn         A Sqn RY (TA)
  2 X Fuchs Tps      2 X PBDS Tps    Comd          (6 MPDS)
  (10 Fuchs)         (9 PBDS)        Log
  1 X MPDS Tp                        Engr          W Sqn RY (TA)
  (6 MPDS)                           Admin         (6 MPDS)
```

Organisation Chart
Challenger 2
386 Challenger 2 available. Crew 4; Length Gun Forward 11.75 m; Height 3.04 m; Width 4.2 m with applique armour; Ground Clearance 0.51 m; Combat Weight 66.5 tonnes- MLC 76; Main Armament 1 × 120 mm L30 CHARM Gun; Ammunition Carried max 49 rounds stowed – APFSDS, HESH and Smoke; Secondary Armament Co-axial 7.62 mm Chain Gun; Loaders pintle mounted 7.62 mm GPMG; Ammunition Carried 4000 rounds 7.62 mm; Engine CV12 12 cylinder – Auxiliary Power Unit 4-stroke diesel; Gearbox TN54 epicyclic – 6 forward gears and 2 reverse; Road Speed 59 kph; Cross-Country Speed 40 kph; Fuel Capacity 1,592 litres usable internal plus 2 × 175 litre external fuel drums.

Challenger 2 was manufactured by Vickers Defence Systems and production was undertaken at their factories in Newcastle-Upon-Tyne and Leeds. At 1999 prices Challenger 2 is believed to cost £4 million per vehicle.

Although the hull and automotive parts of the Challenger 2 are based upon that of its predecessor Challenger 1, the new tank incorporates over 150 improvements which have achieved substantially increased reliability and ease of maintenance. The Challenger 2 turret is, however, of a totally new design. The vehicle has a crew of four-commander, gunner, loader/signaller and driver and is equipped with a 120 mm rifled Royal Ordnance L30 gun firing all current tank ammunition natures plus the new depleted uranium (DU) round with a stick charge propellant system.

The design of the turret incorporates several of the significant features that Vickers had developed for its Mk 7 MBT (a Vickers turret on a Leopard 2 chassis). The central feature is an entirely new fire control system based on the Ballistic Control System developed by Computing Devices Company (Canada) for the US Army's M1A1 MBT. This second generation computer incorporates dual 32-bit processors with a MIL STD1553B databus and has sufficient growth potential to accept Battlefield Information Control System (BICS) functions and navigation aids (a GPS satnav system). The armour is an uprated version of Challenger 1's Chobham armour.

The only export order so far is an Omani order for 38 × Challenger which includes 2 × Driver Training Vehicles and 4 × Challenger Armoured Repair and Recovery Vehicles.

Challenger Repair and Recovery Vehicle (CRARV)
(80 In Service) Crew 3; Length 9.59 m; Operating Width 3.62 m; Height 3.005 m; Ground Clearance 0.5 m; Combat Weight 62,000 kg; Max Road Speed 59 kph; Cross Country Speed 35 kph; Fording 1.07 m; Trench Crossing 2.3 m; Crane – Max Lift 6,500 kg at 4.9 m reach; Engine Perkins CV12 TCA 1200 26.1 V-12 direct injection 4-stroke diesel.

Between 1988 and 1990 the British Army ordered 80 Challenger CRARV in two batches and the contract was completed with the last vehicles bought into service during 1983. A 'Type 58' tank Challenger 2 Regiment has 5 × CRARRV, one with each sabre squadron and one with the REME Light Aid Detachment (LAD).

The vehicle has a crew of three plus additional space in a separate compartment for another two REME fitters. The vehicle is fitted with two winches (main and auxiliary) plus an Atlas hydraulically operated crane capable of lifting a complete Challenger 2 powerpack. The front dozer blade can be used as a stabiliser blade for the crane or as a simple earth anchor.

Fv 107 Scimitar
(Approx 320 available): Armament 1 × 30 mm Rarden L21 Gun; 1 × 7.62 mm Machine Gun; 2 × 4 barrel smoke dischargers; Engine B6 Cummins diesel; Fuel Capacity 423 litres; Max Road Speed 80 kph; Weight loaded 7,750 kg; Length 4.9 m; Height 2.096 m; Width 2.2 m; Ground Clearance 0.35 m; Road Range 644 km; Crew 3; Ammunition Capacity 30 mm –

160 rounds; 7.62 mm – 3,000 rounds; Main Armament Elevation – 10 degrees to + 35 degrees.

CVR(T) Scimitar is the mainstay reconnaissance vehicle with which all Formation Reconnaissance regiments are equipped as well as all Close Reconnaissance troops and platoons of Armoured and Mechanized Battlegroups. The Scimitar is an ideal reconnaissance vehicle, mobile and fast with good communications and excellent viewing equipment.

Fv 102 CVR(T) Striker

(Approx 54 in service) Armament 10 × Swingfire Missiles: 1 × 7.62 mm Machine Gun: 2 × 4 barrel smoke dischargers. Engine: Jaguar J 60 replaced by B6 Cummins diesel: Fuel Capacity 350 litres: Max Road Speed 80 kph: Road Range 483 km: Length 4.8 m: Height 2.2 m: Width 2.2 m: Ground Clearance 0.35 m: Ammunition Capacity 3,000 rounds of 7.62 mm: Main Armament Traverse 53 degrees left, 55 degrees right.

Striker is one of the family of the CVR(T) vehicles (Combat Vehicle Reconnaissance Tracked) which includes Scimitar, Spartan, Sultan, Samson and Samaritan. Striker carries 10 Swingfire anti-tank missiles with a range of up to 4,000 metres. Five of these missiles are carried in bins on top of the vehicle, which can be lowered when the system is not expected to be in action. One significant drawback to the system is the reload operation, which requires a crewman to reload the missile bins from outside the vehicle. There is also a separated sight available which enables the launch vehicle to be hidden in dead ground, and the operator to fire and control the flight of the missile from a position up to 100 m away from the launch vehicle.

The striker system enables a fast, hard hitting anti-tank missile launch platform to keep up with the latest MBTs. Striker is to be found in the Formation Reconnaissance regiment which has a troop of four vehicles in each of its three reconnaissance squadrons. Striker is likely to be replaced by the Future Rapid Effect System (FRES) variant towards the end of the decade.

Swingfire Data

Type – Anti Tank Guided Missile: Wire Guided; Command to line of sight: Length of Missile 1.06 m: Body Diameter 37.3 cm: Warhead Hollow Charge HE: Propellant Solid Fuel: Weight of Missile 37 kg: Minimum Range 150 m: Maximum Range 4,000 m.

Fuchs

(11 In Service) Road Range 800 kms; Crew 2; Operational Weight 17,000 kg; Length 6.83 m; Width 2.98 m; Height 2.30 m; Road Speed 105 kph; Engine Mercedes-Benz Model OM-402A V-8 liquid cooled diesel; Armament 1 × 7.62 mm MG; 6 × Smoke Dischargers.

Manufactured by the German company Thyssen-Henschel, Fuchs can detect gamma radiation and identify either surface deposits of chemical agents or chemical vapour. The vehicle is equipped with a Global Positioning System (GPS) and provides the crew with integral collective protection.

Prototype Biological Detection System (PBDS)

PBDS has been developed as the UK's current system to detect and identify biological agents. It consists of a detection suite contained in a box-body mounted on a Bedford 4 tonne chassis. A generator is towed to power the system. PBDS is equipped with integral collective protection, a communications suite and GPS.

Multi-Purpose Decontamination System (MPDS)

MPDS is a diesel driven, high pressure cleaning and decontamination system. It consists of two KARCHER water pumps, capable of spraying water at various temperatures, ranging from cold through to steam, and a 9000 litre water tank mounted on a DROPS flatrack. The system is capable of drawing water (including seawater) from either an open source or Service sources such as bulk water carriers. The system is operated in conjunction with decontaminents. It can be operated mounted on DROPS or dismounted.

Future Rapid Effect System (FRES)

The FRES requirement is for a family of fighting platforms (including a range of Ground Manoeuvre Reconnaissance roles), which only when integrated with a variety of other capabilities produces a complete system of systems. It will seek to make full use of any intelligence-gathering capabilities that are, or become, available. However, the project is still in the early stages of its Assessment Phase and therefore the precise nature of the interface with other capabilities is not yet determined.

Following acceptance into service it is expected that there will be three FRES-equipped brigades and this will enable the UK to deploy armoured forces more rapidly in support of national and alliance interests. The exact number of FRES type vehicles to be procured has not yet been determined but it is expected to be at least 2,000 if the current fleet of CVR(T), Saxon and FV432 series vehicles are to be replaced.

A major FRES requirement is that it should be able to be transported in a C-130 Hercules aircraft which will place severe constraints on the platform weight and eventual design. As yet there does not appear to have been a decision as to whether FRES will be tracked or wheeled. FRES vehicle groups are based around the following requirements:

Group 1 FRES utility vehicles are expected to include protected mobility, light armoured support, command-and-control, medical, equipment support and possibly a driver-training vehicle.

Group 2 FRES vehicles will cover intelligence, surveillance, target acquisition and reconnaissance (ISTAR) and fire control. This group will include vehicles that also improve indirect fire support, direct-fire support, indirect fire control, engineer reconnaissance, ground-based surveillance, scout, anti-tank guided weapon and an enhanced protected mobility vehicle.

Group 3 FRES vehicles will include the formation communications variants (Falcon) and electronic warfare versions (Soothsayer). Variants of the former are expected to include Bowman gateway and a variety of Falcon and Wasp capable platforms.

Group 4 FRES vehicles will be formation force protection and manoeuvre support and will include an armoured vehicle launched bridge, armoured vehicle engineer, armoured engineer tractor and CBRN reconnaissance and survey.

Group 5 FRES vehicles currently consists of a remotely delivered mine system to replace the current Shielder, based on a Stormer chasis.

If the FRES programme goes ahead we would expect to see the first vehicles accepted into service around 2012.

Panther Command Liaison Vehicle (Panther CLV)

The UK MoD announced in July 2003 that the BAE Systems Land Systems (formerly Alvis) Multirole Light Vehicle (MLV) had been selected as the British Army's Future Command and Liaison Vehicle (FCLV). The first procurement contract was signed in November 2003 for an initial 401 vehicles. The vehicle has been named the Panther Command and Liaison Vehicle (CLV). In June 2004, Thales Defence Optronics was selected to provide the Driver's Vision Enhancer (DVE) for the Panther CLV. Thales' DVE driver's sight is based on an uncooled thermal imager.

Panther CLV is based on a design by Iveco Defence Vehicles Division of Italy and the vehicles will be manufactured during the period 2006 to 2009. A Development and Demonstration contract covers the build and test of seven vehicles by 2005, with a planned in-service date of 2007. Acquisition cost for some 400 vehicles is £193 million spread over five years.

The current gross vehicle weight of a Panther CLV is 7.1 tonnes. The vehicle is to be air transportable, underslung beneath a Chinook helicopter or carried inside C130, C17 and A400M aircraft.

Panther CLV will replace a range of vehicles which are reaching the end of their operational lives, for example the Land Rover, Saxon, some FV432 and a number of Combat Vehicle (Reconnaissance) Tracked. The vehicles will also enter service with the Royal Air Force Regiment.

CHAPTER 5 – INFANTRY

Regiments and Battalions

The British Infantry is based on the well tried and tested Regimental System, which has proved to be repeatedly successful on operations over the years. It is currently based on Regiments, some of which have one or more regular battalions and most have associated TA battalions. The esprit de corps of the Regimental system is maintained in the names and titles of British Infantry Regiments handed down through history, with a tradition of courage in battle. For manning purposes Infantry Regiments are grouped within administrative 'Divisions'. These are no longer field formations but represent original historical groupings based on recruiting geography.

The 'Division' of Infantry is an organisation that is responsible for all aspects of military administration, from recruiting, manning and promotions for individuals in the regiments under its wing, to the longer term planning required to ensure continuity and cohesion. Divisions of Infantry have no operational command over their regiments, and should not be confused with the remaining operational divisions, such as 1(UK) Armoured Division and 3(UK) Division.

Under the terms of the Future Army Structure (FAS) the infantry will be restructured as follows:

a. The number of Regular Line Infantry battalions will reduce by four (from 40 to 36 by April 2008), with the manpower and structure of one of the four being used as the core of a new Joint Special Forces Support Group.
b. A new Regimental system and structure will be adopted over the coming years. This will be based on large, multi battalion regiments within a Divisional structure.
c. Arms Plotting will cease, limited relocations will occur for battalions in particular roles/ locations.
d. There will be an increase from 19 (48%) to 23 (64%) of Infantry battalions in All Arms brigades.
e. The 9th platoon in Armoured Infantry battalions will be decaderised.
f. Enhancements will be made to reconnaissance platoons.
g. Fire Support platoons will be established with a mix of AGL and GPMG.

Infantry Structure in January 2005

During early January 2005 the Administrative 'Divisions' of Infantry were structured as follows:

The Guards Division   – 5 regular battalions
The Scottish Division   – 6 regular battalions
The Queen's Division   – 6 regular battalions
The King's Division   – 6 regular battalions
The Prince of Wales Division   – 7 regular battalions
The Light Division   – 4 regular battalions

Not administered by 'Divisions' of Infantry but operating under their own similar administrative arrangements were the following:

The Parachute Regiment	– 3 regular battalions
The Brigade of Gurkhas	– 2 regular battalions
The Royal Irish Regiment	– 1 regular battalion (plus 3 Home Service battalions)

TA battalions were under the administrative command of the following:

The Guards Division	– Nil
The Scottish Division	– 2 TA battalions
The Queen's Division	– 3 TA battalions
The King's Division	– 3 TA battalions
The Prince of Wales Division	– 3 TA battalions
The Light Division	– 2 TA battalions
The Parachute Regiment	– 1 TA battalions
The Royal Irish Regiment	– 1 TA battalion
The Royal Gibraltar Regiment	– 1 composite battalion

In total the British Army had 40 regular battalions available for service and this total combined with the 15 TA battalions (excluding the Royal Gibraltar Regiment) could have given a mobilisation strength of 55 infantry battalions.

Outside the above listed Regiments are three companies of guardsmen each of 110 men, who are provided to supplement the Household Division Regiments while on public duties in London. This allows Regiments of the Foot Guards to continue to carry out normal training on roulement from guard duties. Gibraltar also has its own single battalion of the Royal Gibraltar Regiment comprising one regular and two volunteer companies.

At the beginning of 2005 the infantry are located as follows:

United Kingdom	31 battalions (4 Resident in Northern Ireland)
Germany	6 battalions
Iraq	5 battalions on detachment
Cyprus	2 battalions
Falkland Islands	1 company group on detachment
Bosnia	1 battalion (-) two companies on detachment
Kosovo	1 company on detachment
Brunei	1 battalion (Gurkha)
Afghanistan	1 battalion on detachment

The establishment and strength of each of the 38 British infantry battalions (i.e. excluding the Gurkhas) are as shown in the following table:

Battalion	Establishment (November 2004)	Strength (November 2004)
The Guards Division		
1 Grenadier Guards	560	650
1 Coldstream Guards	585	660
1 Scots Guards	620	620
1 Irish Guards	560	515
1 Welsh Guards	560	545
The Scottish Division		
1 Royal Scots	560	480
1 Royal Highland Fusiliers	560	515
1 King's Own Scottish Borderers	560	490
1 Black Watch	605	545
1 Argyll and Sutherland Highlanders	580	485
1 Highlanders	620	490
The Queen's Division		
1 Princess of Wales's Royal Regiment	620	615
2 Princess of Wales's Royal Regiment	560	550
1 Royal Regiment of Fusiliers	620	585
2 Royal Regiment of Fusiliers	560	530
1 Royal Anglian Regiment	585	565
2 Royal Anglian Regiment	560	550
The King's Division		
1 King's Own Royal Border Regiment	560	500
1 King's Regiment	620	540
1 Prince of Wales's Own Regiment	585	575
1 Green Howards	560	510
1 Queen's Lancashire Regiment	560	565
1 Duke of Wellington's Regiment	620	515
The Prince of Wales's Division		
1 Devonshire and Dorset Regiment	585	540
1 Cheshire Regiment	585	505
1 Royal Welch Fusiliers	585	550
1 Royal Regiment of Wales	620	585
Royal Gloucestershire, Berkshire and Wiltshire Regiment	560	545
1 Worcestershire and Sherwood Foresters Regiment	560	505
1 Staffordshire Regiment	620	540

The Light Division
1 Light Infantry	620	520
2 Light Infantry	560	530
1 Royal Green Jackets	560	535
2 Royal Green Jackets	560	530

The Parachute Regiment
1 Para	580	570
2 Para	580	540
3 Para	580	540

The Royal Irish Regiment
1 Royal Irish Regiment	560	500
	22095	20630

Note: The establishment figures refer to the number of posts within a battalion that may be filled by infantry personnel (officers and soldiers). Therefore, it excludes posts that are filled by attached personnel of other Arms and Services such as cooks, clerks, etc. Establishments will also vary depending on the particular role of a battalion; for example, armoured infantry battalions have larger establishments than light role infantry battalions. The figures are rounded to the nearest five.

The strength figures refer to actual numbers of trained infantry personnel within a battalion. To allow for direct comparison with the establishment, figures on strength do not include officers and soldiers who are posted to the battalion but who are serving away from the battalion, nor personnel from other Arms and Services who are attached to the battalion.

The excess in strength compared to establishment for the Grenadier Guards, Coldstream Guards and Scots Guards is accounted for by the Public Duty companies currently attached to each of these battalions. (Source UK MoD)

Overall trained infantry strength at 1 July 2004 was:

Rank	Trained Officers
Lt Colonel	360
Lt Colonel (Special List)	5
Major	1,020
Captain	1,025
Lieutenant	495
Second Lieutenant	50
Officer Total	2,995

Other Ranks

WO1	150
WO2	855
SSGT	955
SGT	1,825
CPL	3,615
LCPL	3,765
PTE	11,615
Soldier Total	22,780
Total Infantry Trained Strength	**25,735**

Note: Totals have been rounded to the nearest five and include Gurkhas and infantry soldiers who are not actually serving in infantry battalions. (Source UK MoD)

Future Infantry Structure

Inside the overall Future Army Structure, the Future Infantry Structure has proposed that the reduction of four battalions will be achieved in the following way:

a. One battalion from the Scottish Division by the union of 1 RS and 1 KOSB.

b. One battalion from the King's Division by merging 1 KORBR, 1 KINGS and 1 QLR to form two new battalions of The King's Lancashire and Border Regiment.

c. Merging 1 RGBW with 1 D&D who together become part of the Light Infantry.

d. Removing the 1st Bn The Parachute Regiment from the infantry structure and using it as the core of a new, tri-service Joint Special Forces Support Group (JSFSG).

By 2008 the new regular infantry structure should therefore resemble the following:

The Guards Division

1st Bn Grenadier Guards
1st Bn Coldstream Guards
1st Bn Scots Guards
1st Bn Irish Guards
1st Bn Welsh Guards
Nijmegen Company Grenadier Guards
7 Company Coldstream Guards
F Company Scots Guards

The Scottish Division

1st Bn The Royal Regiment of Scotland (The Royal Scots and King's Own Scottish Borderers)
2nd Bn The Royal Regiment of Scotland (The Royal Highland Fusiliers)
3rd Bn The Royal Regiment of Scotland (The Black Watch)
4th Bn The Royal Regiment of Scotland (The Highlanders)
5th Bn The Royal Regiment of Scotland (The Argyll & Sutherland Highlanders)

The Queen's Division
1st Bn The Princess of Wales's Royal Regiment
2nd Bn The Princess of Wales's Royal Regiment
1st Bn The Royal Regiment of Fusiliers
2nd Bn The Royal Regiment of Fusiliers
1st Bn The Royal Anglian Regiment
2nd Bn The Royal Anglian Regiment

The King's Division
1st Bn The Yorkshire Regiment (Prince of Wales's Own)
2nd Bn The Yorkshire Regiment (Green Howards)
3rd Bn The Yorkshire Regiment (Duke of Wellington's)
1st Bn The King's, Lancashire and Border Regiment
2nd Bn The King's, Lancashire and Border Regiment

The Prince of Wales's Division
1st Bn The Royal Welsh (The Royal Welsh Fusiliers)
2nd Bn The Royal Welsh (The Royal Regiment of Wales)
1st Bn The Mercian Regiment (Cheshires)
2nd Bn The Mercian Regiment (Worcesters and Foresters)
3rd Bn The Mercian Regiment (Staffords)

The Light Division
1st Bn The Light Infantry
2nd Bn The Light Infantry
3rd Bn The Light Infantry
1st Bn The Royal Green Jackets
2nd Bn The Royal Green Jackets

The Royal Gurkha Rifles
1st Bn The Royal Gurkha Rifles
2nd Bn The Royal Gurkha Rifles

The Parachute Regiment
1st Bn The Parachute Regiment (Joint Special Forces Support Group)
2nd Bn The Parachute Regiment
3rd Bn The Parachute Regiment

The Royal Irish Regiment
1st Bn The Royal Irish Regiment

Force Operations and Readiness Mechanism (FORM)
Under the Future Army Structure there is a strategy to deliver both training and commitments known as the Force Operations and Readiness Mechanism (FORM); a replacement for the Formation Readiness Cycle. All Army units, including Infantry battalions, will programme their training and operational commitment activities according

to the principles of FORM. This system enables the Army to meet its outputs (force elements ready for both programmed operations and contingent operations/emergency deployments) from within the force structure. The sequence of activity for any one force element, such as an Infantry battalion, is in five separate six month phases:

◆ Phase 1 – Recuperation
◆ Phase 2 – Unit and battlegroup training
◆ Phase 3 – Formation training
◆ Phase 4 – High readiness
◆ Phase 5 – An operational deployment

Infantry entry 2004–2009
The following tables show the latest UK MoD figures for the number of trained officers and soldiers expected to join the infantry over the next five years.

Officers	Financial year				
Method of entry	2004–05	2005–06	2006–07	2007–08	2008–09
Direct entry	165	165	165	165	165
Late entry	31	28	28	28	28
Total	**196**	**193**	**193**	**193**	**193**

Note: Direct entry relates to those who enter the Royal Military Academy Sandhurst direct from education or civilian life. Late entry refers to those who apply for a commission through the ranks.

Soldiers	Financial year				
Category	2004–05	2005–06	2006–07	2007–08	2008–09
Foot Guards	368	405	418	430	430
Line Regiments	2,004	2,200	2,134	2,036	2,036
Parachute Regiment	230	225	221	234	234
Total	**2,582**	**2,830**	**2,780**	**2,700**	**2,700**

Operational units
As explained in Chapter 3, it would be unusual for the Infantry to fight as battalion units especially in armoured or mechanised formations. If the task is appropriate, the HQ of an infantry battalion will become the HQ of a 'battle group', and be provided with armour, artillery, engineers and possibly aviation to enable it to become a balanced Infantry Battle Group. Similarly Infantry companies can be detached to HQs of Armoured Regiments to make up Armoured Battle Groups.

In the pages that follow, the groupings are based on Unit Establishment figures for peace support operations. For Warfighting a pairing mechanism operates which provides augmentation which allows a unit to meet its role. For example, an Armoured Infantry Regiment will receive additional Manoeuvre Support assets and another rifle company to reach its Warfighting Establishment (WFE) of 4 × Companies, 9 × Mortars and 18 × Medium Range Anti-Tank Guided Weapons (ATGW).

Types of Infantry Battalions

Armoured Infantry Battalion – Equipped with Warrior AFV.
Mechanised Infantry Battalion – Equipped with Saxon APC.
Light Role Infantry Battalion – Equipped for General Service.
Air Assault Infantry Battalion – Equipped for Air Mobile Operations

Future TA Infantry

The future TA Infantry structure will be organised to support and complement the regular regimental structure, thereby restoring a true sense of identity at TA battalion level. There will be 14 TA infantry battalions. These will provide reinforcement of the regular infantry for up to 14 unit HQs or, where necessary individual or smaller unit reinforcements.

In addition the new TA Infantry Structure will provide the manpower to include up to seven Defence Troops for Armoured and Formation Reconnaissance Regiments committed to operations. The affiliation of TA battalions will be driven by the revised Future Infantry Structure (FIS), assigning one TA battalion to each new two or three battalion regular regiments, and two TA battalions to a large regular regiment. Restructuring will be conducted on the basis of a minimum of 400 soldiers per battalion. We expect a finalised structure in late 2005.

Armoured Infantry Battalion

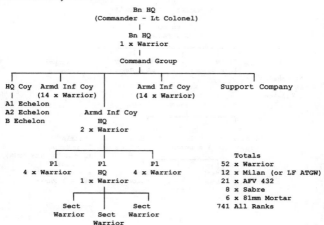

Armoured Infantry Battalion – Support Company

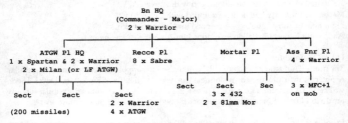

Note: (1) There are 9 × Armoured Infantry Battalions, 6 of which are in Germany with 1 (UK) Armoured Division and the remaining 3 in the UK with 3 (UK) Division. (2) There are plans to replace the remaining AFV 432's on issue to armoured infantry battalions. (3) Another 4 × Milan (or LF ATGW) firing posts are held by the mobilisation section that is only activated in time of deployment for war and personnel will come from the TA.

Mechanised Infantry Battalion

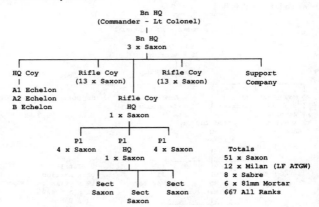

Mechanised Infantry Battalion – Support Company

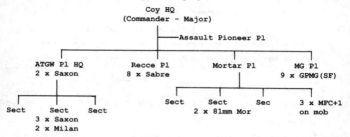

Note: (1) Sabre is a vehicle that has been created by taking a Fox turret, mounting it on a Scorpion chassis and replacing the GPMG with a Chain Gun.

Light Role Infantry Battalion

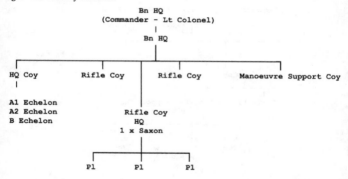

Light Role Infantry Battalion – Support Company

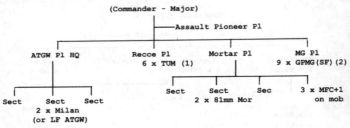

Notes: (1) TUM is the abbreviation for Truck-Utility-Medium; (2) Air Assault Bns have an HMG Pl with 6 × .50 Calibre Machine guns mounted on TUM.

Territorial Army Infantry Battalion

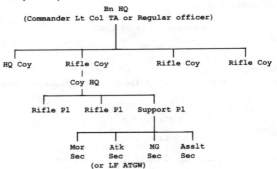

Platoon Organisation

The basic building blocks of the Infantry Battalion are the platoon and the section. Under normal circumstances expect a British infantry platoon to resemble the organisation in the following diagram:

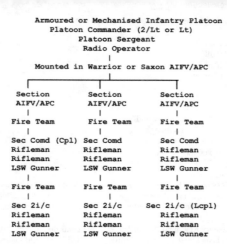

```
              Armoured or Mechanised Infantry Platoon
                   Platoon Commander (2/Lt or Lt)
                        Platoon Sergeant
                        Radio Operator
                              |
                 Mounted in Warrior or Saxon AIFV/APC

    ┌─────────────────────┬─────────────────────┐
  Section               Section               Section
  AIFV/APC              AIFV/APC              AIFV/APC
    |                     |                     |
  Fire Team             Fire Team             Fire Team
    |                     |                     |
  Sec Comd (Cpl)        Sec Comd              Sec Comd
  Rifleman              Rifleman              Rifleman
  Rifleman              Rifleman              Rifleman
  LSW Gunner            LSW Gunner            LSW Gunner
    |                     |                     |
  Fire Team             Fire Team             Fire Team
    |                     |                     |
  Sec 2i/c              Sec 2i/c              Sec 2i/c (Lcpl)
  Rifleman              Rifleman              Rifleman
  Rifleman              Rifleman              Rifleman
  LSW Gunner            LSW Gunner            LSW Gunner
```

Notes:

(1) The whole platoon with the exception of the LSW (Light Support Weapon) gunners are armed with IW SA80 (Individual Weapon).

(2) The APC could be either Warrior or Saxon and possibly AFV 432.

(3) Platoons in armoured or mechanised infantry battalions are armed with the LAW 80 for anti-tank operations. The LAW 80 is issued to other types of infantry battalion when a tank threat exists. LAW 80 is about to be replaced by NLAW.

(4) All riflemen in the Pl carry a rifle grenade sight which can be attached to the SA80. In combat each SA80 user is also issued with two 'Bullet Catcher' rifle grenades. This grenade is simply pushed onto the end of the barrel and an ordinary 5.56 mm round fired into it. The grenade absorbs the bullet without damage and is projected towards the target up to 150 m away.

The Royal Irish Regiment

The Royal Irish Regiment was formed in July 1992 following the merger of the Ulster Defence Regiment and the Royal Irish Rangers. The Royal Irish Regiment is comprised of 1 × General Service, 1 × TA and 3 × Home Service Battalions.

The soldiers of the General Service Battalion (1 Royal Irish) operate as does any other unit of the Regular Army and in early 2003 the battalion was amongst the first British troops that entered Iraq. The Home Service battalions serve only in Northern Ireland except for occasional training overseas and include both full-time and part time soldiers.

Royal Irish Regiment (Home Service) Strength (1 April 2004)

Males	1,910	(Full Time)
Females	190	(Full Time)
Males	1,190	(Part Time)
Females	110	(Part Time)
Total	**3,410**	

General Service	– 1 R Irish
Home Service	– 2 R Irish (Holywood)
	– 3 R Irish (Armagh)
	– 4 R Irish (Omagh)
Territorial Army	– The Rangers (V)

Special Forces

The Special Air Service: The SAS (Special Air Service) whilst not considered as part of the Infantry is established to carry out special operations. SAS soldiers are selected from other branches of the Army after exhaustive selection tests. There are two regiments of TA SAS.

Special Reconnaissance Regiment (SRR): This Regiment was declared operational on 6 April 2005 and has been formed to meet a growing worldwide demand for special reconnaissance capability.

The Regiment will ensure improved support to international expeditionary operations and will provide a wide range of specialist skills and activities related to covert surveillance. The SRR will draw personnel from existing capabilities and recruit new volunteers from serving members of the Armed Forces where necessary. Due to the specialist nature of the unit it will come under the command of Director Special Forces and be a part of the UK Special Forces group.

Joint Special Forces Support Group

Under the Future Army Structuring plans 1 Para will re-role as a 'Ranger' type or Special Forces Support Group available for operations from 2008.

It is believed that the Special Forces Support Group will be located at St Athan, in South Wales, close to the SAS headquarters in Hereford. The force will be composed of around 450 Parachute Regiment soldiers and 200 personnel from both the Royal Marines and the RAF Regiment.

Soldiers wishing to become part of the Special Forces Support Group will need to be able to offer more than the average infantryman but the entrance requirements will be different from those of the SAS.

AFV 432

(Aprox 1,467 in service of which 811 are base line vehicles – models include command vehicles, ambulances, and 81 mm mortar carriers). Crew 2 (Commander and Driver): Weight loaded 15,280 kg: Length 5.25 m: Width 2.8 m: Height 2.28 m: Ground Pressure 0.78 kg km squared: Armament 1 × 7.62 Machine Gun: 2 × 3 barrel smoke dischargers: Engine Rolls Royce K60 No.4 Mark 1–4: Engine Power 240 bhp: Fuel Capacity 454 litres: Max Road Speed 52 kph: Road Range 580 km: Vertical Obstacle 0.9 m: Trench Crossing 2.05 m: Gradient 60 degrees: Carries up to 10 men : Armour 12.7 mm max.

The vehicle is NBC proof and when necessary can be converted for swimming when it has a water speed of 6 kph. Properly maintained it is a rugged and reliable vehicle with a good cross-country performance. The most serious drawback is the lack of vision ports for the crew and their subsequent disorientation after dismounting.

The FV 430 family of vehicles is rapidly approaching the end of its service life.

MCV – 80 Fv 510 (Warrior)

(736 available – possibly 667 in service). Weight loaded 24,500 kg: length 6.34 m: Height to turret top 2.78 m: Width 3.0 m: Ground Clearance 0.5 m: Max Road Speed 75 kph: Road Range 500 km: Engine Rolls Royce CV8 diesel: Horsepower 550 hp: Crew 3 (carries 7 infantry soldiers): Armament L21 30 mm Rarden Cannon: Coaxial EX-34 7.62 mm Hughes Chain Gun: Smoke Dischargers Royal Ordnance Visual and Infra Red Screening Smoke (VIRSS).

Warrior is an armoured infantry fighting vehicle (AIFV) that replaced the AFV 432 in the armoured infantry battalions. The original buy of Warrior was reduced to 789 units. Of this total the vast majority had been delivered by early 1995 and the vehicle is in service with three armoured infantry battalions in the UK with 3 (UK) Div and six armoured infantry battalions in Germany with 1 (UK) Armd Div.

Warrior armed with the 30 mm Rarden cannon gives the crew a good chance of destroying enemy APC's at ranges of up to 1,500 m and the vehicle carries a crew of three and seven dismounted infantry.

The vehicle is NBC proof, and a full range of night vision equipment is included as standard.

The vehicle has seen successful operational service in the Gulf (1991), with British troops serving in the Balkans and more recently in Iraq. The vehicle has proven protection against mines, and there is dramatic BBC TV footage of a Warrior running over a Serbian anti-tank mine with little or no serious damage to the vehicle or crew .

The hull and mechanical components of Warrior are exceptional and few other vehicles in the world can match it for reliability and performance. The Warrior armament fire control system and electronics require upgrading if the vehicle is to remain in service to 2025 as intended.

A Warrior Mid-Life Improvement Programme is due to be implemented between 2007 and 2012. This should provide a new power pack, vehtronics enhancement, a digital fire control system (FCS) and a modern medium calibre cannon system. This extension of capability for Warrior will provide the necessary lead time for the introduction of future advanced capability systems vehicles to replace both Challenger 2 and Warrior.

The future digitisation programme in-service date (ISD) has slid to around 2017. Current thinking suggests that the British Army may replace existing rifle platoon Warrior with the improved Warrior 2000. This would release existing Warrior to be refitted to fulfil roles currently carried out by ageing and obsolescent FV 432s. This plan would create a new Battalion Assault Support Vehicle (BASV) which can carry Manoeuvre Support elements, principally 81 mm mortars, at the same pace as the Warrior fighting vehicles.

Numbers in UK service are believed to include 482 × Warrior Basic; 59 × Warrior RA; 126 × Warrior Rec and Rep. The Kuwait MoD has signed a contract for the purchase of 230 Warrior vehicles some of which are Recce vehicles armed with a 90 mm Cockerill gun.

AFV 103 Spartan
(637 in service) Crew 3: Weight 8,172 kg: Length 5.12 m: Height 2.26 m: Width 2.26 m: Ground Clearance 0.35 m: Max Road Speed 80 kph: Road Range 483 kms: Engine Jaguar J60 No.1 Mark 100B: Engine Power 190 bhp: Fuel Capacity 386 litres: Ammunition Carried 3,000 rounds of 7.62 mm: Armament 1 × 7.62 Machine Gun.

Spartan is the APC of the Combat Vehicle Reconnaissance Tracked (CVRT) series of vehicles, which included Fv 101 Scorpion, Fv 102 Striker, Fv 104 Samaritan, Fv 105 Sultan, Fv 106 Sampson and Fv 107 Scimitar. Spartan is a very small APC that can only carry four men in addition to the crew of three. It is therefore used to carry small specialised groups such as the reconnaissance teams, air defence sections, mortar fire controllers and ambush parties.

Samaritan, Sultan and Sampson are also APC type vehicles, Samaritan is the CVRT ambulance vehicle, Sultan is the armoured command vehicle and Sampson is an armoured recovery vehicle.

Spartan, like FV 432 is likely to be replaced in some roles by the future Multi Role Armoured Vehicle (MRAV) and in other roles by the Future Command and Liaison Vehicle (FCLV).

Spartan is in service with the following nations:
Belgium – 266
Oman – 6
Philippines – 7.

Sabre
(136 in service) As part of the UK MoDs CVR(T) rationalisation programme both the tracked Scorpion with its 76 mm gun and the wheeled Fox with its 30 mm Rarden Cannon were withdrawn from service and a hybrid vehicle – Sabre produced. Essentially Sabre consists of the Scorpion chassis fitted with the turret of a Fox.

In addition to the installation of the manually operated two-man Fox turret, extensive modifications have been carried out by 34 Base Workshops at Donnington. These modifications include redesigned smoke grenade dischargers, replacement of the 7.62 MG with a 7.62 mm Chain Gun, new light clusters and additional side bins. Domed hatches have also improved headroom for both commander and gunner.

We believe that about 136 Sabre vehicles are in service and the vehicle is now in service with the Reconnaissance Platoons of Armoured and Mechanised Infantry Battalions.

AT – 105 Saxon
(605 in service of which 482 are baseline vehicles) Weight 10,670 kg: Length 5.16 m: Width 2.48 m: Height 2.63 m: Ground Clearance (axles) 0.33 m: Max Road Speed 96 kph: Max Road Range 510 km: Fuel Capacity 160 litres: Fording 1.12 m: Gradient 60 degrees: Engine Bedford 600 6-cylinder diesel developing 164 bhp at 2,800 rpm: Armour proof against 7.62 rounds fired at point blank range: Crew 2 + 10 max.

The Saxon was manufactured by GKN Defence and the first units for the British Army were delivered in late 1983. The vehicle, which can be best described as a battlefield taxi is designed around truck parts and does not require the enormous maintenance of track and running gear normally associated with APC/AIFVs.

As a vehicle capable of protecting infantry from shell splinters and machine gun fire in Europe during the Cold War years Saxon was a useful addition to the formerly larger Army. It does not, however, have the speed and agility which the lessons of recent mobile combat suggest will be necessary for infantry to survive in the assault in the future. The vehicle is fitted with a 7.62 mm Machine Gun for LLAD.

Each vehicle cost over £100,000 at 1984 prices and they are on issue to mechanised infantry battalions assigned to 3 (UK) Division.

The Army holds a number of Saxon IS (Patrol) vehicles for service in counter insurgency operations. The IS equipped vehicle has a Cummins BT 5.1 engine instead of the Bedford 6-cylinder installed on the APC version and other enhancements for internal security operations such as roof-mounted searchlights, improved armour, a barricade removal device and an anti-wire device.

Saxon Patrol comes in two versions, troop carrier and ambulance. The troop carrier carries 10 men and the ambulance two stretcher cases. Industry sources suggest that this latest contract was for 137 vehicles at a cost of some £20 million resulting in a unit cost per vehicle of approximately £145,000.

Saxon is in service with the following overseas customers: Bahrain – 10: Brunei – 24: Hong Kong – 6: Malaysia – 40: Oman – 15.

Milan 2
Missile – Max Range 2,000 m; Mix Range 25 m; Length 918 mm; Weight 6.73 Kg; Diameter 125 mm; Wing Span 267 mm; Rate of Fire 3–4rpm; Warhead – Weight 2.70kg; Diameter 115mm; Explosive Content 1.79kg; Firing Post- Weight 16.4kg; Length 900mm; Height 650mm; Width 420mm; Armour Penetration 352mm; Time of Flight to Max Range 12.5 secs; Missile Speed 720kph; Guidance Semi-Automatic command to line of sight by means of wires:

Milan is a second generation anti-tank weapon, the result of a joint development project between France and West Germany with British Milan launchers and missiles built under licence in the UK by British Aerospace Dynamics. We believe that the cost of a Milan missile is currently in the region of £12,000 and that to date the UK MoD has purchased over 50,000 missiles.

The Milan comes in two main portable components which are the launcher and the missile, it then being a simple matter to clip both items together and prepare the system for use. On firing, the operator has only to keep his aiming mark on the target and the SACLOS guidance system will do the rest.

Milan was the first of a series of infantry anti-tank weapons that started to challenge the supremacy of the main battle tank on the battlefield. During fighting in Chad in 1987 it appears that 12 Chadian Milan posts mounted on Toyota Light Trucks were able to account for over 60 Libyan T-55's and T-62's. Reports from other conflicts suggest similar results.

Milan is on issue throughout the British Army and an armoured infantry battalion could be expected to be equipped with up to 20 firing posts and 200 missiles.

LF ATGW

Max Range 2,500 m: Length 1.08 m; Guidance – automatic self guidance; Total weight 21 kg.

The LF ATGW, based on the US Javelin system, is a more sophisticated guided weapon with a range of some 2,500 m. LF ATGW will equip Light Forces, Mechanised and Armoured Infantry, and Formation Reconnaissance units.

A production contract was signed in early 2003 worth over £300 million. Industry sources suggest that up to 5,000 missiles and 300 firing posts have been ordered. First deliveries to the UK have been made and the system will replace Milan.

The US Army and Marine Corps have been using Javelin for some years and the system is either in service, or has been selected by Australia, Ireland, Jordan, Lithuania, New Zealand and Taiwan. The US has used Javelin in both Iraq and Afghanistan.

Although Javelin has been developed mainly to engage armoured fighting vehicles, the system can also be used to neutralise bunkers, buildings, and low-flying helicopters. Javelin's top-attack tandem warhead is claimed to defeat all known armour systems.

In UK service Javelin will have a number of modifications including an enhanced command launch unit (CLU) with a wider field of view, and the ability to recognise targets at longer ranges.

First UK Javelin deliveries will go to rapid-reaction units such as 16 Air Assault Brigade and 3 Commando Brigade Royal Marines. It will then be issued to infantry units in the armoured, mechanised and light roles.

Over 7,000 Javelin launchers have been manufactured since 1995.

LAW 80

Effective Range Up to 500 m: Armour Penetration Up to 650 mm: Impact Sensor – Scrub and Foliage Proof: Launcher Length (Firing Mode) 1.5 m: Launcher Length (Carrying

Mode) 1 m: Carrying Weight 10 kg: Projectile Diameter 94 mm: Temperature Range –46 to +65 degrees C: Rear Danger Area 20 m.

LAW 80 replaced the 84 mm Carl Gustav and the US 66 mm in service with the British Army, and infantry units in armoured and mechanised battalions are equipped down to section level with this weapon that is capable of destroying main battle tanks at ranges of up to 500 m.

NLAW

NLAW is a man-portable, short-range anti-armour weapon. It will provide a capability out to a range of 600 m, against main battle tanks and light armoured vehicles; have the ability to be fired from enclosed spaces and defensive positions and be a means of attack against personnel in structures.

The NLAW prime contractor is SAAB Bofors Dynamics of Sweden, with Thales Air Defence Ltd as the main UK sub-contractor, the Demonstration and Manufacture contract having been placed in June 2002. The final cost of the NLAW contract is in the order of £400M. The system is planned to enter service in 2006 and will replace LAW 80.

The NLAW system is being developed in a collaborative programme with Sweden.

81 mm L16 Mortar

(450 in service including 100 SP) Max Range HE 5,650 m: Elevation 45 degrees to 80 degrees: Muzzle Velocity 255 m/s: Length of barrel 1280 mm: Weight of barrel 12.7 kg: Weight of base plate 11.6 kg: In action Weight 35.3 kg: Bomb Weight HE L3682 4.2 kg: Rate of Fire 15 rpm: Calibre 81 mm.

The 81mm Mortar is on issue to all infantry battalions, with each battalion having a mortar platoon with three or four sections; and each section deploying two mortars. These mortars are the battalions organic Manoeuvre Support Firepower and can be used to put a heavy weight of fire down on an objective in an extremely short period. Mortar fire is particularly lethal to infantry in the open and in addition is very useful for neutralising dug-in strongpoints or forcing armour to close down.

The fire of each mortar section is controlled by the MFC (Mortar Fire Controller) who is usually an NCO and generally positioned well forward with the troops being supported. Most MFCs will find themselves either very close to or co-located with a Task Group Commander. The MFC informs the base plate (mortar position) by radio of the location of the target and then corrects the fall of the bombs, directing them onto the target.

Mortar fire can be used to suppress enemy positions until assaulting troops arrive within 200–300 m of the position. The mortar fire then lifts onto enemy counter attack and supporting positions while the assault goes in. The 81 mm Mortar can also assist with smoke and illuminating rounds.

The mortar is carried in an AFV432 or a Truck (Utility Light or Medium) and if necessary can be carried in two, man portable loads of 11.35 kg and one 12.28 kg respectively. In the past, infantry companies working in close country have carried one 81 mm round per man when operating in areas such as Borneo where wheeled or tracked transport was not available. For Air Mobile and Air Assault operations mortar rounds are issued in twin packs of two rounds per man on initial deployment. These are used as initial ammunition resources until palletted ammunition loads can be flown in.

The L16A2 81 mm Mortar has undergone a mid life upgrade (MLU) to embrace recent technological developments. The inclusion of the new SPGR (Specialised Personal GPS Receiver) and LH40C (Laser) combine to make the new TLE (Target Locating Equipment). This generates a significant enhancement in first round accuracy and the ease, and speed, with which accurate fire missions can be executed. Additionally, the equipment reduces the number of adjustment rounds which will be used and lead to greater dispersal of mortar barrels, thus increasing protection for the mortar crew soldiers. Plans continue to develop further synergies with The Royal Artillery to improve the existing levels of co-ordination between Artillery and Mortars in fighting the indirect fire battle.

Improved performance ammunition with greater lethality against buildings, armour and equipment is expected to be in service within the next two years.

51 mm Light Mortar
(2093 available) Range 750 m: Bomb Weight 800 gms (illum), 900 gms (smk), 920 gms (HE): Rapid Rate of Fire 8 rpm: Length of barrel 750 mm: Weight Complete 6.275 kg: Calibre 51.25 mm

The 51 mm Light Mortar is a weapon that can be carried and fired by one man, and is found in the HQ of an infantry platoon. The mortar is used to fire smoke, illuminating and HE rounds out to a range of approximately 750 m; a short range insert device enables the weapon to be used in close quarter battle situations with some accuracy. The 51 mm Light Mortar has replaced the older l940s 2' mortar.

5.56 mm Individual Weapon (IW) (SA 80 and SA 80A2)
Effective Range 400 m: Muzzle Velocity 940 m/s: Rate of Fire from 610–775 rpm: Weight 4.98 kg (with 30 round magazine): Length Overall 785 mm: Barrel Length 518 mm: Trigger Pull 3.12–4.5 kg:

Designed to fire the standard NATO 5.56 mm × 45 mm round the SA 80 was fitted with an X4 telescopic (SUSAT) sight as standard. The total buy for SA 80 was for 332,092 weapons. Issues of the weapon are believed to have been made as follows:

Royal Navy	7,864
Royal Marines	8,350
Royal Air Force	42,221
MoD Police	1,878
Army	271,779

At 1991/92 prices the total cost of the SA 80 Contract was in the order of £384.16 million. By late 1994 some 10,000 SA 80 Night Sights and 3rd Generation Image Intensifier Tubes for use with SA80 had been delivered.

The SA 80 had a mixed press and following some severe criticism of the weapons mechanical reliability the improved SA 80A2 was introduced into service during late 2001.

SA 80A2: Some thirteen changes were made to weapon's breech block, gas regulation, firing-pin, cartridge extractor, recoil springs, cylinder and gas plug, hammer, magazine and barrel. Since modification the weapon has been extensively trialled.

Mean time before failure (MTBF) figures from the firing trials for stoppages, following rounds fired are as follow:

	SA 80A2	LSW
UK (temperate)	31,500	16,000
Brunei (hot/wet)	31,500	9,600
Kuwait (hot/dry)	7,875	8,728
Alaska (cold/dry)	31,500	43,200

The first SA 80A2 were in operational service during early 2002 and these weapons were in service across the army by late 2004. The cost of the programme was £92 million and some 200,000 weapons should have been modified by the time the programme ends in May 2006.

During late 2001 the British Army Combat Shooting Team took part in the Australian Army's skill at arms meeting in Brisbane using the new SA 80A2. Teams from eight nations took part in the competition and the British Army team won. The team's SA 80s fired 21,000 rounds in nine days without a stoppage.

5.56 mm Light Support Weapon (LSW)
Range 1,000 m: Muzzle Velocity 970 m/s: Length 900 mm: Barrel Length 646 mm: Weight Loaded with 30 round magazine 6.58 kg: Rate of Fire from to 610–775 rpm.

The LSW has been developed to replace the GPMG in the light role and about 80% of the parts are interchangeable with the 5.56 IW (SA 80). A great advantage for the infantryman is the ability of both weapons to take the same magazines. A rifle section will have two, four-man fire teams and each fire team one LSW.

Like the SA 80 the LSW is currently experiencing some difficulty in firing 5.56 ammunition supplied by other NATO countries. This problem is under review.

An Image Intensifier night sight, the CWS, has been produced for LSW which gives excellent night vision out to 400 m.

5.56mm Minimi Light Machine Gun

Effective range 800 m; Calibre 5.56 mm; Weight 7.1 kg; Length 914 mm; Feed 100-round disintergrating belt; Cyclic rate of fire 700 to 1000 rounds per minute.

FN Herstal's Minimi belt fed 5.56mm Light Machine Gun (LMG), is entering service on a scale of one per four-man fire team. The Minimi has been used operationally by British troops in Afghanistan and Iraq and the UK MoD is planning to procure 2,472 weapons. The contract which will boost the firepower within infantry sections will be complete by 2007.

The Minimi is in service with the Australian, Canadian and New Zealand armies as well as the US Armed Forces.

7.62 mm General Purpose Machine Gun (GPMG)

Range 800 (Light Role), 1,800 m (Sustained Fire Role): Muzzle Velocity 538 m/s: Length 1.23 m: Weight loaded 13.85 kg (gun + 50 rounds); Belt Fed: Rate of Fire up to 750 rpm: Rate of Fire Light Role 100 rpm: Rate of Fire Sustained Fire Role 200 rpm.

An infantry machine gun which has been in service since the early 1960s, the GPMG can be used in the light role fired from a bipod or can be fitted to a tripod for use in the sustained fire role. The gun is also found pintle mounted on many armoured vehicles. Used on a tripod the gun is effective out to 1,800 m although it is difficult to spot strike at this range because the tracer rounds in the ammunition belt burns out at 1,100 m.

Machine Gun platoons in air assault battalions remain equipped with the GPMG in the sustained fire role. GPMG performance has recently been enhanced by the issue of a Maxi Kite night image intensification sight giving excellent visibility out to 600 m.

0.5 Inch Heavy Machine Gun

Effective range – up to 2000 m; Calibre 12.7 mm; Weight 38.15 kg (gun only); Length: 1,656 mm; Barrel Length 1,143 mm; Muzzle Velocity 915 m/s; Cyclic rate of fire – 485 – 635 rounds per minute.

The L1A1 12.7 mm Heavy Machine gun (HMG) is an updated version of the Browning M2 'Fifty-cal' – generally recognised as one of the best heavy machine guns ever developed. Currently, the HMG provides integral close-range support from a ground mount tripod or fitted to a Land Rover TUM using a Weapon Mount Installation Kit (WMIK) and a variety of sighting systems. The performance of the HMG has recently been enhanced with a new 'soft mount' (to limit recoil and improve accuracy) and a quick change barrel.

Long Range Rifle (LRR)

The SA 80 is designed to shoot accurately out to 300 m and be easily handled in combat situations. With the disappearance of the .303 the skill of shooting accurately above 400 m has largely died away. The 7.62 Sniper Rifle filled the gap for a while but the vulnerability of the round to wind deflection over longer ranges made it desirable to come up with a weapon which could be fired with some precision in all phases of modern warfare.

The result has been the development by Accuracy International UK of the .338 Long Range Large Calibre Rifle. Capable of shooting accurately out to 1100 m the LCR came into service in early 2000. The weapon has been issued to JRRF (Joint Rapid Reaction Force) units on the basis of 14 per battalion.

CHAPTER 6 – ARTILLERY

Background

The Royal Regiment of Artillery (RA) provides the battlefield fire support and air defence for the British Army in the field. Its various regiments are equipped for conventional fire support using field guns, for area and point air defence using air defence missiles and for specialised artillery locating tasks.

The RA remains one of the larger organisations in the British Army with 15 Regiments included in its regular Order of Battle. Current personnel figures suggest a total of approximately 1,000 officers and 6,500 soldiers.

At the beginning of 2005 the RA had the following structure in both the UK and Germany.

	UK	Germany
Field Regiments (AS 90 SP Guns)	2	3
Field Regiments (Light Gun)	2(1)	–
Depth Fire Regiments (MLRS)	1(2)	–
Air Defence Regiments (Rapier)	1	–
Air Defence Regiment (HVM)	1	1
Surveillance & Target Acquisition Regiment	1	–
Phoenix UAV Regiment	1	–
Training Regiment (School Assets Regt)	1	–
The Kings Troop (Ceremonial)	1	–

Note:
(1) Of these two Regiments one is a Commando Regiment (29 Cdo Regt) and the other is an Air Assault Regiment (7 PARA RHA*). A third Regiment (40 Regiment) is in the process of converting to the Light Gun. Either of these Regiments can be called upon to provide Manoeuvre Support Artillery to the AMF. On deployment of the AMF it is 29 Cdo Regt RA which forms the AMF Arty HQ and the Commanding Officer is CO Force Arty.
(2) A second MLRS Regiment is now a TA Regt with 12 Launch vehicles in peace uprateable to 18 in war.
(3) Although the artillery is organised into Regiments, much of the 'Gunners'' loyalty is directed towards the battery in which they serve. The guns represent the Regimental Colours of the Artillery and it is around the batterys where the guns are held that history has gathered. A Regiment will generally have three or four gun batterys under command.
(4) The Schools Asset Regiment is not included in the totals given for artillery in Chapter 1.

The Royal Horse Artillery (RHA) is also part of the Royal Regiment of Artillery and its three regiments have been included in the totals above.
There is considerable cross posting of officers and soldiers from the RA to the RHA, and some consider service with the RHA to be a career advancement.

Future Army Structure

Under the terms of the Future Army Structure (FAS) the following changes will take place.

a. One AS90 Regiment (40 Regt RA) will re-role as a Light Gun Regiment in support of 19 Light Brigade.
b. The Gun Groups of three AS90 batteries will be cut.
c. An additional UAV battery, a rocket battery and a STA battery will be established. Providing direct support for the activities of the Field Army will be a new surveillance and target acquisition (STA) battery equipped with the MAMBA (Ericsson ARTHUR) weapon locating radar to be formed by redeploying personnel from a ground air defence regiment (22 Regiment RA). Other personnel from 22 Regiment are to be used to form an additional unmanned aerial vehicle (UAV) battery, while the remaining third will be re-allocated to allow the formation of a multiple rocket launcher battery.
d. There will be an overall reduction in Ground Based Air Defence but the Rapier capability will be owned and operated by the RA.
e. Tactical Groups for Formation Reconnaissance regiments and the 4th Light Role Battalion in 16 Air Assault Brigade will be established, and there will be enhancements to the current Aviation Tactical Group to provide better support for the attack helicopter regiments.
f. The FAS documentation also noted the investment being made in HUMINT for fire-support purposes. For this role the Honourable Artillery Company (HAC – a reserve regiment)is devoted to surveillance and target (STA)acquisition patrolling. The HAC provides a number of battery level patrol groupings.

At the beginning of 2005 the Regular Regiments of the Royal Artillery were as follows:

United Kingdom

1 Regiment RHA	155 mm AS 90
3 Regiment RHA	155 mm AS 90
4 Regiment RA	155 mm AS 90
5 Regiment RA	STA & Special Ops (1)
7 Parachute Regiment RHA	105 mm Lt Gun
12 Regiment RA	HVM
14 Regiment RA	All School Equipments
16 Regiment RA	Rapier
19 Regiment RA	AS 90
26 Regiment RA	155 mm AS 90
29 Commando Regiment RA	105 mm Light Gun (2)
47 Regiment RA	HVM
32 Regiment RA	UAVs
39 Regiment RA	MLRS
40 Regiment RA	Light Gun (converting)
The King's Troop RHA	13-Pounders (Ceremonial)

Notes:
(1) STA – Surveillance and target acquistion.
(2) The Regimental HQ of 29 Commando Regiment with one battery is at Plymouth. The other two batterys are at Arbroath and Poole. Those at Poole provide the amphibious warfare Naval Gunfire Support Officers(NGSFO).

TA Artillery Regiments

HAC	London	STA and Special Ops
100 Regt RA (V)	Luton	Light Gun
101 Regt RA (V)	Newcastle	MLRS (12 in peace)
103 Regt RA (V)	Liverpool	Light Gun
104 Regt RA (V)	Newport	HVM
105 Regt RA (V)	Edinburgh	HVM
106 Regt RA (V)	London	HVM

Training

Artillery recruits spend the first period of recruit training (Phase 1 Training, Common Military Syllabus) at the Army Training Regiment – Pirbright. Artillery training (Phase 2) is carried out at the Royal School of Artillery (RSA) at Larkhill in Wiltshire. After Phase 2 training officers and gunners will be posted to RA units worldwide, but all of them will return to the RSA for frequent career and (Phase 3) employment courses.

Divisional Artillery Group (DAG)

The Royal Artillery provides the modern British armoured formation with a protective covering on the battlefield. The close air defence assets cover the immediate airspace above and around the formation, with the field artillery reaching out to 30 kms in front, and 60 kms across the flanks of the formation being supported. An armoured formation that moves out of this protective covering is open to immediate destruction by an intelligent enemy.

An armoured or mechanised division has it own artillery under command. This artillery usually consists of three Close Support Regiments, with a number of units detached from the Corps Artillery and could include TA reinforcements from the UK. In war the composition of the DAG will vary from division to division according to the task. The following is a reasonable example of the possible organisation for a DAG.

Armoured Divisional Artillery Group (DAG)- Organisation for War

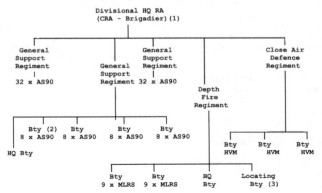

Notes:

(1) This is a diagram of the artillery support which may typically be available to an Armd Div deployed with the ARRC. Expect each brigade in the division to have one Close Support Regiment with AS 90. Artillery regiments are commanded by a Lieutenant Colonel and a battery is commanded by a Major.

(2) The number of batterys and guns per battery in an AS 90 Close Support Regiment has changed post SDR 1999 at four batterys of six guns per battery in the UK Regiments, and three batteries of six in the Germany Regiments. In war all batteries will have eight guns each.

(3) The locating Battery in the Depth Fire Regiment may have the following configuration:

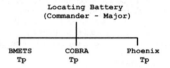

(4) Area Air Defence (AAD) is provided by Rapier.

(5) The staff of an armoured or mechanised division includes a Brigadier of Artillery known as the Commander Royal Artillery (CRA). The CRA acts as the Offensive Support Advisor to the Divisional Commander, and could normally assign one of his Close Support Regiments to support each of the Brigades in the division. These regiments would be situated in positions that would allow all of their batteries to fire across the complete divisional front. Therefore, in the very best case, a battlegroup under extreme threat could be supported by the fire of more than 128 guns.

Artillery Fire Support

A square brigade (of two infantry battalions and two armoured regiments) will probably have a Close Support Regiment of four batterys in support, and the CO of this regiment will act as the Offensive Support Advisor to the Brigade Commander.

It would be usual to expect that each of the four Battlegroups in the brigade would have a Battery Commander acting as the Offensive Support Advisor to the Battlegroup Commander. Squadron/Company Groups in the Battlegroup would each be provided with a Forward Observation Officer (FOO), who is responsible for fire planning and directing the fire of the guns onto the target. The FOO and his party travel in equivalent vehicles to the supported troops to enable them to keep up with the formation being supported and are usually in contact with:

(a) The Gun Positions
(b) The Battery Commander at BGHQ
(c) The Regimental Fire Direction Centre
(d) The Company Group being supported.

Having identified and applied prioritisation of targets, the FOO will call for fire from the guns, and he will then adjust the fall of shot to cover the target area. The FOO will be assisted in this task by the use of a Warrior FCLV OP vehicle containing the computerised fire control equipment which provides accurate data of the target location.

Given a vehicle with its surveillance and target acquisition suite the FOO can almost instantly obtain the correct grid of the target and without calling for corrections, order 'one round fire for effect'.

The next decade
The Revolution in Military Affairs (RMA) has made its impact on the Royal Artillery. As when gunpowder lifted the range of the bow and arrow to that of the cannon, currently modern technology both in space and on the ground is showing signs of yielding ever greater range and accuracy to the artillery.

Greater ability to fix locations in depth and the ability to fire projectiles accurately over longer distances is transforming the horizons for modern artillery. Base bleed ammunition reduces drag by burning chemical compounds at the rear of the projectile and results in greatly increased range. Similarly, technology has discovered that there is an optimum relationship between projectile range, diameter and barrel length. Longer ranges had used to mean greater beaten zone or dispersion of the fall of shot.

Micro technology now makes it possible for onboard computers and navigation systems to provide a long range shell with a once only correction, which brings the round back onto a more precise route to the target. Re-barrelled British Artillery will enter the next decade capable of firing accurately to double present ranges.

Rocket artillery is reaching ever further towards the enemy rear areas. The next generation of rocket artillery rounds is looking beyond a range of 80 kms and designers are also looking at precision guided terminal sub munitions. In addition, unmanned aerial vehicles (UAVs) are flying deeper into enemy territory and sending back ever more accurate target data which will be used by the artillery of the future.

The Indirect Fire Precision Attack (IPFA) project is designed to give the Royal Artillery the ability to strike out to targets at ranges of 150 kms with pinpoint accuracy – up to four times the range of current in service systems. IPFA is one of a number of projects that have been designed to give the artillery dramatically increased range and effect on the target area.

The manned aircraft could carry a man and deliver a weapons load with pinpoint accuracy (in the right conditions) far beyond the range of an artillery observer. This situation is about to be reversed, and there will probably be little support for sending a man where an artillery observation vehicle can go for a fraction of the cost, and a similar likelihood of striking the target. This is likely to happen within the next decade and the term 'Depth Battle' will have real meaning for the Artillery. Once this happens they will have an increasingly important role in shaping the future battlefield. Attacking an enemy with ground troops in the field will be less costly if all his command and control headquarters up to 100 km behind the lines have already been identified and destroyed.

Field Artillery

AS 90

178 available: Crew 5: Length 9.07 m: Width 3.3 m: Height 3.0 m overall: Ground Clearance 0.41 m: Turret Ring Diameter 2.7 m: Armour 17 mm: Calibre 155 mm: Range (39 cal) 24.7 kms (52 cal) 30 kms: Recoil Length 780 mm: Rate of Fire 3 rounds in 10 secs (burst) 6 rounds per minute (intense) 2 rounds per minute (sustained): Secondary Armament 7.62 mm MG: Traverse 6,400 mills: Elevation – 89/+1.244 mills: Ammunition Carried 48 × 155 mm projectiles and charges (31 turret & 17 hull): Engine Cumminis VTA903T turbo-charged V8 diesel 660 hp: Max Speed 53 kph: Gradient 60%: Vertical Obstacle 0.75 m: Trench Crossing 2.8 m: Fording Depth 1.5 m: Road Range 420 kms.

AS 90 was manufactured by Vickers Shipbuilding and Engineering (VSEL) at Barrow in Furness. 179 Guns were delivered under a fixed price contract for £300 million. These 179 guns completely equipped six field regiments replacing the older 120 mm Abbot and 155 mm M109 in British service. At the beginning of 2005 three of these Regiments were under the command of 1(UK) Armoured Division in Germany and three under the command of 3 (UK) Div in the United Kingdom.

AS 90 is currently equipped with a 39 calibre gun which fires the NATO L15 unassisted projectile out to a range of 24.7 kms (Base Bleed ERA range is 30 kms). Funding is available for the re-barreling of 96 × AS 90 with a 52 calibre gun with ranges of 30 kms (unassisted) and 60 to 80 kms with improved accuracy and long range ERA ammunition. The current in service date for the 52 calibre gun is 2002/3 based on a firm programme which will fit 50% of the guns by November 2002 and up to 90% of them by the following April 2003.

AS 90 has been fitted with an autonomous navigation and gunlaying system (AGLS), enabling it to work independently of external sighting references. Central to the system is an inertial dynamic reference unit (DRU) taken from the US Army's MAPS (Modular Azimuth Positioning System). The bulk of the turret electronics are housed in the Turret Control Computer (TCC) which controls the main turret functions, including gunlaying, magazine control, loading systems control, power distribution and testing.

Artillery has always been a cost effective way of destroying or neutralising targets. When the cost of a battery of guns, (approx £20 million) is compared with the cost of a close air support aircraft, (£40 million) and the cost of training each pilot, (£4 million +) the way ahead for governments with less and less to spend on defence is clear.

227 mm MLRS

63 launchers in service – 54 operational in 3 Regiments: Crew 3: Weight loaded 24,756 kg: Weight Unloaded 19,573 kg: Length 7.167 m: Width 2.97 m: Height (stowed) 2.57 m: Height (max elevation) 5.92 m: Ground Clearance 0.43 m: Max Road Speed 64 kph: Road Range 480 km: Fuel Capacity 617 litres: Fording 1.02 m: Vertical Obstacle 0.76 m: Engine Cummings VTA-903 turbo-charged 8 cylinder diesel developing 500 bhp at 2,300 rpm: Rocket Diameter 227 mm: Rocket Length 3.93 m: M77 Bomblet Rocket Weight 302.5 kg: AT2 SCATMIN Rocket Weight 254.46 kg: M77 Bomblet Range 11.5 –32 kms: AT2 SCATMIN Rocket Range 39 kms: One round 'Fire for Effect' equals one launcher firing 12 rockets: Ammunition Carried 12 rounds (ready to fire).

The MLRS is based on the US M2 Bradley chassis and the system is self loaded with 2 × rocket pod containers, each containing 6 × rockets. The whole loading sequence is power assisted and loading takes between 20 and 40 minutes. There is no manual procedure.

A single round 'Fire for Effect' (12 rockets) delivers 644 bomblets or 336 scatterable mines and the coverage achieved is considered sufficient to neutralise a 500 m × 500 m target or produce a minefield of a similar size. Currently the weapon system accuracy is range dependent and therefore more rounds will be required to guarantee the effect as the range to the target increases. Future smart warhead sub munitions currently under development will enable pinpoint accuracy to considerably extended ranges. Ammunition for the MLRS is carried on the DROPS vehicle which is a Medium Mobility Load Carrier. Each DROPS vehicle with a trailer can carry 8 × Rocket Pod Containers and there are 15 × DROPS vehicles supporting the 9 × M270 Launcher vehicles within each MLRS battery.

The handling of MLRS is almost a military 'art form' and is an excellent example of the dependence of modern artillery on high technology. Getting the best out of the system is more than just parking the tubes and firing in the direction of the enemy. MLRS is the final link in a chain that includes almost everything available on the modern battlefield, from high speed communications, collation of intelligence, logistics and a multitude of high technology artillery skills and drills. Unmanned aerial vehicles (UAVs) can be used to acquire targets, realtime TV and data links are used to move information from target areas to formation commanders and onward to the firing positions. Helicopters can be used to dump ammunition and in some cases to move firing platforms. The refining of this capability is an interesting and dynamic future development area in which available technologies are currently being harnessed and applied.

MLRS is deployed as independent launcher units, using 'shoot-and-scoot' techniques. A battery of nine launchers will be given a battery manoeuvre area (BMA), within which are allocated three troop manoeuvre areas (TMA). These TMAs will contain close hides, survey points and reload points. In a typical engagement, a single launcher will be given its fire mission orders using burst data transmission.

An important initial piece of information received is the 'drive on angle'; the crew will drive the launcher out of the hide (usually less than 100 m) and align it with this angle. Using the navigation equipment, its location is fed into the ballistic computer which already has the full fire mission details. The launcher is then elevated and fired and the process can take as little as a few minutes to complete.

As soon as possible after firing, the vehicle will leave the firing location and go to a reload point where it will unload the empty rocket pods and pick up full ones; this can be done in less than five minutes. It will then go to a new hide within the TMA via a survey point to check the accuracy of the navigation system (upon which the accuracy of fire is entirely dependent). The whole of this cycle is co-ordinated centrally, and details of the new hide and reload point are received as part of the fire mission orders. The complete cycle from firing to being in a new hide ready for action might take half an hour.

In a typical day, a battery could move once or twice to a new BMA but this could impose a strain upon the re-supply system unless well planned (bearing in mind the need for the ammunition to be in position before the launcher vehicle arrives in a new BMA). The frequent moves are a result of security problems inherent in MLRS's use. In addition to attack by radar-controlled counterbattery fire, its effectiveness as an interdiction weapon makes it a valuable target for enemy special forces units. Although MLRS will be hidden amongst friendly forces up to 15 km behind the FEBA, its firing signature and small crew (three) will force it to move continually to avoid an actual confrontation with enemy troops.

There are currently (early 2005) one Regular and one TA MLRS Regiments. The Regular Regiment operates 18 launcher vehicles and the TA Regiment 12 in peace and 18 in war.

Under development is the GMLRS rocket which will have a range of over 70 km and be fitted with a 90 kg plus unitary warhead. This warhead would be insensitive munitions compliant. In addition, it would feature inertial measurement unit (IMU) guidance and be global positioning system (GPS) aided.

The US Army is currently operating 857 MLRS, the French have 58, the West Germans 154 and the Italians 21.

105 mm Light Gun
112 service – possibly another 95 in store: Crew 6: Weight 1,858 kg: Length 8.8 m: Width 1.78 m: Height 21.3 m: Ammunition HE, HEAT, WP, Smoke, Illuminating, Target Marking: Maximum Range (HE) 17.2 kms: Anti Tank Range 800 m: Muzzle Velocity 709m/s: Shell Weight HE 15.1 kg: Rate of Fire 6 rounds per minute.

The 105 mm Light Gun has been in service with the Royal Artillery for 25 years and has just received its first and only major upgrade in that time. The enhancement is an Auto Pointing System (APS) which performs the same function as the DRU on the AS 90. The APS is based on an inertial navigation system which enables it to be unhooked and into action in 30 seconds. The APS replaces the traditional dial sight and takes into account trunion tilt without the requirement to level any spirit level bubbles as before.

A touch screen display tells the gun controller when his gun is laid onto the correct target data provided. This enhancement improves the accuracy of the fall of shot to a greater degree of accuracy than possible with the dial sight. User trials will begin in early 2000 with a proposed in service date across all Light Gun Batteries of May 2001.

The Light Gun is in service with the UK Parachute/Air Assault and Commando Field Artillery Regiments as a go-anywhere, airportable weapon which can be carried around the battlefield underslung on a Puma or Chinook.

The gun was first delivered to the British Army in 1975 when it replaced the 105 mm Pack Howitzer. A robust, reliable system, the Light Gun proved its worth in the Falklands, where guns were sometimes firing up to 400 rounds per day. Since then the gun has seen operational service in Kuwait, Bosnia, Afghanistan and Iraq.

During March 2005 the UK MoD placed a contract for an advanced and more effective light artillery shell. This contract for 105 mm Improved Ammunition awarded to BAE Systems will, subject to successful qualification, lead to an initial buy of 50,000 High Explosive shells, and will be worth around £17 Million.

The new High Explosive munitions will be more effective against a range of targets than current shells and will incorporate the latest Insensitive Munitions (IM) technology, making them even safer to transport and handle. Under the programme, planned deliveries will commence late in 2006 and will be spread over three years, with possible future buys until 2017.

The Light Gun has been extremely successful in the international market with sales to Australia (59), Botswana (6), Brunei (6), Ireland (12), Kenya (40), Malawi (12), Malaysia (20), Morocco (36), New Zealand (34), Oman (39), Switzerland (6), UAE (50), United States (548) and Zimbabwe (12).

Lightweight Mobile Artillery Weapon System (LIMAWS)
The next generation lightweight artillery weapon system LIMAWS will provide an indirect fire capability to support light and rapid effect forces. Initial studies showed that the requirement is likely to be best met by a mix of lightweight towed 155 mm gun systems – LIMAWS(Gun) – and lightweight rocket launchers – LIMAWS(Rocket). The two main elements of LIMAWS are currently at different stages – the Gun is in Assessment, whilst the Rocket Launcher is in the Concept Phase.

The LIMAWS(G) requirement was reviewed in March 2001, when it was recognised that a 155 mm gun would not satisfy the entire light artillery requirement. Further work was therefore programmed to assess whether 105 mm ammunition with improved lethality, for use with the Army's Light Gun, could fill the remaining capability gap. In February 2002, the entire programme was reviewed, in the light of changed priorities and tighter financial constraints. The result was the deferral of the LIMAWS(G) programme, slipping the In-Service Date (ISD) from 2006 to 2009, and a reduction in the number of guns from 40 to 32. Funds were also earmarked for the procurement of enhanced 105 mm ammunition. At the same time, the LIMAWS(R) in service date was brought forward from 2008 to 2007.

The main investment decision regarding the appropriate mix of gun and rocket platforms was deferred until June 2004, after completion of the LIMAWS(R) Assessment Phase. This will be followed by a LIMAWS(G) Demonstration and Manufacture approval in May 2006.

The total acquisition costs for the LIMAWS systems is £750 million.

Air Defence

Starstreak HVM
(135 Fire Units on Stormer and 145 on Light Mobile Launcher) Missile Length 1.39 m: Missile Diameter 0.27 m: Missile Speed Mach 3+: Maximum Range 5.5 kms:

Short Missile Systems of Belfast were the prime contractors for the HVM (High Velocity Missile) which continues along the development path of both Blowpipe and Javelin. The system can be shoulder launched or fired from a mounting on the LML (lightweight multiple launcher) or vehicle borne on the Alvis Stormer APC. The Stormer APC has an eight round launcher and 12 reload missiles can be carried inside the vehicle.

HVM has been optimised to counter threats from fast pop-up type strikes by attack helicopters and low flying aircraft. The missile employs a system of three dart type projectiles which can make multiple hits on the target. Each of these darts has an explosive warhead. It is believed that the HVM has an SSK (single shot to kill) probability of over 95%.

12 Regiment RA stationed at Sennelager in Germany is equipped with HVM and supports 1 (UK) Division. The UK HVM Regiment is 47 Regiment RA stationed at Thorney Island. There are three TA HVM regiments. 12 Regiment is believed to be configured as follows:

12 Regiment RA

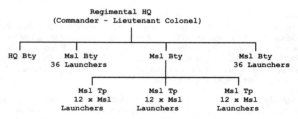

Note: The Regiment has 108 launchers divided amongst the three missile batteries. An HVM detachment of four is carried in a Stormer armoured vehicle and in each vehicle there are four personnel. Inside the vehicle there are twelve ready to use missiles with a further eight stored inside as reloads.

In mid 2001 Thales Air Defence was awarded a £66 million order for an Identification Friend-or-Foe (IFF) system for the Starstreak HVM.

Rapier (FS'C')

(57 fire units in service) Guidance Semi Automatic to Line of Sight (SACLOS): Missile Diameter 13.3 cm: Missile Length 2.35 m: Rocket Solid Fuelled: Warhead High Explosive: Launch Weight 42 kg: Speed Mach 2+: Ceiling 3,000 m: Maximum Range 6,800 m: Fire Unit Height 2.13 m: Fire Unit Weight 1,227 kg: Radar Height (in action) 3.37 m: Radar Weight 1,186 kg: Optical Tracker Height 1.54 m: Optical Tracker Weight 119 kg: Generator Weight 243 kg: Generator Height 0.91 m.

The Rapier system provides area 24 hour through cloud, Low Level Air Defence (LLAD) over the battlefield. The two forms of Rapier in service are as follows:-

Rapier Field standard C (FSC) incorporates a range of technological improvements over its predecessor including an advanced three dimensional radar tracker acquisition system designed by Plessey. The towed system launcher mounts eight missiles (able to fire two simultaneously) which are manufactured in two warhead versions. One of these is a proximity explosive round and the other a kinetic energy round. The total cost of the Rapier FS'C' programme is £1,886 million.

The UK's future Rapier air defence capability will be 16 Regiment Royal Artillery and the Royal Air Force Regiment and the capability of 16 Regiment is being enhanced by the creation of a fourth battery. The possible configuration of 16 Regiment will then be four batterys each of two troops with four fire units per troop.

Rapier in all of its versions has now been sold to the armed forces of at least 14 nations. We believe that sales have amounted to over 25,000 missiles, 600 launchers and about 350 radars.

ARTILLERY LOCATING DEVICES

MSTAR

Weight 30 kg: Wavelength J – Band: Range in excess of 20 kms.

MSTAR is a Lightweight Pulse Doppler J – Band All Weather Radar that has replaced the ZB 298 in the detection of helicopters, vehicles and infantry. Powered by a standard army field battery this radar will also assist the artillery observer in detecting the fall of shot. The electroluminescent display that shows dead ground relief and target track history, also has the ability to superimpose a map grid at the 1:50000 scale to ease transfer to military maps. MSTAR can be vehicle borne or broken down into three easily transportable loads for manpacking purposes.

MSTAR is used by Forward Observation Officers. There are believed to be around 100 MAOV (Warrior Mechanised Artillery Observation Vehicles) equipped with MSTAR. MSTAR is believed to cost about £50,000 pounds per unit at mid 1999 prices and in total about 200 MSTAR equipments are in service throughout the British Army.

COBRA

Cobra (Counter Battery Radar)is a 3-D Phased Array Radar that has been developed for West Germany, France and the UK. Cobra came into service with 5 Regt RA in mid 1999. The dominant cost element of the Cobra Radar is the antenna, which probably accounts for about 70% of the unit price. There are believed to be about 20,000 Gallium Arsenide integrated circuits in each antenna. This enables the equipment to produce the locations of multiple enemy artillery at extremely long ranges, and the radar is able to cope with saturation type bombardments. In addition there is be a high degree of automated software, with high speed circuitry and secure data transmission to escape detection from enemy electronic countermeasures.

Cobra therefore appears to be an ideal equipment for operation in conjunction with MLRS. 5 Regt is believed to field three Cobra Troops, each Troop consisting of three radars.

Cymbeline Mortar Locating Radar
(possibly 10 available) Range 20 kms: Weight of Radar 390 kgs: Frequency I/J Band:

Cymbeline is a mortar locating radar which has been used by by General Support Regiments in both Germany and the UK since the mid 1970s. Cymbeline is mounted on an AFV 432.

Cymbeline detects the flight path of a mortar bomb at two points in the trajectory as it passes through the radar beam(s), rapid computing then enables the grid reference of the enemy base plate to be identified and engaged with artillery. An 81 mortar bomb can be detected at a range of about 10 kms while a 120 mm bomb is detectable at about 14 kms.

In 1994 Cymbeline was deployed by the British Army in support of United Nations operations in the Sarajevo area of the Former Yugoslavia to identify gun and mortar positions around the city. The equipment appears to have been extremely successful in this role and provided much valuable intelligence for the UN Command Staff. The equipment was used extensively during the late 1995 UN bombardment of Serb artillery positions.

At the beginning of 1999 we believe that there were over 325 Cymbeline in service with 18 nations, including Singapore, Norway, Denmark, Finland, Oman, Saudi Arabia, Egypt, Kuwait, Nigeria, South Africa, Malawi, Switzerland and New Zealand.

MAMBA – Mobile Artillery Monitoring Battlefield Radar (Ericsson ARTHUR)
(possibly eight available)

This is an artillery hunting radar which was deployed operationally for the first time in April 2002. MAMBA automatically detects, locates and classifies artillery, rockets and mortars and carries carry out threat assessment based on weapon or impact position. All acquired data is automatically transmitted to a combat control centre. The equipment also incorporates its own basic command, control and communications system for direct control of counter-battery fire.

Mamba's detection range is 20 km (howitzer) and 30 km (rockets) with a circular error probable (CEP) of around 30 metres at extreme range.

Phoenix UAV

Phoenix is an all weather, day or night, realtime surveillance system which consists of a variety of elements. The twin boom UAV (unmanned air vehicle) provides surveillance through its surveillance pod, the imagery from which is datalinked via a ground data terminal (GDT) to a ground control station (GCS). This controls the overall Phoenix mission and is used to distribute the UAV provided intelligence direct to artillery forces, to command level, or to a Phoenix troop command post (TCP). The principle method of communication from the GCS to artillery on the ground is via the battlefield artillery engagement system (BATES).

Powered by a 19kW (25hp) Target Technology 342 two stroke flat twin engine, the Phoenix air vehicle (with a centrally mounted fuel tank) is almost entirely manufactured from composites such as Kevlar, glass fibre, carbon reinforced plastics and Nomex honeycomb. The principal subcontractor was Flight Refueling of Christchurch in Dorset.

The modular design UAV can be launched within one hour of reaching a launch site and a second UAV can be dispatched within eight minutes from the same launcher. The wing span is 5.5 m and the maximum launch weight 175 kgs. The manufacture, GEC states that "Flight endurance is in excess of four hours, radius of action 50 kms and the maximum altitude 2,700 m (9,000 feet)."

A flight section consists of a launch and recovery detachment and a ground control detachment. The launch and recovery detachment consists of three vehicles; the launch support vehicle, with several UAVs and mission pods in separate battlefield containers, plus operational replacement spares and fuel; the launch vehicle, which features a pallet-mounted lifting crane, the hydraulic catapult and launch ramp, a pre-launch detonator device, built-in test equipment, and the Land Rover recovery vehicle which is fitted with cradles for the air vehicle and mission pod. The ground-control detachment consists of two vehicles, the ground control station and the Land Rover towed ground data terminal.

The British Army has one regiment (32 Regiment) equipped with Phoenix. Each of the three Phoenix batterys in 32 Regiment are believed to be equipped with 27 × UAV, with associated ground support equipment and a battery has enough resources to launch 72 flights. The total cost of the programme was £227 million and each Phoenix aircraft is believed to cost approximately £300,000.

Watchkeeper UAV

The Watchkeeper UAV capability (part of the UK's plans for a Network Enabled Capability) will provide UK commanders with accurate, timely and high quality information, including imagery. Watchkeeper will be fully integrated into the wider command and control digitised network, passing data quickly to those who need it. Watchkeeper will be operated and deployed by 32 Regt Royal Artillery to meet the information requirements of HQ Land Manoeuvre Commanders.

The introduction into service of Watchkeeper is expected to offer a significant new capability to Land manoeuvre commanders. The requirement is for greater levels of capability beyond that currently provided by the Phoenix UAV system (the current UAV in service with the UK's Armed Forces). It is anticipated that the role currently fulfilled by Phoenix will be subsumed by Watchkeeper and it remains a possibility that elements of Phoenix may continue in service as part of the overall capability transition.

Watchkeeper will form a significant element of the ISTAR (Intelligence, Surveillance, Target & Reconnaissance) collection capability available within the Land Component. The particular strengths and flexibility of Tactical Unmanned Air Vehicles (TUAV) mean that they can support many of the information gathering tasks of ISTAR.

Watchkeeper in contributing to Network Enabled Capability will have many interfaces to other assets and be dependent upon the Command, Control, Communications, Computer & Information (C4I) infrastructure for the achievement of maximum capability.

The Watchkeeper system is currently completing the Assessment phase and is due to be considered later in 2005. No decision has been made on platform numbers, this will be determined once the preferred option has been finalised and confirmed at project approval.

Watchkeeper capability has an aspired in-service date of 2008 (likely to slip significantly). Current programme acquisition cost estimate is some £1.4bn.

Thales Defence Limited have been selected as the preferred bidder to take the Watchkeeper project into the Demonstration and Manufacture phase of the programme.

Sound Ranging
Sound Ranging is now obsolescent in all but one or two situations. Sound Ranging (SR)locates the positions of enemy artillery from the sound of their guns firing. Microphones are positioned on a line extending over a couple of kilometres to approximately 12 kilometres. As each microphone detects the sound of enemy guns firing, the information is relayed to a Command Post which computes the location of the enemy battery. Enemy locations are then passed to Artillery Intelligence and counter battery tasks fired as necessary. Sound Ranging can identify an enemy position to within 50 metres at 10 kms. The only Sound Ranging assets remaining in the Royal Artillery are those with 5 Regt RA at Catterick.

The UK has one battery equipped with HALO 2A, an accoustic weapons locating equipment specifically for use in out of area or sensitive operations where flying UAVs might be sensitive.

BMETS
The Battlefield Meteorological System BMETS came into service in 1999 and replaces AMETS which entered service in 1972 and provided met messages in NATO format. However, with AMETS there was only one system for each division resulting in a high radius of data application and the system was vulnerable because it used an active radar.

With the extreme range of modern artillery and battlefield missiles, very precise calculations regarding wind and air density are needed to ensure that the target is accurately engaged. BMETS units can provide this information by releasing hydrogen filled balloons at regular intervals recording important information on weather conditions at various levels of the atmosphere.

To benefit from current technology BMETS uses commercially available equipment manufactured by VAISALA linked to the Battlefield Artillery Target Engagement System (BATES). It is a two vehicle system with a detachment of five in peace, six in war. It is deployed with all regular field artillery and MLRS regiments.

BMETS can operate in all possible theatres of conflict world wide where the Meteorological Datum Plain (MDP) varies from 90 m below to 4000 m above sea level, and can be used with a variety of radiosonde types to sound the atmosphere to a height of up to 20 km. Measurements are made by an ascending radiosonde. This is tracked by a passive radiotheodolite which provides wind data, air temperature, atmospheric pressure and relative humidity from the datum plan for each sounding level, until flight termination. In addition virtual temperature, ballistic temperature and ballistic density are calculated to a high degree of accuracy. Cloud base is estimated by observation. The data is then processed by receiver equipment in the troop vehicles to provide formatted messages to user fire units via the existing military battlefield computer network

Air Defence Alerting Device (ADAD)
An infra-red thermal imaging surveillance system that is used by close air defence units, to detect hostile aircraft and helicopter targets and directs weapon systems into the target area. The air defence missile operators can be alerted to up to four targets in a priority order. This passive system which is built by Thorn EMI has an all weather, day and night capability.

CHAPTER 7 – ARMY AVIATION

Aviation Support

Battlefield helicopters have played a major role in UK military operations since the 1960s. The AAC battlefield helicopter fleet has accumulated a vast amount of operational experience in recent years, and is arguably a more capable force than that possessed by any other European nation.

The flexibility of battlefield helicopters was demonstrated in 2003 during Operation TELIC in Iraq. Here 3 Regiment, Army Air Corps, with two Pumas from the Support Helicopter Force attached, was deployed forward as a combined-arms battlegroup, initially within 16 Air Assault Brigade and later in conjunction with 7 Armoured Brigade. The battlegroup had responsibility for an area that extended over 6,000 square kilometres, and provided a versatile combat arm during the warfighting phase. In the immediate aftermath of hostilities, helicopters proved to be the most efficient means of covering the vast operational area allocated to British forces, and also in distributing humanitarian aid to isolated villages.

Force structure

The Army obtains its aviation support from Army Air Corps (AAC), which is an organisation with six separate regiments and a number of independent squadrons. The AAC also provides support for Northern Ireland on a mixed resident and roulement basis and the two squadrons concerned are sometimes referred to as the seventh AAC Regiment, although the units would disperse on mobilisation and have no regimental title.

AAC manpower is believed number some 1,650 personnel of all ranks, including 480 officers and 1,400 soldiers. Unlike the all-officer Navy and Air Force helicopter pilot establishments, almost two-thirds of AAC aircrew are non-commissioned officers. The AAC is supported by REME and RLC personnel numbering some 2,600 all ranks. Total AAC-related manpower is believed to be some 4,400 personnel of all ranks.

With certain exceptions, during peace, all battlefield helicopters come under the Joint Helicopter Command (JHC). Under strategic planning guidelines released by the MoD in 2004, the core operational formation of the AAC will remain the Air Assault Brigade – currently 16 Air Assault Brigade.

The introduction into AAC service of the WAH-64D Apache Longbow attack helicopter between 2004 and 2007 is transforming AAC doctrine, organisation, and order of battle. The British Army designation of the type is Apache AH Mk1. As of early 2005, the AAC was in a process of organisational transformation with the UK Army having taken the decision to concentrate the Apache AH Mk 1 into three Attack Regiments.

The AAC is to equip these three Aviation Attack Regiments with a total of 48 × Apache AH Mk 1 attack helicopters. Pilot training on Apache is well under way, and AAC and RAF Support Helicopter Squadrons are being forged into a new Air Manoeuvre Arm within 16 Air Assault Brigade which includes two Battalions of the Parachute Regt. The three newly equipped Attack Regiments will be 9 Regt at Dishforth in Yorkshire, and 3 and 4 Regts at Wattisham in Suffolk – with a full operating capability expected by June 2007.

Each attack regiment will have 2 × attack squadrons equipped with 8 × Apache AH Mk1 attack helicopters and 1 × support squadron equipped with 8 × Lynx. The Gazelle Helicopter has already started to be phased out by several units as the Apache AH Mk 1 is being introduced. The capability gap left will be filled by introducing the Battlefield Light Utility Helicopter (BLUH) in this capacity. Several Gazelle Helicopters will, however, continue to be retained for specialist tasks as required. The Lynx Helicopter will also be phased out as the Apache AH Mk 1 will replace it in its attack helicopter role. Ultimately, however, the Lynx will be replaced by the BLUH (which may be Lynx-based, according to indications in 2005).

The current (2005) AAC Regimental and Squadron locations are shown below. The Attack Regiments equipping with Apache AH Mk 1s are forming, and it is not at present clear whether the new regiments will retain existing squadron numbers.

Army Air Corps force structure and helicopters in 2005

Regiment	Squadron	Location	Helicopter/aircraft	Fleet
1 Regiment	652,661	Germany	Lynx, Gazelle	16
3 Attack Regiment	653,662 & 663	Wattisham	Apache, Lynx (forming)	24
4 Attack Regiment	654,659 & 669	Wattisham	Apache, Lynx (forming)	24
5 Regiment	655,665	Aldergrove	Lynx, Gazelle, Islander	43
9 Attack Regiment	656,664,672	Dishforth	Apache, Lynx	24
2 Regiment (Training)	670, 671,673	Middle Wallop	Apache, Lynx, Gazelle	36

Independent units

Joint Special Forces				
Aviation Wing	657	Odiham	Lynx	12
Development & Trials	667	Middle Wallop	Lynx	6
Initial Training	660	Shawbury	Squirrel HT 1	12
7 Regiment (TA)	658, 666	Netheravon	Gazelle	12

Flights include 3 (TA) Flight (Leuchars), 6 (TA) Flight (Shawbury)
7 Flight (Brunei), 12 Flight (Germany), 25 Flight (Belize), 29 BATUS Flight – Canada

The AAC Centre at Middle Wallop in Hampshire acts as a focal point for all Army Aviation, and it is here that the majority of corps training is carried out. Although the AAC operates some fixed-wing aircraft for training and liaison flying, the main effort goes into providing helicopter support for the land forces. About 200 AAC helicopters are believed to be in operational service in early 2005.

Employment of aviation

Following significant development during World War II, Army Aviation formally joined the Army order of battle in the early 1950s. Since then its place on the battlefield has developed rapidly as an integral element of the Army's manoeuvre forces. The introduction of attack helicopters clearly identifies the shift of emphasis from combat support towards the combat role, particularly within air manoeuvre operations, and establishes the AAC as the sixth combat arm of the British Army. However, despite this changing emphasis, the Army also has a continuing essential requirement for army aviation to provide both combat support and combat service support roles.

Army Aviation doctrine

Army aviation operations rely for their effect on integration into combined arms groupings (e.g. brigades and battlegroups) of which army aviation forms an element, the most pivotal of which is its place within air manoeuvre forces.

In the context of Land Operations, Air Manoeuvre seeks decisive advantage through the exploitation of the third dimension by combined-arms forces centred on rotary-wing aircraft, but within an overall joint operations framework.

Until 2004, the Army Lynx was the main AAC battlefield helicopter, and the only one with a combat role. Consequently, the AAC has had no previous experience of what some might describe as true Attack Helicopter operations. With the introduction of the Apache AH Mk 1 into service, doctrine must therefore evolve and be promulgated in an orderly, top-down fashion and to agreed assumptions. The experience of other Apache operators (particularly the US Army) will be invaluable. The fielding of the Attack Helicopter will require to be aligned with the wider development of Air Manoeuvre.

The Aviation Mission

Combat Aviation: To find, fix and strike, either independently, or as the lead element, or as a constituent of combined arms groupings, throughout the depth of the battlefield and the 24-hr battle, and throughout the full spectrum of operations.

Combat Support Aviation: To provide enabling capabilities for combined arms operations, throughout the depth of the battlefield and the 24-hr battle, and throughout the full spectrum of operations.

Roles of Army Aviation

In a Combat Role: To conduct air manoeuvre using direct fire and manoeuvre, as part of the land battle component.

In a Combat Support Role: To provide ISTAR (intelligence, surveillance, target acquisition and reconnaissance) as a collection asset in its own right or potentially as a platform for other sensors, including ECM (electronic countermeasures): NBC (nuclear, chemical and biological) reconnaissance: ESM (electronic support measures): radar and other electronic systems.

Other tasks may include:

◆ To provide direction of fire support (ground/air/maritime/special forces).
  To provide mobility for combat forces.
◆ To assist in command and control, including acting as airborne command posts.
◆ To provide a limited extraction capability.

In a Combat Service Support Role: To provide movement for personnel and materiel including casualty evacuation (CASEVAC).

Joint Helicopter Command (JHC)

The combined operations environment of ground and air elements created by the formation of 16 Air Assault Brigade resulted in a need to merge the Command and Control elements of AAC regiments and RAF troop and vehicle carrying Support Helicopters in the forward combat zone (FCZ). The integration of Aviation Attack and Combat Support assets was made possible by the formation of the Joint Helicopter Command.

Peacetime command and control of 16 Air Assault Brigade is provided by the Joint Helicopter Command which was formed as a result of the Strategic Defence Review on 1 October 1999. This joint headquarters is commanded by a two star commander. It is under full command of HQ LAND Command, and is situated with it at Wilton, in Wiltshire. The role of the JHC is to deliver and sustain effective Battlefield Helicopter and Air Assault assets, operationally capable under all environmental conditions, in order to support UK defence missions and tasks. The JHC is responsible for the Commando Helicopter Force (CHF), all Army Aviation Units, RAF Support Helicopter Force, 16 Air Assault Brigade, the Joint Helicopter Force Northern Ireland and the Joint Helicopter Command and Standards Wing (Army).

The JHC provides a unified command structure for the integration of Battlefield Helicopters and Air Assault combat, combat support and combat service support units. This enables doctrine, structures, training, support and working practices to be harmonised across the three Services. As of 2005, the estimated current helicopter fleet under the JHC is shown in the table.

Joint Helicopter Command: Helicopter Fleet as of 1 Jan 2005

	AAC	RAF	RN	Total
Apache AH Mk 1	48			48
Lynx AH-7/9	110		6	116
Gazelle	105		8	113
Sea King HC 4		33	33	
Chinook HC2/2A		31		31
Puma		34		34
EH-101 Merlin HC3		18		18
Total	**263**	**83**	**47**	**393**

Notes:

1. Apache AH Mk 1 introduction into service due for completion by mid-2007
2. Some Gazelles and Lynx are to be withdrawn as Apache enters service
3. Figures exclude 8 × Chinook HC 3 not due to enter service until 2007
4. JHC also operates 6 × Islander fixed-wing aircraft and 6 × Contractor Owned Bell 212 helicopters

The Joint Helicopter Command was mandated a total of over 100,000 flying hours in 2003-04 by the Defence Logistics Organisation for its Lynx, Gazelle, Chinook, Puma, and Sea King fleets. With the exception of Lynx, each individual aircraft is resourced to fly approximately 400 hours per year. The Lynx fleet is resourced for 23,900 hours, which averages 206 hours per aircraft.

Future Helicopter Fleet Requirements
During 2004, the MoD identified the future helicopter fleet requirements for Army mission tasks under three contingency levels, as shown in the table.

Future helicopter force structure – Army component

	Small-scale contingency	Medium-scale contingency	Large-scale contingency
Attack helicopters	34	36	48
Support helicopters	44	65	110
Total	**78**	**101**	**158**

AAC organisation

We would expect an AAC Regiment to be organised on the lines shown in the diagrams below.

Army Air Corps – Attack Regiment

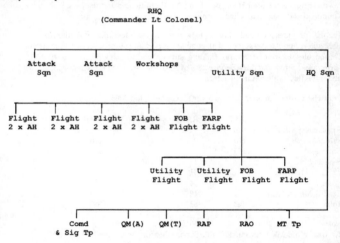

Totals: 8 × LUH (Light Utility Helicopters) 16 × AH (Attack Helicopters)

Notes: FOB – Forward Operating Base: FARP- Forward Arming and Refuelling Point.

Army Air Corps – Divisional Aviation Regiment

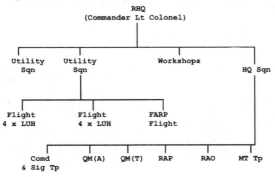

Total: 16 × LUH (Light Utility Helicopters)

Army Aviation Training

The School of Army Aviation at Middle Wallop in Hampshire trains Army pilots using the Army's front line aircraft, the Islander, the Gazelle, the Lynx and the Apache AH Mk 1. It also trains soldiers to support these aircraft on the ground, to protect its operating bases, to provide communications between the ground and aircraft, and to arm and refuel them. The training activity conducted by SAAvn is divided into ground training and flying training.

Ground training is conducted by 2 Regiment AAC and consists of:

◆ Phase 2 training to provide special to arm training for recruits on completion of their basic training at Winchester Army Training Regiment, and,
◆ Phase 3 training to provide career progress courses for trained soldiers.

Flying training is conducted by Flying Wing and consists of:

◆ Army Flying Grading
◆ Operational Training Phase of the Army Pilots Course
◆ Conversion to the Army Air Corps operational aircraft

The AAC Centre at Middle Wallop is under the ownership of the Army Training and Recruitment Agency (ATRA). There is also a detachment of 132 Aviation Support Squadron, Royal Logistics Corps, which comes under the Joint Helicopter Command, based at the AAC Centre. The Headquarters of the Director of Army Aviation is also based at Middle Wallop. There are 12 Attack Helicopters allocated to the School of Army Aviation for training purposes.

HQ DAAvn (Director Army Aviation) is responsible for providing advice and support on Army Aviation and AAC training matters. In this regard HQ DAAvn is responsible for the training policy for both aircrew and groundcrew. The School of Army Aviation (SAAvn) undertakes AAC Special-to-Arm training. AAC Soldier Basic Training takes place at ATR Winchester.

The AAC recruits pilots from three main sources:

◆ Direct Entry (Officers only)
◆ The ranks of the AAC (Corporals and above)
◆ Officers and soldiers from other arms and branches of the Service (Corporal and above)

Officers join the Corps after completing the Commissioning course at the Royal Military Academy Sandhurst. Unlike the all-officer Navy and Air Force helicopter pilot establishments, almost two-thirds of AAC aircrew are non-commissioned officers. Within the Army, NCOs, of at least LCpl rank with a recommendation for promotion, from within the AAC and from the remainder of the Army may also apply for pilot training. NCO pilots spend the majority of their service flying and many go on to be commissioned as Officers, normally to fill specialist flying appointments such as flying instructors.

There are three phases to selection for Army pilot training:

Aircrew Selection tests are conducted at RAF College Cranwell. These tests are common to the three Services and last two days. Army candidates require a minimum aircrew aptitude score of 80/180 to progress onto the next phase. RAF/RN require higher scores, but the Army is able to accept a lower score at this point, as Army candidates also have to pass Army Flying Grading which the AAC considers a far more accurate indicator of potential to be an Army pilot.

Army Flying Grading (AFG) is conducted at Middle Wallop. This consists of 13 hours, over a three week period, in a Slingsby Firefly 160. The aim of this course is to test aptitude in a live flying environment and to identify whether students have the capability to become an Army pilot.

Students who have successfully demonstrated the necessary flying potential at AFG will progress onto the final phase at the Pilot Selection Centre. This is run by HQ SAAvn and selection includes aptitude tests, a medical, and finally a selection interview.

Flying training
There are several stages in AAC flying training.

Groundschool
The Army Flying Course starts with four weeks of groundschool instruction at RAF College Cranwell. Students learn the basic building blocks of aviation – such as Meteorology, Principles of Flight, Aircraft Operations, Navigation and Technical instruction.

Elementary Flying Training (EFT)
EFT is the first element of Army Flying Training at RAF Barkston Heath. This phase consists of 40 flying hours of elementary fixed- wing flying training over 14 weeks on the Slingsby Firefly (260).

Aeromedical and Survival Training

After EFT, students complete a week of aeromedical and survival training at RNAS Yeovilton, Lee-on-Solent and Plymouth.

Defence Helicopter Flying School

The Defence Helicopter Flying School (DHFS) at RAF Shawbury provides basic single-engine helicopter training for the three Services and some overseas countries. The DHFS also provides advanced twin-engine helicopter training for RAF aircrew and other special courses for the three Services.

At the DHFS, much of the training effort is contracted out to FBS Ltd – a consortium of Flight Refuelling Aviation, Bristow Helicopters Ltd and Serco Defence. All DHFS military and civilian instructors are trained by the Central Flying School (Helicopter) Squadron. The single-engine basic flying course incorporates some 36 flying hours over nine weeks on the Squirrel helicopter with the instructors of No 660 Squadron. Army students complete nine weeks training before they leave to start their Operational Training Phase at Middle Wallop.

Operational Training Phase (OTP)

The penultimate phase is conducted at the School of Army Aviation at Middle Wallop. Training is focused on converting helicopter pilots into Army pilots. It starts with a week of tactics training, preparing students for the military part of the course. The OTP phase involves 82 flying hours in 18 weeks, and is conducted on the Squirrel helicopter.

Conversion to Type (CTT)

The final phase is conducted at the School of Army Aviation at Middle Wallop. Before being posted to a regiment, students have to convert onto an operational helicopter type. The Conversion to Type (CTT) course takes around nine weeks. At Middle Wallop, Apache aircrew and ground crew training is conducted by Aviation Training International Limited (ATIL).

Conversion to Role (CTR)

Once a pilot has been converted onto type at Middle Wallop, he or she will proceed to a Regiment. At the Regiment a special CTR course will be held to bring the pilot up to combat ready status.

AAC Aircraft

In 2005, the AAC aircraft fleet comprises four types: Apache AH Mk1, Lynx AH7/9, and Gazelle helicopters, and the fixed-wing BN-2 Islander/Defender aircraft. Contractor-owned Bell 212s are also used by the Army flight in Brunei as a utility and transport helicopter.

Over the next ten years, the MoD plans to invest some £3bn in helicopter platforms to replace and enhance the existing capability. In light of the improved security situation in Northern Ireland, the MoD plans to make some reductions in overall helicopter numbers.

Apache (AH Mk1)

(67 ordered and delivered) Gross Mission Weight 7,746 kgs (17,077 lb): Cruise Speed at 500 meters 272 kph: Maximum Range (Internal Fuel with 20 minute reserve) 462 kms: General

Service Ceiling 3,505 metres (11,500 ft): Crew 2: Carries – 16 × Hellfire II missiles (range 6,000 metres approx): 76 × 2.75" CRV-7 rockets: 1,200 30mm cannon rounds: 4 × Air-to-Air Missiles: Engines 2 × Rolls Royce RTM-332.

The UK MoD ordered 67 Apache based on the US Army AH-64D manufactured by Boeing in 1995. Boeing built the first eight aircraft, and partially assembled the other 59. The UK Westland helicopter company undertook final assembly, flight testing and programme support at their Yeovil factory. Full operating capability for all three Apache Attack Regiments is expected by June 2007.

We believe that there will be 48 operational aircraft in three regiments (each of 16 aircraft). The remaining 19 aircraft will be used for trials, training and a war maintenance reserve (WMR).

The Apache can operate in all weathers, day or night, and can detect, classify and prioritise up to 256 potential targets at a time. Apart from the 'Longbow' mast-mounted fire control radar, the aircraft is equipped with a 127 × magnification TV system, 36 × magnification thermal imaging, and 18 × magnification direct view optics. The missile system incorporates Semi-Active Laser and Radio Frequency versions of the Hellfire missile, whose range is at least 6 kms. Apart from the Rolls-Royce engines, specific British Army requirements include a secure communications suite and a Helicopter Integrated Defensive Aids System (HIDAS). Programme cost is some £3 billion.

It is believed that an air-to-air weapon capability will continue to be investigated and trials of the Shorts Starstreak missile onboard an AH-64 have continued in the US. Any longer term decision to proceed will be based on the results of these US Army trials.

The night vision system of 67 Apache AH Mk1 attack helicopters is to be upgraded in the near future. The M-TADS/PNVS, which is designated Arrowhead, will replace the existing forward-looking infra-red (FLIR) and daylight television image intensifier with new sensors to provide improved target identification over longer ranges, better pilot performance and reduced life-cycle costs. Army Air Corps (AAC) aviators are said to have been keen to proceed with the upgrade, because the damp UK climate significantly degrades the effectiveness of the existing Target Acquisition and Designation Sight/Pilot Night Vision Sensor

The Apache AH Mk 1 presents a completely new capability for the AAC with significant implications for Air Manoeuvre doctrine in Land and Joint Operations. The Apache certainly gives the British Army the 'punch' necessary for operations during the next decade.

Lynx AH – Mark 7/9
(110 in service). Length Fuselage 12.06 m: Height 3.4 m: Rotor Diameter 12.8 m: Max Speed 330 kph: Cruising Speed 232 kph: Range 885 km: Engines 2 Rolls-Royce Gem 41: Power 2

× 850 bhp: Fuel Capacity 918 litres(internal): Weight (max take off) 4,763 kg: Crew one pilot, one air-gunner/observer: Armament 8 × TOW Anti-Tank Missiles: 2–7.62 mm machine guns: Passengers-able to carry 10 PAX: Combat radius approximately 100kms with 2 hour loiter.

Until the introduction of Apache, Lynx was the helicopter used by the British Army to counter the threat posed by enemy armoured formations. Armed with 8 × TOW missiles the Lynx was the mainstay of the British armed helicopter fleet. However, in addition to its role as an anti-tank helicopter, Lynx can be used for fire support using machine guns, troop lifts, casualty evacuation and many more vital battlefield tasks.

As an armed helicopter, during hostilities, we would expect Lynx to operate on a section basis, with two or three Lynx aircraft armed with TOW directed by a Section Commander possibly flying in a Gazelle. The Section Commander would control what is in reality an airborne tank ambush and following an attack on enemy armour decide when to break contact. Having broken contact, the aircraft would return to a forward base to refuel and rearm. Working from forward bases, some of which are within 10 kms of the FEBA, it is suggested that a Lynx section could be 'turned around' in less than 15 minutes. Lynx with TOW replaced SCOUT with SS11 as the British Army's anti-tank helicopter.

We believe that there are 86 Lynx Mark 7 in British service and that there are also 23 Lynx Mark 9 (the latest version) in the inventory.

TOW 2B
(Tube Launched, Optically Tracked, Wire Guided, Anti-Tank Missile). Length 1.17 m: Diameter 15 cm: Maximum Range 3750 m: Speed 1127 khp (200mps): Warhead 3.9 kg shaped charge high explosive HEAP : Missile Weight 28.1 kg: Guidance Automatic command to line of sight: Armour Penetration 800 mm.

TOW is the US system that has been adopted for use on the Lynx anti-tank helicopter. First seen in US service in l965 TOW is a very powerful system that can defeat the armour on all conventional MBTs. It is also a second generation missile in that the operator no longer 'flies' the missile to the target using a control stick. All the operator needs to do is keep the aiming mark on the target and the guidance system will do the rest. AAC Lynx are fitted with the roof-mounted stabilised M65 sight.

TOW 2B is the top attack version of the missile system and these systems in AAC service are being upgraded under the Further Improved Tow Programme which enhances both range (possibly 5,000 m) and armour penetration.

Gazelle
(Approximately 120 in AAC service). Fuselage Length 9.53 m: Height 3.18 m: Rotor Diameter 10.5 m: Maximum Speed 265 kph: Cruising Speed 233 kph: Range 670 km:

Engine Turbomeca/Rolls-Royce Astazou 111N: Power 592 shp: Fuel Capacity 445 litres: Weight 1,800 kg (max take off): Armament 2 × 7.62 mm machine guns (not a standard fitting).

Gazelle is the general purpose helicopter in use by the AAC, and it is capable of carrying out a variety of battlefield roles. Gazelle is a French design built under licence by Westland Aircraft. It is equipped with a Ferranti AF 532 stabilised, magnifying observation aid. The fleet is now some 30 years old, and due to be withdrawn progressively by 2008 – being replaced by the Battlefield Light Utility Helicopter (BLUH). Some Gazelles are expected to remain in service in some non-battlefield roles beyond 2008.

BN-2 Islander

(6 In Service) Crew 2: Length Overall 12.37 m: Max Take Off Weight 3,630 kg: Max Cruising Speed at 2,135 m (7,000 ft and 75% of power) 257 kph (154 mph): Ceiling 4,145 m (13,600 m): Range at 2,137 m (7,000 ft and 75% of power) 1,153 km (717 miles): Range with Optional Tanks 1,965 kms (1,221 miles).

This type is the only fixed-wing aircraft that the AAC operates. The AAC BN-2 Islanders carry the Thorn EMI CASTOR (Corps Airborne Stand Off Radar) that is designed to provide intelligence information in the forward edge of the battlefield (FEBA) and beyond while operating well within friendly territory. The radar, located in the nose cone of the aircraft has a 360 degree scan and offers wide coverage against moving and static targets.

The Islander has been routinely deployed with 1 Flight AAC in Northern Ireland, and also deployed with British Army SFOR contingents in the former Yugoslavia. More recently, the Army acquired three more of the type under an Urgent Operational Requirement (UOR) for service in Iraq. The first of these was delivered in October 2004. Defensive aids system dispensers are installed in pods under the aircraft wings to improve survivability when flying into high-threat airfields in Iraq, such as Baghdad International, Basra and Al Amara. The new aircraft have the designation BN2T-4S AL.1 Defender

Battlefield Light Utility Helicopter (BLUH)

The Battlefield Light Utility Helicopter (BLUH) will replace the capability currently provided by 45 Gazelle AH 1 and 109 Lynx Mk 7 and Mk 9. BLUH capability will include Intelligence, Surveillance, Target Acquisition and Reconnaissance (ISTAR), direction of fire, mobility support, assistance in command and control, and casualty evacuation. An option was taken in April 2002 to reduce BLUH numbers from 102 to 85.

As of early 2005, the BLUH programme focus hinges on a proposal from Westland Helicopters Ltd (WHL) – since 2004 owned by the Italian Finmeccanica Agusta helicopter company – with its Future Lynx (FLynx). Potential competitors to Flynx include the Agusta AB139, European collaborative NH90, Sikorsky UH-60M and Eurocopter EC655 helicopters. The current In-Service Date is October 2008. The BLUH programme has an estimated cost of £1.1bn for 85 helicopters.

If the Westland Flynx is selected to meet the BLUH requirement, it would signify that some of these 85 helicopters would replace Lynxes and Gazelles in the three newly forming AAC attack regiments, as well as all the Lynx AH7s and most of the Gazelles in other AAC squadrons.

RAF Support

The second agency that provides aviation support for the Army is the Royal Air Force. In general terms, the RAF provides helicopters that are capable of moving troops and equipment around the battlefield, and fixed-wing fighter ground attack (FGA) aircraft that provide close air support to the troops in the vicinity of the Forward Edge of the Battlefield Area (FEBA). The RAF also provides the heavy air transport aircraft that will move men and material from one theatre of operations to another. In general terms, the RAF support (other than helicopters) available is as follows:

RAF Support Helicopters

Squadron	Aircraft	Location
7 Squadron	5 × Chinook HC2, 1 × Gazelle	Odiham
18 Squadron	18 × Chinook HC2	Odiham
27 Squadron	12 × Chinook HC2	Odiham
28 Squadron	18 × Merlin	Benson
33 Squadron	15 × Puma HC1	Benson
78 Squadron	1 × Chinook HC2, 2 × Sea King HAR 3	Mount Pleasant, Falkland Islands
84 Squadron	3 × Bell 412 Griffon HAR 2	Akrotiri, Cyprus
230 Squadron	18 × Puma HC1	Aldergrove

Puma

(34 in Service) Crew 2 or 3: Fuselage Length 14.06 m: Width 3.50 m: Height 4.38 m: Weight (empty) 3,615 kg: Maximum Take Off Weight 7,400 kgs: Cruising Speed 258 km/ph (192 mph): Service Ceiling 4,800 m: Range 550 kms: 2 × Turbomeca Turmo 111C4 turbines.

The Puma is powered by 2 × Turbomeca Turmo 111C4 engines mounted side by side above the main cabin. Capable of many operational roles Puma can carry 16 fully equipped troops, or 20 at light scales. In the casualty evacuation role (CASEVAC), six stretchers and six sitting cases can be carried. Underslung loads of up to 3,200 kgs can be transported over short distances and an infantry battalion can be moved using 34 Puma lifts. Deliveries of the RAF Pumas started in 1971. The RAF Puma fleet is now over 30 years old, and we believe that there is a planned out of service date of 2010.

Chinook

(34 in Service – possibly 7 in reserve + 14 on order with an expected ISD of 2007) Crew 3:
Fuselage Length 15.54 m: Width 3.78 m: Height 5.68 m: Weight (empty) 10,814 kgs:
Internal Payload 8,164 kgs: Rotor Diameter 18.29 m: Cruising Speed 270 km/ph (158 mph):
Service Ceiling 4,270 m: Mission Radius(with internal and external load of 20,000 kgs
including fuel and crew) 55 kms: Rear Loading Ramp Height 1.98 m: Rear Loading Ramp
Width 2.31 m: Engines 2 × Avco Lycoming T55L11E turboshafts.

The Chinook is a tandem-rotored, twin-engined medium lift helicopter. It has a crew of
four (pilot, navigator and 2 × crewmen) and is capable of carrying 45 fully equipped
troops or a variety of heavy loads up to approximately 10 tons. The first Chinooks entered
service with the RAF in 1982. The triple hook system allows greater flexibility in load
carrying and enables some loads to be carried faster and with greater stability. In the ferry
configuration with internally mounted fuel tanks, the Chinook's range is over 1,600 kms
(1,000 miles). In the medical evacuation role the aircraft can carry 24 × stretchers.

Chinook aircraft have been upgraded to the HC2/2A standard. The first of the 32 aircraft
being upgraded was delivered to the RAF in the Spring of 1993, with the remaining
aircraft modified by the end of 1995. The HC2 upgrade, for which a total of £145 million
was allocated, allowed for the aircraft to be modified to the US CH-47D standard with
some extra enhancements. These enhancements include fitting infra-red jammers, missile
approach warning indicators, chaff and flare dispensers, a long range fuel system and
machine gun mountings. A further upgrade involved the addition of the Night
Enhancement Package to some Chinook HC2/2As, to improve pilots' night-time
situational awareness and provide secure communications, was completed in nine months,
at a cost of approximately £70 million.

The RAF Chinook costs upwards of £5,200 per flying hour to operate.
This is a rugged and reliable aircraft. During the Falklands War reports suggest that, at one
stage 80 fully equipped troops were carried in one lift and, during a first Gulf War mission
a single Chinook carried 110 Iraqi POWs. The Chinook mid-life update significantly
enhances the RAF's ability to support the land forces during the next 20 years.

Since 1995, the RAF has had 14 more Chinooks on order, whose delivery has been delayed
by lengthy problems with the design specification and performance of the new types. The
original contract for the 14 × Chinooks was signed in early September 1995 at a price of
£259 million – for delivery in 1998/99. These new Chinooks (6 × Chinook MSH/HC2A
and 8 × Chinook MSH/HC3)were to be fitted with in-flight Refuelling capability, forward-
looking infrared and extra fuel because they are to be capable of self-deployment. None of
the new Chinooks have so far been accepted into service by the MoD. Continuing
technical problems mean that an ISD will not be achievable prior to mid-2007. When they
enter service, it is believed that the 8 × Chinook Mk3s will be based at RAF Odiham in

direct support of 16 Air Assault Brigade, releasing the Chinook HC 2s currently earmarked for this task to return to the support role.

EH101 Merlin Mk3

(18 + 4 believed to be in reserve) Crew 2: Length 22.81 m: Rotor Diameter 18.59 m: Max Speed 309 k/ph (192mph): Engine 3 × Rolls Royce/Turbomeca RTM 322 three-shaft turbines of 2,312 shp each: Up to 35 fully equipped troops can be carried or 16 stretchers and a medical team.

The RAF ordered 22 EH101 (Merlin) support helicopters in March 1995. Merlin was a direct replacement for the Westland Wessex and it was to operate alongside the Puma and Chinook in the medium lift role. Its ability to carry troops, artillery pieces, light vehicles and bulk loads, means that the aircraft will be ideal for use with the UK Army's 16 Air Assault Brigade.

The aircraft can carry a maximum load of 35 troops with support weapons. The maximum payload is 4,000 kg and Merlin has a maximum range of 1,000 km, which can be extended by external tanks or by air-to-air refuelling. The Merlin Mk 3 has sophisticated defensive aids and the aircraft is designed to operate in extreme conditions with corrosion-proofing for maritime operations. All weather, day/night precision delivery is possible because of GPS navigation, a forward-looking infra-red sensor and night vision goggle compatibility.

In the longer term the aircraft could be fitted with a nose turret fitted mounting a .50 calibre machine gun. It is claimed that the noise level inside the aircraft is no higher than that of a commercial turboprop aircraft.

RAF TRANSPORT AIRCRAFT

Hercules C1/C3

Crew 5/6: Capacity 92 troops or 64 paratroops or 74 medical litters: Max freight capacity 43,399 lb/19,685 kg: Length C1 29.79 m C3 34.69 m: Span 40.41 m: Height 11.66 m: Weight Empty 34,287 kg: Max All-up Weight 45,093 kg: Max speed 374 mph/602 kph: Service Ceiling 13,075 m: Engines 4 × Allison T-56A-15 turboprops.

The C-130 Hercules is the workhorse of the RAF transport fleet. Over the years it has proved to be a versatile and rugged aircraft, primarily intended for tactical operations including troop carrying, paratrooping, supply dropping and aeromedical duties. The Hercules can operate from short unprepared airstrips, but also possesses the endurance to mount long-range strategic lifts if required. As a troop carrier, the Hercules can carry 92 fully armed men, while for airborne operations 62 paratroops can be dispatched in two simultaneous 'sticks' through the fuselage side doors. Alternatively, 40 paratroops can jump from the rear loading ramp. As an air ambulance the aircraft can accommodate 74 stretchers.

Freight loads that can be parachuted from the aircraft include: 16 × 1 ton containers or 4 × 8,000 pound platforms or 2 × 16,000 pound platforms or 1 × platform of 30,000 pounds plus. Amongst the many combinations of military loads that can be carried in an air-landed operation are: 3 × Ferret scout cars plus 30 passengers or 2 × Land Rovers and 30 passengers or 2 × Gazelle helicopters.

Of the original 66 C1 aircraft, some 31 have been given a fuselage stretch producing the Mark C3. The C3 'stretched version' provides an additional 37% more cargo space. Refuelling probes have been fitted above the cockpit of both variants and some have received radar warning pods under the wing tips.

The C-130 LTW (RAF Lyneham Transport Wing) appears to have a total of 49 aircraft (including five in reserve).

Hercules C-130J C4/C5

The RAF has replaced some of its Hercules C1/C3 aircraft with second-generation C-130Js on a one-for-one basis. Twenty-five Hercules C4 and C5 aircraft were ordered in December 94, and the first entered service in 2000. Deliveries were completed by 2003 at a total cost of just over £1bn. The C4 is the same size as the older Hercules C3 which features a fuselage lengthened by 4.57 m (15ft 0 in) than the original C1. The Hercules C5 is the new equivalent of the shorter model. With a flight deck crew of two plus one loadmaster, the C-130J can carry up to 128 infantry, 92 paratroops, eight pallets or 24 CDS bundles. The Hercules C4/C5s have new Allison turboprop engines, R391 six-bladed composite propellers and a Full Authority Digital Engine Control (FADEC). This propulsion system increases take off thrust by 29% and is 15% more efficient. Consequently, there is no longer a requirement for the external tanks to be fitted. In addition there is an entirely revised 'glass' flight deck with head-up displays (HUD) and four multi-function displays (MFD) replacing many of the dials of the original aircraft. These displays are compatible with night-vision goggles (NVG).

Tristar

(8 in service) Crew 3: Passengers 265 and 35,000 pounds of freight: Length 50.05 m: Height 16.87 m: Span 47.35 m: Max Speed 964 km/ph (600 mph): Range 6,000 miles (9,600 kms): Engines 3 × 22,680 kgs thrust Rolls Royce RB 211–524B4 turbofans.

The Tristar normally cruises at 525mph and with a payload of 50,000 pounds has a range in excess of 6,000 miles. The aircraft entered service in early 1986 with No 216 Sqn which reformed at RAF Brize Norton on 1 Nov 1984.

VC-10

(18 in service) Crew 4: Carries 150 passengers or 78 medical litters: Height 12.04 m: Span 44.55 m : Length 48.36 m: Max Speed (425 mph): Range 7596 kms: All Up Operational Weight 146,513 kgs: Engines 4 × Rolls Royce Conway turbofans.

The VC-10 is a fast transport aircraft which is the backbone of Strike Command's long-range capability, providing flexibility and speed of deployment for British Forces. This multi-purpose aircraft can be operated in the troop transport, freight and aeromedical roles in addition to maintaining scheduled air services.

C-17 Globemaster

(4 in service) Crew of 2 pilots and 1 loadmaster. Capacity Maximum of 154 troops. Normal load of 102 fully-equipped troops, up to 172,200lb (78,108 kg) on up to 18 standard freight pallets or 48 litters in the medevac role: Wingspan 50.29 m: Length overall 53.04m: Height overall 16.8 m: Loadable width 5.5m: Cruising speed 648 kph (403 mph): Range (max payload) 4,444 km (2,400 miles): Engines 4 × Pratt and Whitney F117 turbofans.

The C-17 meets an RAF requirement for an interim strategic airlift capability pending the introduction of Future Transport Aircraft (A400). The decision to lease four C-17 aircraft for some £771m from Boeing was taken in 2000, and the aircraft entered service in 2001. The lease is for a period of seven years, with the option of extending for up to a further two years. The C-17 fleet is capable of the deployment of 1,400 tonnes of freight over 3,200 miles in a seven day period. The aircraft is able to carry one Challenger 2 MBT, or a range of smaller armoured vehicles, or up to three WAH-64 Apache aircraft at one time. Over 150 troops can be carried. Inflight refuelling increases the aircraft range. No 99 Sqn has some 158 flight crew and ground staff.

A400

The UK MoD is committed to 25 × Airbus A400M in 2000 to meet the Future Transport Aircraft (FTA) requirement for an air lift capability to replace the remaining Hercules C-130K C1/C3 fleet. The A400 is a collaborative programme involving eight European nations (Germany, France, Turkey, Spain, Portugal, Belgium, Luxembourg and United Kingdom), procuring a total of 196 aircraft. The expected UK cost is some £2.4bn for 25 aircraft. The projected in-service date has slipped from 2007 to 2010.

The most commonly quoted argument in favour of the A400M over the C-130J is that this aircraft could carry a 25-ton payload over a distance of 4,000 km. Thus, it is argued that a fleet of 40 × FLA could carry a UK Brigade to the Gulf within 11.5 days, as opposed to the 28.5 days required to make a similar deployment with 40 × C-130s. In any event, the RAF seems likely to retain its C-17s, and to operate a mixed transport fleet comprising the C-130J, A-400 and C-17.

RAF Attack Aircraft

Squadron	Aircraft	Location
1 Squadron	13 × Harrier GR7	Cottesmore
3 Squadron	13 × Harrier GR7	Cottesmore
4 Squadron	13 × Harrier GR7	Cottesmore
20(R)Squadron	9 × Harrier GR7	Cottesmore
9 Squadron	12 × Tornado GR4	Marham
12 Squadron	12 × Tornado GR4	Lossiemouth
14 Squadron	12 × Tornado GR4	Lossiemouth
31 Squadron	12 × Tornado GR4	Marham
617 Squadron	12 × Tornado GR4	Lossiemouth
6 Squadron	11 × Jaguar GR3	Coltishall
54 Squadron	11 × Jaguar GR3	Coltishall
16 (R) Squadron	8 × Jaguar GR3	Coltishall

Note: (R)denotes a reserve squadron.

We would expect the AAC armed helicopter to deal with the localised armoured threats to a British force on operations, with RAF aircraft (such as the Harrier and Tornado) being used on larger target at a great distance from the forward edge of the battle area. However, high performance modern aircraft are very expensive and fast jet pilots take up to three years to train. It would only be sensible to risk such valuable systems when all other options had failed. In addition, the strength of enemy air defences would probably allow only one pass to be made over the target area. A second pass by fixed- wing aircraft after ground defences had been alerted would be problematical.

Harrier

(48 in RAF operational service) Crew (GR7, GR7A, GR9, GR9A) 1: (T Mark 10, T12) 2: Length (GR7, GR7A,GR9) 14.1 m: Length (T10, T12) 17 m: Wingspan (normal) 9.2 m: Height (GR7) 3.45 m: Height (T10) 4.17 m: Max Speed 1,065 k/ph (661 mph) at sea level: All Up Operational Weight approx 13,494 kg: Engine (GR7, GR9, T10, T12) 1 × Rolls-Royce Pegasus Mk 105 (GR7A, GR9A) 1 × Rolls-Royce Pegasus Mk 107: Ferry Range 5,382 km (3,310 miles) with 4 × drop tanks. Armament on seven available wing stations: 2 × 30 mm Aden guns, 4 × wing weapon pylons and 1 × under-fuselage weapon pylon, conventional or cluster bombs: 2 × Sidewinder AIM-9L AAM, ASRAAM: up to 16 × Mk 82 or six Mk 83 bombs: 4 × Maverick air-to-ground anti-armour missiles, Paveway II and III laser-guided bombs: Brimstone anti-armour missiles, CRV-7 rocket pods: 2 × Storm Shadow CASOM.

The Harrier fleet is to receive a number of upgrades in the near future. These are expected to cost some £500m. New Pegasus 107 engines giving more thrust at higher temperatures as well as reduced maintenance costs will be fitted to 30 aircraft, these becoming Harrier GR7As. Also, a major upgrade to the aircraft's avionics and weapons systems will enable the Harrier to carry a variety of current and future weapons. These include Maverick air-surface missiles, Brimstone anti-armour missiles and AIM-9L Sidewinder air-to-air missiles for self-defence. A new, stronger composite rear fuselage will also be fitted. These 40 aircraft will become Harrier GR9s, whilst those with the uprated engines and weapons systems will be Harrier GR9As. The programme also includes an upgrade of the two-seater T10 aircraft to the equivalent GR9 standard known as the Harrier T12.

All three Harrier squadrons from RAF Cottesmore were deployed for the 2003 Iraq War in Operation Telic. The Harrier fleet is expected to be replaced by the Joint Strike Fighter in 2012-2015. Expect a Harrier GR7 Squadron to have 17 established crews.

Royal Navy Support Helicopters

Squadron	Aircraft	Location
845 Squadron	11 × Sea King HC4	Yeovilton
846 Squadron	11 × Sea King HC4	Yeovilton
848 Squadron	11 × Sea King HC4	Yeovilton
847 Squadron	6 × Lynx AH7	Yeovilton
	8 × Gazelle	

Helicopters in UK service

During March 2005 the UK MoD produced the following figures for helicopters in service with all three armed services, and the length of in-service life.

Helicopter type	Fleet size	In-service date	Planned out of service date
Attack Helicopter	67	2001	2030
Chinook Mk 2	34	1993	2015
Chinook Mk 2a	6	2000	2025
Lynx Mk 7	86	1977	2012
Lynx Mk 9	23	1992	2012
Lynx Mk 3	33	1976	2012
Lynx Mk 8	34	1994	2014
Merlin Mk 1	42	1999	2029
Merlin Mk 3	22	2000	2030
Puma Mk 1	45	1971	2010
Gazelle Mk 1	127	1973	2018
Sea King Mk 3	19	1978	2017
Sea King Mk 3a	6	1996	2017
Sea King Mk 4	37	1979	2012
Sea King Mk 5	16	1981	2017
Sea King Mk 6	4	1988	2006
Sea King Mk 6c	5	2004	2008
Sea King Mk 7	11	2002	2017
Agusta A109	4	1984	2008

In addition to the aircraft above, the UK MoD contracts for a Commercially Owned Military Registered (COMR) fleet of helicopters. These helicopters are on the Military Register and flown by military aircrew, but are owned and maintained by commercial operators.

Helicopter type and location	Number	Contract let	Contract expires
Bell 412/Shawbury	11	1997	2012
Bell 412/Cyprus	4	2003	2008
Bell 212/Belize	3	2003	2008
Bell 212/Brunei	3	1993	2008
Bell 212/Middle Wallop	1	2004	2007
Dauphin/Plymouth	2	1996	2007
Single Squirrel/Shawbury	27	1997	2012
Single Squirrel/Middle Wallop	10	1997	2012
Twin Squirrel (AS355F)/ Northolt	3	1995	2005
Twin Squirrel (AS355N)/ Northolt	4	2006	2011
Sikorski S61N/Falklands	2	1983	2011

Although planned out of service and contract expiry dates have been given, the UK MoD has emphasised that no decisions have yet been taken on the shape of the future helicopter programme, or the individual components within it.

CHAPTER 8 – ENGINEERS

Background
The engineer support for the Army is provided by the Corps of Royal Engineers (RE). Known as Sappers, the Royal Engineers are one of the Army's six combat arms, and are trained as fighting soldiers as well as specialist combat engineers. The Corps of Royal Engineers performs highly specialised combat and non-combat, and is active all over the world in conflict and peacetime. The Corps has no battle honours, its motto *'ubique'* (everywhere), signifies that it has taken part in every battle fought by the British Army in all parts of the world.

Force structure
As of September 2004, the RE had a regular Army establishment of some 9,160 personnel and a strength of 8,850 personnel. These figures are for UK trained regular army, and therefore exclude Gurkhas, Full Time Reserve Service Personnel, and mobilised reservists. The figures also exclude those with the rank of Colonel and above who are held against staff strength and requirement.This large corps comprises 15 regular regiments (including two training regiments) and five TA regiments – presently organised as follows:

Royal Engineers: Regular Army units and locations during early 2005

Unit	Location	Country	Notes
21 Engineer Regiment	Osnabruck	Germany	4 Armoured Brigade
22 Engineer Regiment	Perham Down	UK	1 Mechanised Brigade
23 Engineer Regiment	Waterbeach	UK	16 Air Assault Brigade (Woodbridge from 2006)
25 Engineer Regiment	Antrim	UK	Supports Headquarters Northern Ireland
26 Engineer Regiment	Ludgersall	Germany	To deploy to Iraq in 2005
28 Engineer Regiment	Hameln	Germany	Amphibious Engineers, 1 Armoured Division
32 Engineer Regiment	Hohne	Germany	7 Armoured Brigade
33 Engineer Regiment	Wimbish	UK	EOD
35 Engineer Regiment	Paderborn	Germany	20 Armoured Brigade
36 Engineer Regiment	Maidstone	UK	3 Division
38 Engineer Regiment	Ripon	UK	19 Mechanised Brigade, 16 Air Assault Brigade
39 Engineer Regiment	Waterbeach	UK	RAF Support
42 Engineer Regiment	Hermitage	UK	Geographic survey

The former Gurkha Engineer Regiment QGE (Queen's Gurkha Engineers) now forms part of 36 Engineer Regiment, comprising 50 Headquarters Squadron, two wheeled field squadrons (20 Field Squadron and 69 Gurkha Field Squadron) and an engineer logistic squadron (70 Gurkha Field Support Squadron). The listing of Regiments by role is as follows:

	Germany	UK
Engineer Regiments	5	6
EOD Regiment	–	1
Resident N Ireland Regiment	–	1

Training Regiments	–	2	
TA Engineer Regiments	–	5	

There are also a number of independent engineer squadrons in the UK, as shown in the next table:

Royal Engineers: Specialist units and locations during early 2005

Unit	Location	Country	Notes
12 (Air Support) Engineer Brigade	Waterbeach	UK	Air support
29 (Corps Support) Engineer Brigade	Aldershot	UK	Corps support
59 Independent Commando Squadron	Barnstaple	UK	Commando
62 Cyprus Support Squadron	Cyprus	Cyprus	Cyprus
Military Works Force, Queen's Gurkha Engineers	Nottingham	UK	Gurkhas
Works Group RE (Airfields)	Wallingford	UK	Airfields
Engineer Resources	Bicester	UK	Logistics
Engineer Training Advisory Team (ETAT)	Sennelager	Germany	Training
Geographic Engineer Group	Hermitage	UK	Geographic survey
Band of the Corps of Royal Engineers	Chatham	UK	Band

Territorial Army Royal Engineer regiments and independent units are shown below:

Royal Engineers: Territorial Army units and locations in 2005

Unit	Location	Country
71 Engineer Regiment (V)	Fife	UK
73 Engineer Regiment (V)	Nottingham	UK
75 Engineer Regiment (V)	Manchester	UK
Royal Monmouthshire RE (Militia)	Monmouth	UK
101 Engineer Regiment (V) EOD	Catford	UK
131 Independent Commando Sqn (V)	London	UK
135 Independent Commando Sqn (V)	Ewell	UK
HQ RE Territorial Army	Aldershot	UK
Central Volunteer HQ RE	Minley	UK
Military Works Force	Minley	UK

Contingents of Royal Engineers (including Volunteer Reservists) are likely to be deployed in all combat zones, including most recently Afghanistan, Iraq, Balkans, Democratic Republic of Congo, Georgia, Liberia and Sierra Leone.

Future Army Structure (FAS)

Under the late 2004 FAS proposals the following enhancements to the Royal Engineers will be implemented:

a. A new Commando Engineer Regiment (24 Commando Engineer Regiment) will be established.

b. An Air Support RHQ and associated HQ and Support Squadron will be established by the re-roling of 25 Engineer Regiment's RHQ and HQ and Support Squadron following Northern Ireland Normalisation.

c. An additional EOD squadron will be formed.

d. Two additional Close Support (CS) squadrons will be generated in order to provide support to all battlegroups within the armoured and mechanised brigades.

e. The resources cells in Field Support Squadrons will be decaderised.

f. The geographic capability will be enhanced.

g. Counter mobility support will be established within the specialist brigades.

h. Engineer reconnaissance will be embedded into formation reconnaissance regiments.

i. The Military Work Force will be enhanced and 535 Specialist Team Royal Engineers transferred from NI on NI Normalisation.

Combat engineering roles Combat engineer support to military operations may be summarised under the following headings:

◆ Mobility
◆ Counter-mobility
◆ Protection

Mobility

The capability to deliver firepower, troops and supplies to any part of the battlefield is crucial to success. Combat engineers use their skills to overcome physical obstacles both natural and man-made, ensuring that armoured and mechanised troops can reach their targets and fight effectively.

Combat Engineers employ a wide variety of equipment, including tank-mounted, amphibious and girder bridges, to cross physical barriers. This equipment can be rapidly deployed to any part of the battlefield to ensure minimum interruption to progress.

Combat engineers are trained and equipped to clear enemy minefields which block or hinder movement. All combat engineers are trained to clear minefields by hand with the minimum risk. They also employ a number of explosive and mechanical devices to clear paths through minefields.

Combat engineers are also trained to detect and to destroy booby traps.

Improving the mobility of own and friendly forces may include the following tasks:

◆ Route clearance and maintenance
◆ Construction and maintenance of diversionary routes
◆ Routes to and from hides
◆ Bridging, rafting and assisting amphibious vehicles at water obstacles
◆ Detection and clearance of mines and booby traps
◆ Assisting the movement of heavy artillery and communications units
◆ Preparation of landing sites for helicopters

Counter-mobility

Counter-mobility is the term used to describe efforts to hinder enemy movement. Combat engineers aim to ensure that hostile forces cannot have freedom of mobility. Combat engineers are trained in the use of explosive charges to create obstacles, crater roads and destroy bridges. In this role, the combat engineer may be required to delay detonation until the last possible moment to allow the withdrawal of friendly forces in the face of an advancing enemy.

Combat engineers are also responsible for laying anti-tank mines, either by hand or mechanically, to damage vehicles and disrupt enemy forces. Combat engineers are trained to handle these devices safely and deploy them to maximum effect. Combat engineers are also trained for setting booby traps.

Earthwork defences, ditches and obstacles – one of the earliest forms of battlefield engineering – are also used to prevent the advance of enemy vehicles. Hindering enemy movement may include the following tasks:

- ◆ Construction of minefields
- ◆ Improvement of natural obstacles by demolitions, cratering, and barricades
- ◆ Nuisance mining and booby traps
- ◆ Route denial
- ◆ Construction of obstacles to armoured vehicle movement, such as tank ditches

Protection

Construction of field defences is a core task for combat engineers. The capability to protect troops, equipment and weapons is critical. Combat engineers provide advice and assistance to the other parts of the Land Forces and the other services on the best methods of concealment and camouflage, and use mechanised plant to construct defensive positions and blast-proof screens.

Protection for troops in defensive positions may include field defences, minefields, wire, and other obstacles. Because of their commitment to other primary roles, there may be little engineer assistance available for the construction of defensive positions. What help can be given would normally be in the form of earth-moving plant to assist in digging, and advice on the design and methods of construction of field defences and obstacles.

Combat Engineers Military Works units have design and management teams that can provide military infrastructure support to all armed services and other government departments. Secondary protection roles include:

- ◆ Water and power supply in forward areas
- ◆ Technical advice on counter-surveillance with particular reference to camouflage and deception
- ◆ Destruction of equipment
- ◆ Intelligence

A major Engineer commitment in the forward area is the construction, maintenance and repair, of dispersed airfields for aircraft and landing sites for helicopters.

Non-Combat Engineering

Combat engineers also perform non-combat tasks during national peacetime contingencies and multilateral peace support operations in foreign countries, including:

◆ General support engineering, including airfield damage repair and repair of ancillary installations for fuel and power, construction of temporary buildings, power and water supplies, repair and construction of POL pipelines and storage facilities, and construction and routine maintenance of airstrips and helicopter landing sites
◆ Survey – including maps and aeronautical charts
◆ Explosive Ordnance Disposal – including terrorist and insurgent bombs
◆ Traffic Movement Lights for mobilisation and exercises
◆ Postal and courier services for all the Armed Forces

Recent coalition and peace support operations have highlighted the importance of combat engineers in all spheres of military activity. During the period 1993-2005, the multitude of tasks for which engineer support has been requested has stretched the resources of the Corps to its limit. Engineers are almost always among the first priorities in any call for support: tracks must be improved, roads built, accommodation constructed for soldiers and refugees, clean water provided and mined areas cleared. For example, during 2003 22 Engineer Regiment (operating in Iraq) was tasked to supply a quick fix to problem areas along the diesel pipeline for the Oil Security Force (OSF), and to ensure regular supplies of water for the Iraqi population in Basra and the surrounding urban areas.

Organisation

The smallest engineer unit is the Field Troop which is usually commanded by a Lieutenant and consists of approximately 44 men. In an Armoured Division, a Field Troop will have up to four sections, each mounted in an APC. Some Engineer Regiments in UK may have only three sections and may be mounted in wheeled vehicles such as Land Rovers and 4-Ton Trucks. An engineer troop will deploy with most of its equipment scale (known as G1098), stores and explosives to enable it to carry out its immediate battlefield tasks.

Armoured Engineer Regiment (1)

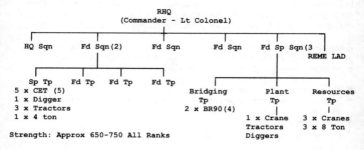

Strength: Approx 650-750 All Ranks

(1) This Regiment would send most of its soldiers to man the engineer detachments that provide support for a Division's battlegroups; (2)A Field Squadron will have approximately 68 vehicles and some 200 men; (3)Field Support Squadron; (4) or Medium Girder Bridge; (5) Combat Engineer Tractor.

This whole organisation is highly mobile and built around the AFV 432 and Spartan series of vehicles. In addition to the Regimental REME LAD, each squadron has its own REME section of some 1215 men.

An Engineer Field Troop assigned to work in support of a battlegroup operating in the area of the FEBA would normally resemble the following:

Field Troop Organisation

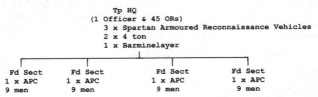

```
                    Tp HQ
              (1 Officer & 45 ORs)
           3 x Spartan Armoured Reconnaissance Vehicles
           2 x 4 ton
           1 x Barminelayer

   Fd Sect      Fd Sect          Fd Sect       Fd Sect
   1 x APC      1 x APC          1 x APC       1 x APC
   9 men        9 men            9 men         9 men
```

Engineer amphibious capability and specialist support is provided by elements of 28 Engineer Regiment in Germany and a TA Regiment with 227 Amph Engr Sqn in the UK. The current organisation of 28 Regiment incorporates five squadrons, and resembles the following:

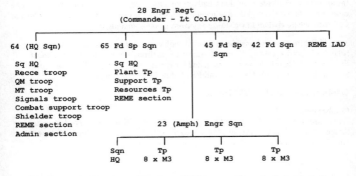

```
                         28 Engr Regt
                   (Commander - Lt Colonel)

 64 (HQ Sqn)   65 Fd Sp Sqn       45 Fd Sp   42 Fd Sqn   REME LAD
                                  Sqn
 Sq HQ         Sq HQ
 Recce troop   Plant Tp
 QM troop      Support Tp
 MT troop      Resources Tp
 Signals troop REME section
 Combat support troop
 Shielder troop
 REME section              23 (Amph) Engr Sqn
 Admin section

               Sqn        Tp          Tp          Tp
               HQ         8 x M3      8 x M3      8 x M3
```

The UK Engineer Field Regiment (Regular and TA) is generally a wheeled organisation that would normally have 2 × Field Squadrons, a Support Squadron and possibly an Airfield Damage Repair (ADR) Squadron. Engineer regiments supporting 3(UK) Division are likely to be structured along the lines of the Armoured Divisional Engineer Regiment.

33 Engineer Regiment (EOD) is currently configured as follows: 3 Field Squadrons (EOD) which each have a unique operational role and one Headquarters and Support Squadron (EOD) who hold specialist EOD support equipment. Additionally there is an Explosive Ordnance Clearance (EOC) Group who work as independent teams:

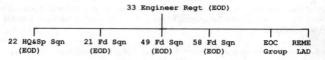

Combat engineer training

All RE officers undergo officer training at RMA Sandhurst (44 weeks) before taking the Royal Engineers Troop Commanders Course (RETCC) with 1 and 3 RSME Regiments. The RETCC is 27 weeks long. All RE officers are expected to have or to obtain university degree-level engineering qualifications, and many qualify for higher degrees in the course of their career.

Recruit training for other ranks involves three phases:

◆ Soldier training (12 to 32 weeks)
◆ Combat engineer training (10 weeks)
◆ Trade training (10 – 49 weeks)

For both officers and other ranks, specialist engineer training is mainly conducted by 1 and 3 Royal School of Military Engineer (RSME) Regiments based at Chatham and Blackwater. 1 RSME Regiment is the support regiment for training. During a year, some 8000 students may pass through 1 RSME Regiment, many of whom have recently joined the army and who have arrived at Chatham for a long engineering course lasting, in some cases, up to 44 weeks. 1 RSME Regiment incorporates the Construction Engineer School at Chatham, where civil and mechanical engineering skills are taught.

3 RSME Regiment is responsible for combat engineer training. The Combat Engineer School is located at Minley. 55 and 57 Training Squadrons are responsible for Combat Engineer and Assault Pioneer training, and Driver Training Troop, 63 Training Support Squadron, is responsible for ABLE and RE Module Driver training.

COMBAT ENGINEERING VEHICLES

Combat Engineer Tractor

(140 in service) Weight 17,010 kg: Length 7.54 m: Height 2.67 m: Road Speed 56 kph: Road Range 480 kms: Fuel Capacity 430 litres: Engine Rolls-Royce C6TCR: Engine Power 320 bhp: Crew 2: Armament 1 × 7.62 mm machine gun.

The FV180 Combat Engineer Tractor (CET), which entered service in 1977, is a versatile tracked AFV that can clear obstacles, dig pits, prepare barriers and recover other vehicles that become stuck or damaged. In short, it is an armoured vehicle that can assist in a variety of engineer battlefield tasks, and has an impressive amphibious capability. The 100 m winch cable can be fired from the CET by rocket and, using an anchor, can assist in dragging the vehicle up steep slopes and over river banks. CET is found mainly in the Divisional Engineer Regiments and the UK Engineer Regiments. India has 39 × CET in service and Singapore is believed to have another 18.

Terrier

Terrier is a lightly armoured highly mobile, general support engineer vehicle optimised for battlefield preparation in the indirect fire zone. It will replace the existing FV180 Combat Engineer Tractor from 2008, providing mobility support (obstacle and route clearance), counter-mobility (digging of anti-tank ditches and other obstacles) and survivability (digging of trenches and Armoured Fighting Vehicle slots). Terrier is claimed to be faster, more mobile and with more effective armour and mine protection than the FV-180 CET.

Terrier will be operated by a crew of two – or may be operated remotely in particularly hazardous environments. The vehicle must also be able to tow a trailer carrying fascines, trackway and the GIAT Viper minefield breaching system; clear scatterable mines; remove or enhance obstacles, and establish routes whilst keeping pace with other armoured vehicles such as the Challenger 2 MBT and the Warrior ICV. Terrier will be fitted with day and night vision systems and, although (at 30 tonnes) twice as heavy as CET, it will be air-portable in An-124, C17 or A400M transport aircraft. The Terrier manufacturer (OEM) is BAe Systems. Current indications are that some 100 vehicles could be required. Over the life of the Terrier the contract is believed to be worth some £700 million.

Trojan and Titan

The Trojan and Titan are new armoured engineer vehicles based on a common tank chassis – the Challenger 2 MBT. The replacement of the Chieftain AVRE and AVLB systems by the ETS means that the British Army has a common heavy armour fleet based on the Challenger 2 MBT chassis. Both vehicles are manufactured by the Alvis subsidiary of BAe Systems. These vehicles represent the first armoured engineer vehicles specifically designed (rather than adapted from battle tank chassis) for their role and incorporate the very latest mobility and survivability features, many of which are also planned for Challenger 2. Improved visibility is achieved by incorporating direct and indirect vision devices with low light, image intensifying and thermal imaging capabilities. The interior, and to some extent the exterior, of the vehicles have been designed around the crew station positions.

A contract worth £250 million was awarded during early 2001 for the supply of 66 vehicles – 33 × Trojan and 33 × Titan. Deliveries to the RE are expected to start in late 2005.

Trojan Armoured Vehicle Royal Engineers (AVRE)

(33 on order, in service from late 2005): Crew 3: Weight (est) 62,500 kg: Max Road Speed 59 kph: Road Range 450 km: Powerpack comprises Perkins CV12 diesel engine, David Brown TN54 enhanced low-loss gearbox, and the OMANI cooling group: Auxiliary Power Unit(APU)is also fitted: Engine Power 1,200 bhp: Armament 7.62 mm GPMG: Stowage for crew man-portable Light Anti-Tank Weapons: Fitted with NBC protection system.

Trojan is designed to open routes through complex battlefield obstacles and clear a path through minefields. Standard equipment includes a winch and a knuckle-arm excavator shovel. A Pearson Engineering Full-Width Mine Plough can be mounted at the front to clear mines and a Pearson Engineering Pathfinder clear lane-marking system can also be fitted. It can also carry fascines to drop into ditches and tow a trailer-mounted Python rocket-propelled mine-clearing system. Trojan has the flexibility to support a wide range of operations, including humanitarian missions.

In March 2004, the first prototype Trojan was delivered to the Royal Engineers Trials and Development Unit (RETDU) at Bovington. The vehicle, was to undergo a 10-month demonstration trials period – with a second vehicle due to be delivered to British units in Germany for climatic trials.

Titan Armoured Vehicle Launcher Bridge (AVLB)
(33 on order, in service from 2005): Crew 3: Weight (est) 62,500 kg: Max Road Speed 59 kph: Road Range 450 km: Powerpack comprises Perkins CV12 diesel engine, David Brown TN54 enhanced low-loss gearbox and the OMANI cooling group: Auxiliary Power Unit(APU)is also fitted: Engine Power 1,200 bhp: Carries BR-90 Close Support Bridges: No. 10 (length 26 m, span 21-24.5 m); No. 11 (length 16 m, span 14.5m); & No.12 (length 13.5 m, span 12 m): Armament 7.62 mm GPMG: Stowage for crew man-portable Light Anti-Tank Weapons: Fitted with NBC protection system.

Titan is designed to cross gaps of up to 60 ms, laying a selection of close support bridges. It can carry and lay the current range of In-Service No 10, 11 and 12 Close Support Bridges, providing ground manoeuvre formations with improved operation of the bridges enabling them to be laid in a greater range of terrain conditions.

BRIDGING EQUIPMENT

BR90
The RE BR-90 family of bridges are built from a range of seven modular panels of advanced aluminium alloy fabrication. These are interchangeable through the various bridge types, to form two interconnecting trackways with a 4 m overall bridge width and a 1 m girder depth.BR90 is deployed with Royal Engineer units in both Germany and the UK. The production order was valued at approximately £140 million in 1993. These bridges entered service from 1999, and comprise the following elements:

◆ General Support Bridge
◆ Close Support Bridge
◆ Two Span Bridge
◆ Long Span Bridge

Close Support Bridge – This consists of three tank-launched bridges capable of being carried on a tank bridgelayer and a Tank Bridge Transporter truck.
There are three basic Tank Launched Bridges (also known as Close Support or Assault Bridges): the No 10, No 11 and No 12.

General Support Bridge – This system utilises the Automated Bridge Launching Equipment (ABLE) that is capable of launching bridges up to 44 m in length. The ABLE vehicle is positioned with its rear pointing to the gap to be crossed and a lightweight launch rail extended across the gap. The bridge is then assembled and winched across the gap supported by the rail, with sections added until the gap is crossed. Once the bridge has crossed the gap the ABLE launch rail is recovered. A standard ABLE system set consists of an ABLE vehicle and 2 × TBT carrying a 32 m bridge set. A 32 m bridge can be built by 10 men in about 25 minutes

Spanning Systems – There are two basic spanning systems. The long span system allows for lengthening a 32 m span to 44 m using ABLE and the two span system allows 2 × 32 m bridge sets to be constructed by ABLE and secured in the middle by piers or floating pontoons, crossing a gap of up to 60 ms

BR-90 carrier – The Unipower 8x8 TBT is an improved mobility transporter for the BR 90 bridging system. It can carry one No 10 bridge or two No 12 bridges. The TBT can self load from, and off-load to, the ground. The TBT task is to re-supply the Chieftain and Titan AVLB with replacement bridges.

Medium Girder Bridge (MGB)

The MGB is a simple system of lightweight components that can be easily manhandled to construct a bridge capable of taking the heaviest AFVs. The MGB has been largely replaced by the BR90 system, although some MGB have been retained for certain operational requirements. Two types of MGBs are fielded: Single span bridge – 30 m long which can be built by about 25 men in 45 minutes; Multi span bridge – a combination of 26.5 m spans: a two span bridge will cross a 51 m gap and a three span bridge a 76 m gap. If necessary, MGB pontoons can be also be joined together to form a ferry.

Class 16 Airportable Bridge

In service since 1974 and a much lighter bridge than the MGB, the Class 16 can be carried assembled under a Chinook helicopter or in 3 × 3/4 ton vehicles with trailers. A 15 m bridge can be constructed by 15 men in 20 minutes. The Class 16 can also be made into a ferry which is capable of carrying the heaviest AFVs. In the near future, the British Army will replace the Class 16 bridge with the Future Light Bridge (FLB) systems. This bridge will also be capable of being used as a ferry.

M3 Ferry

Weight 24,500 kg: Length 12.74 m: Height 3.93 m: Width 3.35 m: Width (bridge deployed) 6.57 m: Max Road Speed 80 kph: Water Speed 14 kph: Road Range 725 kms: Crew 3.

The M3 can be driven into a river and used as a ferry or, when a number are joined together from bank to bank, as a bridge, capable of taking vehicles as heavy as the Challenger MBT. The M3 has a number of improvements over the M2 which it has

replaced (the M2 was in service for over 25 years). The M3 can deploy pontoons on the move, in or out of water; it needs no on-site preparation to enter the water; it can be controlled from inside the cab when swimming and its control functions have been automated allowing the crew to be reduced from four to three.

A single two-bay M3 can carry a Class 70 tracked vehicle, where two M2s would have been required for this task with additional buoyancy bags. Eight M3 units and 24 soldiers can build a 100 m bridge in 30 minutes compared with 12 M2s, 48 soldiers and a construction time of 45 minutes. The M3 is only 1.4 m longer and 3,300 kg heavier than the M2. It is still faster and more manoeuvrable on land and in water. A four-wheel steering facility gives a turning diameter of 24 m.

By early 1999, 38 × M3 rigs had been delivered and 30 of these (including four of seven pre-production vehicles) went to 28 Engineer Regiment in Germany. The unit cost was believed to be in the region of £1.2 million.

MINE CLEARANCE

Python
Trailer Weight: 136 kg; Hose Length: 230 m; Cleared Zone: 180 m × 7.3 m wide Python is a minefield breaching system that replaces the Giant Viper in RE service. The Python has the ability to clear a much longer 'safe lane' than its predecessor. It is also faster into action and far more accurate. It can clear a path 230 m long and 7 m wide through which vehicles are safe to pass.

The system works by firing a single rocket from a newly designed launcher trailer which has been towed to the edge of a mined area. Attached to the rocket is a coiled 230 m long hose packed with one and a half tons of powerful explosive. After the hose lands on the ground it detonates and destroys or clears any mines along its entire length. It is claimed that in a cleared lane, over 90% of anti-tank mines will have been destroyed.

Mine Warfare
Anti-tank minefields laid by the Royal Engineers will usually contain Barmines (anti-tank) or Mk.7 (anti-tank) mines and anti-disturbance devices may be fitted to some Barmines. Minefields will always be recorded and marked; they should also be covered by artillery and mortar fire to delay enemy mine clearance operations and maximise the attrition of armour. ATGWs are often sited in positions covering the minefield that will give them flank shoots onto enemy armour; particularly the ploughs or rollers that might spearhead a minefield breaching operation.

Shielder
Shielder provides the facility to create anti-tank barriers quickly and effectively. The system consists of modular dispensers of anti-tank mines which can be fired to either side or to the rear, mounted on a flatbed version of the Stormer Armoured Personnel Carrier. The anti-tank mines have a programmable life, at the end of which they self-destruct.

Ordered in 1995, Shielder is derived from the US Alliant Techsystems M163 Volcano system. It is believed that the total value of the order was approximately £110 million for

29 × Volcano systems, anti-tank mines, training, spares and the Stormer flatbed carrier. The first vehicles entered service in 1999.

Barmine (Anti-Tank)
Weight 11 kg: Length 1.2 m: Width 0.1 m: Explosive Weight 8.4 kg.

The Barmine is usually mechanically laid by a plough-type trailer that can be towed behind an AFV 432 or Warrior. The Barmines are manually placed onto a conveyor belt on the layer from inside the APC. The minelayer automatically digs a furrow, lays the mines into it at the correct spacing and closes the ground over them. Up to 600 mines can be laid in one hour by one vehicle with a three man crew. A full width attack (FWAM) fuse and an anti-disturbance fuse are available for Barmine; these are secured on the ends of the mine, adjacent to the pressure plate.

Claymore Mine (Anti-Personnel)
Weight 1,58 kg: Length 210 mm: Width 30 mm: Charge Weight 0.68 kg.

The Claymore Mine has a curved oblong plastic casing mounted on a pair of bipod legs. The mine is positioned facing the enemy and fired electrically from distances up to 300 m away. On initiation, the mine scatters about 700 ball-bearings out to a range of 50 m across a 60 degree arc. First purchased from the US in 1963, the Claymore is an effective anti-infantry weapon that is likely to remain in service for many years to come.

Off-Route Mine (Anti-Tank)
Length 0.26 m: Weight 12 kg: Diameter 0.2 m: Range 75 m.

This French mine is designed for vehicle ambush. The mine is placed at the side of the road and a thin electric 'breakwire' laid out across the vehicle's path. The mine is initiated when the vehicle breaks the wire; a shaped charge known as a 'Misznay Schardin Plate' fires an explosively formed projectile into the side of the vehicle.

Mine Detection

L77A1 Mine Detectors
Weight Packed with all accessories 6.5 kg: Weight Deployed ready for use 2.2 kg: Approximate Battery Life 45 hrs: Detection Depth (metal AT mine) 0.6 – 0.7 m.

The 4C, the standard mine detector of the British Army since 1968, has been replaced by the Ebinger EBEX-420PB. The Army have designated the detector L77A1 and assigned it the NATO Stock Number 6665-99-869-3649. The L77A1 is a lightweight modular design which uses pulse induction technology to locate the metallic content of mines. The battery compartment and electronics are built into the tubular structure, and an audible signal provided to the operator via a lightweight earpiece. The sensitivity is such that even modern plastic mines with a minimal metallic content can be detected to a depth of 15 cm.

CHAPTER 9 – COMMUNICATIONS

The Royal Corps of Signals

The Royal Corps of Signals (R Signals) is the combat arm that provides the communications throughout the command system of the Army. Individual battlegroups are responsible for their own internal communications, but in general terms, all communications from Brigade level and above are the responsibility of the Royal Signals.

Information is the lifeblood of any military formation in battle and it is the responsibility of the Royal Signals to ensure the speedy and accurate passage of information that enables commanders to make informed and timely decisions, and to ensure that those decisions are passed to the fighting troops in contact with the enemy. The rapid, accurate and secure employment of command, control and communications systems maximises the effect of the military force available and consequently the Royal Signals act as an extremely significant 'Force Multiplier'.

Force structure

The Royal Corps of Signals provides about 9% of the Army's manpower with nine Regular regiments(with a tenth forming), one training regiment, and 11 Territorial Army regiments, each generally consisting of between three and up to six Squadrons with between 600 and 1,000 personnel. As of September 2004, the Royal Signals had a regular establishment of some 8,630 personnel, and a regular strength of some 8,580 personnel. Principal roles of the regular and reserve regiments are believed to be as shown in the table.

Royal Corps of Signals: Regular and territorial units (principal roles)

Role	Regular Regiments	Territorial Regiments
Strategic satellite communications	1	
Ptarmigan tactical area communications	4	3
Cormorant tactical area communications	1	
Euromux regiments		2
Electronic Warfare	1	
Ground to Air helicopter communications	1	
National Communications		6
Training	1	
Total	9	11

Royal Signals personnel are found wherever the Army is deployed including every UK and NATO headquarters in the world. The Headquarters of the Corps is at the Royal School of Signals (RSS) located at Blandford in Dorset.

Royal Signals units based in the United Kingdom provide command and control communications for forces that have operational roles both in the UK itself, including Northern Ireland, and overseas including mainland Western Europe and further afield wherever the Army finds itself. There are a number of Royal Signals units permanently based in Germany, Holland and Belgium from where they provide the necessary command and control communications and Electronic Warfare (EW) support for both the British Army and other NATO forces based in Europe. Royal Signals personnel are also based in Cyprus, the Falkland Islands, Belize and Gibraltar. Regular Army Royal Signals units are shown in the following table:

Royal Signals: Regular Army units during early 2005

Unit	Location	Notes
1 Sig Bde	Germany	Supports Allied Rapid Reaction Corps (ARRC)
2 (NC) Sig Bde	Corsham HQ	Mainly TA, national communications during contingencies
11 Sig Bde	Donnington HQ	1,000 Regular and 2,500 TA personnel, communications for JRRF
3(UK)Div HQ & Sig Regt	Bulford	Divisional command and control communications
2 Sig Regt	York	With 11 Signal Bde, currently equipping with Cormorant system
10 Sig Regt	Forming	To form part of 2 Sig Bde
14 Sig Regt (EW)	Brawdy	Electronic Warfare
15 Sig Regt	N.Ireland	Command & Control communications
21 Sig Regt (Air Sp)	JHF	Communications for the RAF Support Helicopter Force and AAC Apache
30 Sig Regt	Bramcote	Strategic satellite communications to Land & Joint Task Forces
1(UK)AD and Sig Regt	Germany	Communications for 1st (UK) Armd Div HQ and Bdes
7 (ARRC) Sig Regt	Germany	Part of 1 Sig Bde, supports Allied Rapid Reaction Corps (ARRC)
16 Sig Regt	Germany	Part of 1 Sig Bde, supports Allied Rapid Reaction Corps (ARRC)
11 Signal Regt	Blandford	Training Regt, responsible for Phase 2 and 3 signals training
Queens Gurkha Signals	Various	Support 2 Gurkha Inf Bns, 2 and 30 Sig Regts, and others
209 Sig Sqn	Catterick	Independent Sqn, supporting 19 Light Brigade HQ
213 Sig Sqn	Lisburn	Independent Sqn, supporting 39 Infantry Brigade HQ
215 Sig Sqn	Tidworth	Independent Sqn, supporting 1 Mechanised Bde within 3 Div
216 Sig Sqn	Colchester	Independent Sqn, supporting 16 Air Assault Bde HQ
218 Sig Sqn	Londonderry	Independent Sqn, supporting 8 Inf Bde HQ
228 Sig Sqn	Bulford	Independent Sqn, supporting 12 Mech Bde HQ
238 Sig Sqn	London	Independent Sqn, supports London Military District
242 Sig Sqn	Edinburgh	Independent Sqn, supports Army in Scotland & Northern England
261 Sig Sqn	Aldershot	Independent Sqn, supports 101 Logistics Bde HQ

264 Sig Sqn	Hereford	Independent Sqn, supports SAS
200 Sig Sqn	Germany	Independent Sqn, supporting 20 Armd Brigade HQ
204 Sig Sqn	Germany	Independent Sqn, supporting 4 Armd Brigade HQ
207 Sig Sqn	Germany	Independent Sqn, supporting 7 Armd Brigade HQ
262 Sig Sqn	Germany	Independent Sqn, supporting 102 Logistics Brigade HQ
628 Sig Tp	Netherlands	Independent Tp, supports AFNORTH HQ
CCU & JSSU	Cyprus	Cyprus Communications Unit and Joint Service Signal Unit
JCU (FI)	Falklands	Joint Communications Unit (Falkland Islands)

TA Units

Major Royal Signals Territorial Army (TA) units are shown in the next table.

Royal Signals : Territorial Army units during early 2005

Unit	Location
2 (NC) Sig Bde	Corsham HQ
11 Sig Bde	Donnington HQ
31 Sig Regt (V)	London
32 Sig Regt	Scotland
33 Sig Regt (V)	Lancashire & Cheshire
34 Sig Regt (V)	Yorkshire, Durham & Northumberland
35 Sig Regt (V)	South Midlands
36 Sig Regt (V)	East Anglia and Essex
37 Sig Regt (V)	Wales, Midlands, Lancashire
38 Sig Regt (V)	Yorkshire, Notts, Derbyshire, Leicester
39 Sig Regt (V)	Somerset, Gloucester, Home Counties, Oxon
40 Sig Regt (V)	Ireland
32 Sig Regt (V)	
Central Volunteer Headquarters Royal Signals (CVHQ)	London
63 Sig Sqn (V)	Independent Sqn, supports TA SAS units
81 Sig Sqn (V)	Part of CVHQ
97 Sig Sqn (V)	Independent Sqn, formed from 38 Sig Reg
98 Sig Sqn (V)	Independent Sqn, formed from 11 Sig Bde

Future Army Structure (FAS)

Under the FAS proposals the Regular Units of the Royal Signals will be enhanced as follows:

a. A new Signal Regiment (22 Signal Regiment) will be established, equipped initially with Ptarmigan and then Falcon.
b. Deployable unit structures (operational Divisional Signal Regiments and Brigade Signal Squadrons) will be made more robust.
c. Enhancements will be made to strategic communications.

The Royal Signals TA will be structured as follows:

a. There will be three Ptarmigan regiments based within 11 Signal Brigade, providing a composite Ptarmigan Regiment to the Allied Rapid Reaction Corps.
b. Within 2(NC) Signals Brigade, a total of eight signals regiments (including 36 and 40 Signal Regiments) and four sub-units will provide NC (National Communications) units in support of the Home Defence MACA (Military Aid to the Civil Authority). In addition these units will provide bespoke support to other government departments.
c. 63 Signals Squadron (SAS) will continue to support Director Special Forces.
d. An Air Support Signal Troop will be provided for Joint Headquarters.
e. Royal Signals TA will continue to provide individual reinforcements to the Regular regiments attributed to LSDI.

Functions of military communications

Military communications roles undertaken by the Royal Signals may be divided into three separate functions:

Strategic communications

Communications between the political leadership, military high command, and military administrative and field commands at the divisional level. In terms of capability as opposed to function, modern communications systems increasingly blur the distinction between strategic and tactical systems as a consequence of technological advance.

Tactical communications

Communications between field formations from corps to division through brigade down to battalion level.

Electronic Warfare

The security of own forces and friendly forces communications, and the penetration, compromise and degradation of hostile communications.

Roles of military communications

Communications have enabling capabilities that support all military operations in war and peace. These roles may be summarised under the following headings:

Command and Control

Communications enable commanders at all levels to exercise command and control over their own forces. Communications enable commanders receive information, convey orders and move men and materiel, and select and position their attacking and defensive forces to maximum effect in order to take advantage of their own strengths and enemy weaknesses.

The capacity to deliver firepower, troops and supplies to any part of the battlefield is crucial to success. From the earliest days of messengers, flags, bugles and hand signals, this has been vital to successful command. Modern electronic communications systems have vastly added to this capacity, increasing the distances over which Command and Control can be exercised – from line of sight or hearing to any geographical area where forces are deployed.

Computerised Command Information

Communications enables commanders receive information from the field and rear to build up a picture of the state and disposition of their own forces as well as enemy forces. Commanders have always sought to have the fullest possible information on the dispositions and states of both their own and enemy, forces – but were typically limited by restraints of time, space and information carrying capacity.

Computer hardware and software – allied to the geographical spread, bandwidths and data-carrying capacity of modern military networks - have removed many of these constraints. Computer processing power enables information received from all sources to be sorted into meaningful patterns of use to commanders.

Such sources include:

- ◆ Voice and data reports from troops in the field
- ◆ Intelligence reports
- ◆ Mapping
- ◆ Battlefield sensors
- ◆ Multi-spectral imaging from ground reconnaissance units
- ◆ Reconnaissance and surveillance satellites, aircraft, helicopters and unmanned aerial vehicles
- ◆ Electronic Warfare systems on ground, air and sea platforms

In modern war, to capture the full scope of computer information systems, this communications effect is typically described as Command, Control, Communications, Computers, Intelligence, Surveillance and Reconnaissance (C4ISR)

Electronic Warfare

Secure communications deny the enemy knowledge of own and friendly force activities, capabilities and intelligence (Communications Security). Communications enable the penetration, compromise and destruction of enemy communication systems (Electronic Warfare).

Royal Signals Missions

Royal Signals units have three principal missions:

Communications Engineering

Communications units design, build and dismantle the tactical communications networks at division and brigade levels.

Communications Operations

Communications units operate the tactical communications networks at division and brigade levels, and also battalion and battalion group level in the case of a detached formation.

In conventional divisional and brigade level operations, battalions will typically be responsible for their own communications.

Communications Management

Communications units are responsible for the management of the whole communications nexus at division and brigade level.

These missions will need to be performed in all phases of battle:

Offensive

In the offensive: setting up command posts, setting up area communications networks and setting up wire networks to connect battalions to brigades and elsewhere as far as possible. Can set up air portable communications systems shortly after a foothold is secured on air base.

Advance

In the advance: continuing to keep forward and area communications running and providing logistics and maintenance needs for company and brigade forces as appropriate. Running wire forwards as far as possible with the advance, Setting up alternate Brigade HQs. Relocating and maintaining relay and retransmission points and ensuring communications to rear and flanks remain open.

Defensive

In the defence: re-enforcing command posts and relay points. Increasing the complexity and robustness of wire networks. Providing alternate and redundant communications for all users.

Withdrawal

In the withdrawal: Preventing communications assets falling into enemy hands, setting up alternate command posts on the line of withdrawal, running wire networks backwards to rear. Keeping nodes open and supplying logistics and maintenance support as required.

Non-Combat missions

Communications perform non-combat roles during peacetime, including national peacetime contingencies and multilateral peace support operations in foreign countries.

Training

All Royal Signals officers undergo officer training at RMA Sandhurst (44 weeks) before taking the Royal Signals Troop Commanders Course at the Royal School of Signals at Blandford Camp. Royal Signals officers are expected to have or to obtain university degree-level engineering qualifications.

Recruit training for other ranks involves two phases:

◆ Phase 1 – Soldier training (11 to 21 weeks: apprentices 6 months)
◆ Phase 2 – Trade training (7 – 50 weeks)

Every Royal Signals soldier, whether from the Army Training Regiment Bassingbourn, the Army Technical Foundation College Arborfield, or the Army Apprentices College Arborfield, carries out trade training at the Royal School of Signals at Blandford Camp. The length of the course depends on the trade chosen, varying from seven weeks up to 50.

All trades will carry out a common module of Basic Signalling Skills and a computer literacy module before specialising. Special Operators attend an introductory course of two weeks at the Royal School of Signals before completing their training at the Defence Special Signal School in Chicksands.

11 Signal Regiment is responsible for the special to arm training for both officers and other ranks. The Royal School of Signals at Blandford Camp conducts approximately 144 different types of courses and numbering over 714 courses run per year. There are in excess of 5,250 students completing courses throughout the year with about 1,070 here at any one time. These figures equate to approximately some 470,000 Man Training Days a year.

Organisation
We would expect the organisation of a Signal Regiment supporting an armoured division to be as follows:

Armoured Divisional Signal Regiment Organisation

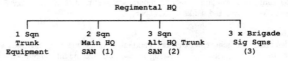

Notes: (1) SAN – Secondary Access Node (2) A Divisional HQ will have two HQs to allow for movement and possible destruction. The main HQ will be set up for approx 24 hrs with the alternate HQ (Alt HQ) set up 20–30 kms away on the proposed line of march of the division. When the Main HQ closes to move to a new location the Alt HQ becomes the Main HQ for another 24-hour period. (3) Expect a Brigade Sig Sqn to have a Radio Troop and a SAN Troop.

Equipment
Royal Signals units are currently operating the following types of major equipment:

- Static strategic communications
- Mobile strategic satellite communications
- Fixed and mobile electronic warfare (EW) systems
- Tactical Area Communications – corps to brigade down to battalion HQ
- VHF Combat Net Radios – battalion and sub-units
- Tactical HF and UHF radios – battalion and sub-units
- Radio Relay (carrying telephone & teleprinter links)
- Teleprinters, Fax, CCTV and ADP Equipment
- Computer Information Sytems
- Local area networks (LAN) and wide area networks (WAN) for computers
- Line

Tactical Area Communications
The principal tactical role of the Royal Signals is to provide corps to brigade level communications that link higher commands to battalion HQs. The area communications systems used by the Royal Signals include:

Ptarmigan

Ptarmigan is a mobile, secure battlefield system that incorporates the latest technology and has been designed to improve communications reliability, capacity and interoperability. Ptarmigan remains the core equipment for the British Army Tactical Trunk Communications System, and has undergone a number of upgrades to be better prepared to meet the challenges of changing deployments and new operational requirements. This has included the introduction of an Air Portable Secondary Access Node (SAN) for 16 Air Assault Brigade. The General Purpose Trunk Access Port (GPTAP) software enhancement will allow improved Interconnectivity to other nations tactical systems.

Bowman is shortly to replace the HQ infrastructure element of Ptarmigan. In time, Ptarmigan is due to be replaced by Falcon, which is in the early process of project definition, and will not be in service for several years. Falcon is expected to build on the lessons learned from the current introduction of Cormorant.

Built by Siemens-Plessey Christchurch (now part of BAe Systems) in the mid 1980s, Ptarmigan is a user-friendly, computer controlled communications system which was initially designed to meet the needs of the British Army in Germany. The system consists of a network of electronic exchanges or Trunk Switches that are connected by satellite and multi-channel radio relay (Triffid) links that provide voice, data, telegraph and fax communications.

The Trunk Switch, radio and satellite relays together with their support vehicles, comprise a 'Trunk Node' and all field headquarters include a group of communications vehicles that contain an Access Switch which can be connected to any Trunk Switch giving access to the system. This ensures that headquarters have flexibility in both siting and facilities and trunk communications then present no constraints on operations. Additionally Ptarmigan has a mobile telephone or Single Channel Radio Access (SCRA) which gives isolated or mobile users an entry point into the entire system.

Euromux

EUROMUX is a trunk system manufactured by Racal (now part of the French Thales group), which is similar in principle to the Ptarmigan system, and is interoperable with the trunk systems of other NATO armies. Triffid is used to provide the relay links within the system.

Cormorant

As of early 2005, this new system is entering service with 2 Signal Regiment. Cormorant will deliver new area communications capabilities to British Forces and the prime contractor for the Cormorant programme is the European EADS company. Cormorant will comprise two primary equipments: a local access component, based on an ATM switch, which will provide digital voice subscriber facilities and a high speed data LAN for over 20 Headquarters; and a wide area component will allow the interconnection of these Headquarters, on a 'backbone' communications network across a large geographical area as well as the means to interconnect with single service and multinational systems.

Designed to link all components of a Joint Force, the system will enable the force to deploy and operate its Wide Area Network (WAN) communications system in either peacekeeping roles or in a fully operational military deployment. The system is fully containerised and can be operated in either vehicle mounted or dismounted mode. Each small HQ is designed to scale up in line with the requirements of a particular operation.

A Cormorant network can consist of the following vehicle-mounted (or dismounted) installations:

- Local Area Support module
- Core Element
- Bearer Module
- Long-Range Bearer Module (Tropo)
- Management Information Systems
- Interoperable Gateways
- Tactical Fibre Optic cabling
- Short-Range Radio

Triffid
Radio relay links within Ptarmigan are provided by Triffid, which is a radio equipment that has three interchangeable radio frequency modules known as 'heads'. Each Triffid link carries the equivalent of up to 32 voice circuits at a data rate of 512 kb/s plus an engineering circuit.

Promina
Promina networks deliver pulse code modulation (PCM) and compressed digital voice analogue voice, video conferencing, Internet Protocol (IP) frame relay, asynchronous transfer mode (ATM) and legacy Synchronous and Asynchronous data services over satellite, microwave, radio and leased line services.

It is extensively used to multiplex Ptarmigan, ATacCS, and JOCS systems alongside traditional voice, video and fax services over a common bearer. Promina networks form the core of NATO and Joint Force HQs, and are deployable for rapid reaction corps.

Combat Net Radio
VHF Combat Net Radios (CNR) provide the main tactical communications for battalions and battlegroups with their sub-units down to section level. CNR communications are the responsibility of the units themselves, and the Royal Signals have no direct role in supporting these networks. Like other combat arms, Royal Signals units are equipped with CNR for their own tactical communications.

Bowman
Bowman is the Combat Net Radio that is currently replacing the Clansman series radios in service with the British Army. The Bowman project covers all the VHF and HF radio configurations used as manpacks or installed in land, sea and air platforms. Bowman is also to replace the HQ infrastructure element of the Ptarmigan area communication system. Bowman will for the first time give tactical units at all levels secure voice and data communications as well as an integrated Global Positioning System (GPS).

The Royal Signals is playing a major role in the introduction into service of Bowman. 228 Signal Sqn – supporting 12 Mechanised Brigade serving in Aldershot – has been the first

Signal unit to train on the Bowman system. By 2005 the whole of 12 Mechanised Brigade will be equipped. Following the conversion of 12 Mechanised Brigade other brigades will be equipped as follows:

2005–2006: 4 Armoured and 7 Armoured Brigades; 1 Mechanised Brigade; 16 Air Assault Brigade and 3 Commando Brigade.

2007–2008: 19 Light Brigade and 20 Armoured Brigade

Clansman was due to be replaced by Bowman in 1996 but there have been a series of problems with both contracting and development. Since July 2001, the programme prime contractor has been Computer Devices Canada (CDC) – a subsidiary of the US company General Dynamics (GD).

As well as being man-portable, BOWMAN equipment will be fitted to:

◆ Some 22,000 military vehicles, from Land Rover to the Challenger 2 Main Battle Tank
◆ Collective training facilities in the UK and overseas
◆ Five of the Royal Navy's capital ships; the frigate and destroyer fleet; and minor naval vessels
◆ The major helicopter types supporting land operations – Chinook and Merlin.

Around 45,000 Personal Role Radios, 47,000 manpack and vehicle radios, and 26,000 computer terminals are to be acquired. Some 75,000 British Army personnel will be trained to use Bowman. The cost of the supply and initial support phase for Bowman is approximately £1.9 billion and the current acquisition cost of the whole project is £2.4 billion.

Satellite Communications (SATCOM)
30 Signal Regiment deploys transportable and manpack satellite ground stations – VSC501, Talon, and in the future Reacher - to provide communications links for headquarters or small groups located in remote parts of the world via its SKYNET 4B satellite system and the new Skynet 5 satellites.

Skynet 5 satellite series
A new series of SKYNET 5 satellites is expected to enhance SATCOM facilities in the future. In 2003, the Skynet 5 contract was awarded to Paradigm. The company is tasked with delivering secure military satellite communications to UK armed forces around the world. The contract is worth around £2 billion over 20 years. This is one of the largest private finance initiatives (PFI) of its kind. Skynet 5 is expected to be fully operational in 2007.

At least two new satellites are due to be launched towards the end of the decade with the majority of satellite construction being done at Stevenage and Portsmouth. The satellites will be controlled from the UK and the service management will take place from a MoD site in Wiltshire. Skynet 5 will deliver military satellite communication services to the Armed Forces until 2018.

The capacity of Skynet 5 is expected to be about 2.5 times greater than the existing system. Users will be able to send and receive information much more quickly.

VSC501 satellite ground terminal

The VSC501 Enhanced is a Land Rover based mobile satellite ground terminal, which has recently been upgraded to automatically track satellites in their figure of eight orbit. Its first major deployment was to Iraq during the first Gulf War and it is currently in service in Iraq on Operation Telic.

Talon satellite ground terminal

Talon is a lightweight deployable terminal to fulfil both tactical and strategic roles. Talon is easily transported and set up, by a crew of two trained operators within 30 minutes. Talon has been successfully used by the ARRC (Allied Rapid Reaction Corps) in Germany for one year, and used extensively in the harsh conditions experienced during Operation Telic in Iraq.

Reacher satellite ground terminal

Reacher is designated as the replacement for the VSC 501, and will be provided in three types:

Reacher Medium – a land terminal specifically designed for X-Band Military Satellite Communications. Designed to operate with a Forward Operating Headquarters Unit, it is mounted on a Bucher Duro 6 x 6 vehicle and has a detachable Intermediate Group cabin and associated trailer.

Reacher Large – mounted on the same vehicle as the Reacher Medium, this unit has a larger antenna.

Reacher All Terrain – mounted on 2 BV206 vehicle and associated trailers.

All Reacher terminals are transportable using Chinook helicopters, C130 Aircraft, sea and rail.

NCRS

The NCRS HF communications system was accepted into service in 1995, and is known to be operated by 32 Signal Regiment (V) in Scotland. A total of 104 NCRS stations were made, consisting of 89 trailer-mounted mobile stations and 15 static, transportable stations. All the stations are identical with the exception of five mobile stations which have high power radios.

NCRS can provide a powerful national network capable of operating in the most extreme circumstances. The network can be deployed at short notice to support a wide range of national operations. NCRS stations include a variety of mobile, static, high and low powered types. Each detachment has a crew of six.

MOULD

Mould is an insecure VHF radio system that uses hilltop sites to provide national radio coverage. The radios are normally grouped together to form regional radio nets.

Army Fixed Telecommunications Systems

The peacetime management of the Army depends heavily on effective communications. The Royal Signals Army Fixed Telecommunication System (AFTS) provides all the telephone, telegraph, facsimile, data systems and radio and line links for the Army in the United Kingdom. AFTS is operated and maintained by 2 (National Communications) Brigade and the system serves over 40,000 subscribers. The staff required to operate the AFTS is approximately 1,100 of whom 40% are military personnel who are located all over the UK in six (Fixed Service) Signal Squadrons supported by operational, engineering, planning and co-ordination staff at Headquarters 2 (NC) Brigade at Corsham in Wiltshire.

One of the ADP systems in the UK is MAPPER, which stands for Maintenance, Preparation and Presentation of Executive Reports. This system is used both as a peacetime management aid to staffs in major headquarters but also for command and control of Military Home Defence and was expanded for use in the Gulf War when MAPPER stations were deployed to Saudi Arabia and linked back to the United Kingdom. Its success in the Gulf has led to the system being used in post-Gulf War operations including the Balkans.

In Germany the Telecommunications Group Headquarters based at Rheindahlen provides a sophisticated fixed communications system based on the Integrated Services Digital Network (ISDN). Project Rodin which is intended to modernise the fixed communications system for both the Army and the RAF in Germany will, when introduced, use state of the art digital technology and will be able to interact with other German and British military and civilian networks.

The Communications Projects Division (CPD) provides engineering support for military fixed communications systems worldwide. CPD is part of the Royal School of Signals at Blandford in Dorset.

BRAHMS

This is a voice encryption terminal equipment that provides secure speech over a civil or military phone system.

DUST

An encrypted telegraph system providing secure telegraph over a civil or military bearer system.

COMPUTER INFORMATION SYSTEMS (CIS)

ATacCS

The Army Tactical Computer System (ATacCS) provides the British Army with a LAN (Local Area Network) and WAN (Wide Area Network) based command and control system for in and out of barracks use across the whole battlespace. The majority of system managers and maintainers for this system are Royal Signals personnel.

JOCS

The formation of the Joint Rapid Reaction Force led to a requirement for a joint computer system. The Joint Operational Command System (JOCS) was brought into service during

1999. This system provides a sophisticated operational picture, along with staff tools for controlling joint operations.

DCM

Deployable CIS Modules (DCM) are a combination of Local Area Network and Wide Area Network (LAN/WAN), Integrated Digital Exchanges, fibre optic connections and a satellite interface capability.

Wavell

Wavell is a battlefield automatic data processing computer system, designed to accept information from all the battlefield intelligence agencies, and produce this information on request in hard copy or on a VDU. Information is then used to assist commanders and their staff with the analysis of intelligence and subsequent conduct of operations. Each headquarters from Corps down to Brigade level is equipped with its own Wavell computers that are linked to the Ptarmigan system. Wavell was continually upgraded during the 1990s.

Slim

Slim has been developed to complement Wavell.

Vixen

Vixen has been designed to provide an automated system for processing of electronic intelligence. It is probably mounted in soft-skinned vehicles and deployed with the 14 Signal Regiment (EW) which amongst its many tasks listens to enemy signal traffic and passes vital intelligence to the operational staff. Vixen became operational in late 1992 and it is probable that the system is linked to the existing electronic direction finding equipment subsequently feeding results into the battlefield artillery target engagement system (BATES)and Wavell ADP systems. The cost of the Vixen system was believed to be in the region of £36.5 million.

CHAPTER 10 – COMBAT SUPPORT

Logistic Support

In the British Army logistic support is based upon the twin pillars of service support (the supply chain) and equipment support (the maintenance of equipment).

Combat Service Support within the British Army is provided by the Royal Logistic Corps (RLC), the Royal Electrical and Mechanical Engineers (REME) and the Royal Army Medical Corps (RAMC).

Within any fighting formation logistic units from these Corps typically represent about 30% of the manpower total of an Armoured Division, and with the exception of certain members of the RAMC all are fully trained fighting soldiers. In November 2004 the total RLC personnel strength was 15,540.

The task of the logistic units on operations is to maintain the combat units in the field which entails:

a. SUPPLY AND DISTRIBUTION – of ammunition, fuel, lubricants, rations and spare parts.
b. RECOVERY AND REPAIR – of battle damaged and unserviceable equipment.
c. TREATMENT AND EVACUATION – of casualties.

In an Operational Division the commanders of the logistic units all operate from a separate, self contained headquarters under the command of a Colonel who holds the appointment of the Division's Deputy Chief of Staff (DCOS). This headquarters, usually known as the Divisional Headquarters (Rear), co-ordinates the whole of the logistic support of the Division in battle.

Supplies, reinforcements and returning casualties pass through an area located to the rear of the Division where some of the less mobile logistic units are located. This area is known as the Divisional Admin Area (DAA) and its staff are responsible for co-ordinating the flow of all materiel and personnel into and out of the Divisional area.

The Royal Logistic Corps (RLC)

The RLC is the youngest Corps in the Army and was formed in April 1993 as a result of the recommendations of the Logistic Support Review. The RLC results from the amalgamation of the Royal Corps of Transport (RCT), the Royal Army Ordnance Corps (RAOC), the Army Catering Corps (ACC), the Royal Pioneer Corps (RPC) and elements of the Royal Engineers (RE). The Corps makes up about 16% of the Army with about 16,000 regular personnel and 12,000 Territorial Army soldiers wearing its cap badge.

There are 22 Regular RLC Regiments (20 operational and two training regiments)and under the terms of the Future Army Structure the RLC TA will probably be structured around 15 regiments plus Catering Support Regiment RLC (V).

The RLC has very broad responsibilities throughout the Army including the movement of personnel throughout the world, the Army's air dispatch service, maritime and rail transport, operational re-supply, explosive ordnance disposal, which included hazardous bomb disposal duties. Other areas of responsibility include the operation of numerous very large vehicle and stores depots both in the UK and overseas, the training and provision of cooks to virtually all units in the Army, the provision of pioneer labour and the Army's postal and courier service.

The principal field elements of the RLC are the Close Support and the General Support Regiments whose primary role is to supply the fighting units with ammunition, fuel and rations (Combat Supplies).

A division has an integral Close Support Regiment which is responsible for manning and operating the supply chain to Brigades and Divisional units.

Close Support Regiment RLC

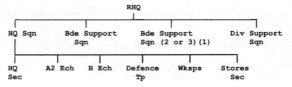

Note:
(1) A regiment could have two or three brigade support squadrons depending upon the size of the division being supported.
(2) Some of these regiments may have a Postal and Courier Sqn.

Brigade Support Squadron

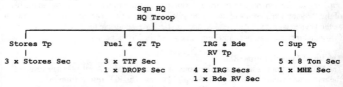

Divisional Support Squadron

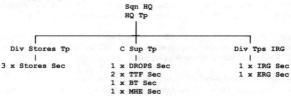

The General Support Regiment's role is primarily to supply ammunition to the Royal Artillery using DROPS vehicles, and to provide tank transporters that move armoured vehicles more rapidly and economically than moving them on their own tracks.

General Support Regiment RLC

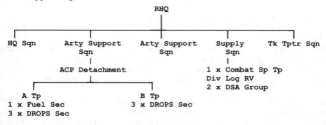

Both types of Regiment have large sections holding stores both on wheels and on the ground. A division will typically require about 1,000 tons of Combat Supplies a day but demand can easily exceed that amount in high intensity operations.

Battlegroups in contact with the enemy can carry a limited amount of C Sups, particularly ammunition As ammunition is expended, it is replenished from RLC vehicles located immediately to the rear of battlegroups in an Immediate Replenishment Group (IRG) area. As the IRG vehicles are emptied they return to the RLC Squadron location and fully loaded replacements are automatically sent forward. This system ensures that a constant supply is always available to the battlegroup.

Ammunition and spares are generally carried on NATO standard pallets. These pallets are loaded to meet the anticipated requirements of particular units and if required, bulk consignments are broken down at the IRG location. Fuel is usually carried in bulk fuel tankers (TTFs) which top-up battlegroup vehicles direct. However there is still a requirement for a large number of the traditional jerricans. Within the NATO area large amounts of fuel can be delivered to the forward areas through the NATO Central European Pipeline System (CEPS).

Artillery ammunition constitutes by far the largest single element in the logistic pipeline. The bulk of this ammunition is delivered directly to the Royal Artillery guns, rocket and missile launchers by RLC Demountable Rack Off Loading and Pickup System (DROPS) vehicles from the General Support Regiment. DROPS vehicles are capable of meeting the requirement of even the highest intensity consumption.

RLC miscellaneous units
Apart from the RLC units that provide direct support the operational formations the RLC is either directly responsible for or co-located with other agencies at the following:

♦ Army School of Mechanical Transport
♦ Base Ordnance Depots

◆ Base Ammunition Depots
◆ Army School of Ammunition
◆ Army Petroleum Centre
◆ Army Base Vehicle Organisation
◆ Armoured Vehicle Sub Depot
◆ Army School of Catering (Aldershot)
◆ Royal Logistic Corps Training Centre (Deepcut)

Vehicles

Although many of the vehicles operated by the RLC are common to all arms RLC units are in the main the majority users. During April 2005 a £1 billion contract was awarded to MAN ERF, will see the delivery from 2007 of over 5,000 modern, versatile and robust support vehicles, with an option to buy thousands more under consideration.

The vehicles, will be capable of transporting large quantities of bulk equipment to front-line troops wherever they are operating. The new fleet will consist of a mix of cargo and recovery vehicles. They will replace the MOD's tri-service fleet of four, eight and 14 tonne cargo vehicles and recovery trucks.

The current (April 2005) British Army vehicle fleet is based around the following vehicles:

Vehicle type	Army
Bedford 4 Tonne	5,002
Bedford 8 Tonne	1,460
Bedford 14 Tonne	900
Leyland-Daf Trucks	3,796
Ambulances operational	780
Ambulances non-operational	11
Land Rover operational	12,191
Land Rover non-operational	148

Daily Messing Rates

The allowances per day for catering purposes are based on a ration scale costed at current prices and known as the daily messing rate (DMR). The ration scale is the same for all three services, and contrary to popular army belief the RAF are not supplied with wine etc at public expense. The rate per day is the amount that the catering organisation has to feed each individual serviceman or servicewoman.

The scale is costed to the supply source of the food items. When the source of supply is more expensive due to local conditions the DMR is set higher to take account of local costs. A general overseas ration scale exists for overseas bases and attachments. This scale has a higher calorific value to take into account the conditions of heat, cold or humidity that can be encountered.

The UK ration scale is designed to provide 2,900 kilo calories nett – that is after loss through preparation and cooking. The general overseas ration scale includes an arduous duty allowance to allow for climate and provides some 3,400 kilo-calories nett. In field conditions where personnel are fed from operational ration packs 3,800 kilo calories are provided.

RLC Catering Units feed the Army generally using detachments of cooks attached to units.

Postal

The Central Army Post Office (APO) is located at Mill Hill in North London and there are individual British Forces Post Offices (BFPO) wherever British Forces are stationed. During the period 17 November-15 December 2004 approximately 112,000 kg of packets (approximately 110 tons) were successfully processed by the British Forces Post Office Depot at Mill Hill so that they would reach service personnel deployed worldwide in time for Christmas

The Royal Electrical & Mechanical Engineers REME

Equipment Support remains separate from the other logistic pillar of Service Support and consequently the REME has retained not only its own identity but expanded its responsibilities. Equipment Support encompasses equipment management, engineering support, supply management, provisioning for vehicle and technical spares and financial management responsibilities for in-service equipment.

The aim of the REME is "To keep operationally fit equipment in the hands of the troops" and in the current financial environment it is important that this is carried out at the minimum possible cost. The equipment that REME is responsible for ranges from small arms and trucks to helicopters and main battle tanks. All field force units have some integral REME support (1st line support) which will vary, depending on the size of the unit and the equipment held, from a few attached tradesmen up to a large Regimental Workshop of over 200 men. In war REME is responsible for the recovery and repair of battle damaged and unserviceable equipment.

The development of highly technical weapon systems and other equipment has meant that REME has had to balance engineering and tactical considerations. On the one hand the increased scope for forward repair of equipment reduces the time out of action, but on the other hand engineering stability is required for the repair of complex systems.

Seven REME Equipment Support Battalions have been established. Six of these battalions provide second line support for the British contribution to the ACE Rapid Reaction Corps (ARRC) and formations in the UK. Three battalions are based in the UK and three battalions are based in Germany to support 1(UK) Armoured Division. An Equipment Support Aviation Battalion in the UK supports the Army Air Corps units assigned to the Joint Helicopter Command.

There are currently four TA REME Equipment Support Battalions but under the Future Army Structure proposals, each armoured and mechanised brigade will be supported by a REME Battalion.

REME Equipment Support Battalion (Outline)

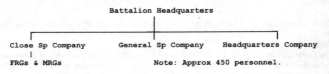

The Close Support Company will normally deploy a number of FRG's (Forward Repair Groups) and MRGs (Medium Repair Groups) in support of brigades. The company is mobile with armoured repair and recovery vehicles able to operate in the forward areas, carrying out forward repair of key nominated equipment often by the exchange of major assemblies. It is also capable of carrying out field repairs on priority equipment including telecommunications equipment and the repair of damage sustained by critical battle winning equipments.

The role of the General Support Company is to support the Close Support Companies and Divisional Troops. Tasks include the regeneration of fit power packs for use in forward repair and the repair of equipment backloaded from Close Support Companies. The General Support Company will normally be located to the rear of the divisional area in order to maximise productivity and minimise vulnerability.

In manpower terms the REME support available to the units of a division might resemble the following:

Armoured Regiment	120
Armoured Recce Regiment	90
Armoured Infantry Battalion	90
Close Support Engineer Regiment	85
General Support Engineer Regiment	110
Field Regiment Royal Artillery	115
Air Defence Regiment Royal Artillery	160
Army Air Corps Regiment	130
Signals Regiment	60
RLC Close Support Regiment	75
RLC General Support Regiment	95
REME Equipment Support Battalion	450

ARMY MEDICAL SERVICES

The Royal Army Medical Corps (RAMC)

In peace, the personnel of the RAMC are based at the various medical installations throughout the world or in field force units and they are responsible for the health of the Army.

On operations, the RAMC is responsible for the care of the sick and wounded, with the subsequent evacuation of the wounded to hospitals in the rear areas. Each Brigade has a medical squadron which is a regular unit (in some cases this may be a TA unit) that operates in direct support of the battlegroups. These units are either armoured, airmobile or parachute trained. There are generally extra medical squadrons that provide support at the divisional level; once again these squadrons can be either regular or TA. These divisional squadrons provide medical support for the divisional troops and can act as manoeuvre units for the forward brigades when required.

All medical squadrons have medical sections that consist of a medical officer and eight Combat Medical Technicians. These sub-units are located with the battlegroup or units being supported and they provide the necessary first line medical support. In addition, the field provides a dressing station where casualties are treated and may be resuscitated or stabilised before transfer to a field hospital. These units have the necessary integral ambulance support, both armoured and wheeled to transfer casualties from the first to second line medical units.

Field hospitals may be regular or TA and all are 200 bed facilities with a maximum of eight surgical teams capable of carrying out life saving operations on some of the most difficult surgical cases. Since 1990 regular medical units have been deployed on operations either in the Persian Gulf, the Former Yugoslavia, Sierra Leone, Afghanistan and Iraq.

Casualty Evacuation (CASEVAC) is by ambulance either armoured or wheeled and driven by RLC personnel or by helicopter when such aircraft are available. A Chinook helicopter is capable of carrying 44 stretcher cases and a Puma can carry six stretcher cases and six sitting cases.

In early 2005 there are 5 × regular medical regiments and three hospitals. The TA provide 10 × independent field hospitals and 1 × specialist field hospital. The early 2005 estimate of the RAMC personnel total is approximately 2,700.

During early 2005 there were some 335 UK medically trained staff in Iraq. (Defined as personnel that have medical, nursing or paramedical training and whose primary role when deployed is the co-ordination or delivery of medical care).

British casualties from Iraq are aeromedically evacuated to the United Kingdom. The clinical decision as to which hospital they should be treated is made in conjunction with the Department of Health (DoH) on the basis of clinical need and bed availability. However the majority are treated at Selly Oak hospital in Birmingham. Those requiring specialist treatment will be referred to the most appropriate facility for their needs.

The Queen Alexandra's Royal Army Nursing Corps (QARANC)
The QARANC is an all-nursing and totally professionally qualified Corps. Its male and female, officer and other rank personnel, provide the necessary qualified nursing support at all levels and covering a wide variety of nursing specialities. QARANC personnel can be found anywhere in the world where Army Medical services are required.

The mid 2004 QARANC personnel total is approximately 805.

Royal Army Dental Corps (RADC)

The RADC is a professional corps that in mid 2004 consisted of 395 officers and soldiers. The Corps fulfils the essential role of maintaining the dental health of the Army in peace and war, both at home and overseas. Qualified dentists and oral surgeons, hygienists, technicians and support ancillaries work in a wide variety of military units – from static and mobile dental clinics to field medical units, military hospitals and dental laboratories.

The Adjutant General's Corps (AGC)

The Adjutant General's Corps formed on 1 April 1992 and its sole task is the management of the Army's most precious resource, its soldiers. The Corps absorbed the functions of six existing smaller corps; the Royal Military Police, the Royal Army Pay Corps, the Royal Army Educational Corps, the Royal Army Chaplains Department, the Army Legal Corps and the Military Provost Staff Corps.

The Corps is organised into four branches, Staff and Personnel Support (SPS) Provost, Educational and Training Services and Army Legal Services. In early 2005 the estimate of the AGC personnel total is just under 7,000.

The Role of SPS Branch

The role of SPS Branch is to ensure the efficient and smooth delivery of Personnel Administration to the Army. This includes support to individual officers and soldiers in units by processing pay and Service documentation, first line provision of financial, welfare, education and resettlement guidance to individuals and the provision of clerical skills and information management to ensure the smooth day to day running of the unit or department.

AGC (SPS) officers are employed throughout the Army, in direct support of units as Regimental Administrative Officers or AGC Detachment Commanders. They hold Commander AGC(SPS) and SO2 AGC(SPS) posts in district/Divisional and Brigade HQs and fill posts at the Adjutant General's Information Centre (AGIC) and general staff appointment throughout the Army headquarters locations.

AGC(SPS) soldiers are employed as Military Clerks in direct support of units within the AGC Field Detachments, in fixed centre pay offices, in headquarters to provide staff support and in miscellaneous posts such as embassy clerks, as management accountants or in AGIC as programmer analysts.

The principal functional tasks of AGC(SPS) personnel on operations are:

a. The maintenance of Field Records, including the soldiers Record of Service, casualty reporting and disciplinary documentation.
b. Clerical and staff support to Battle Group HQs and independent Sub Units such as Engineer and Logistic Squadrons.
c. The issue of pay and allowances to personnel.
d. The maintenance of Imprest Accounts (the MoD Public Accounts) which involve paying local suppliers for services, receiving cash from non-Army agencies such as NAAFI and Forces Post Office receipts.
e. The deployment of a Field Records Cell which co-ordinates all personnel administration in the field.

f. AGC(SPS) personnel play a full part in operational duties by undertaking such tasks as local defence, guards and command post duties. In addition, Command Officers can employ any soldier in their unit as they see fit and may require AGC(SPS) personnel to undertake appropriate additional training to allow them to be used in some specialist roles specific to the unit, or as radio operators or drivers.

Currently, about 70% of AGC(SPS) soldiers are based in UK, 20% in Germany and 10% elsewhere. The majority, currently 70% are serving with field force units, with the remaining 30% in base and training units or HQs, such as MoD.

Members of AGC(SPS) are first trained as soldiers and then specialise as Military Clerks. AGC(SPS) officers complete the same military training as their counterparts in other Arms and Services, starting as the Royal Military Academy, Sandhurst. They are required to attend all promotion courses such as the Junior Command and Staff Course, and to pass the standard career exams prior to promotion to the rank of Major.

Outline Organisation of a Regimental Administrative Office

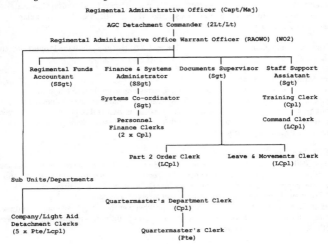

The Role of the Provost Branch
The Provost Branch was formed from the formerly independent Corps of Royal Military Police (RMP) and the Military Provost Staff Corps (MPSC). Although they are no longer independent they are still known as the AGC (PRO) and AGC (MPS) thus forming the two parts of the Provost Branch.

Royal Military Police

To provide the police support the Army requires the RMP has the following functions:

a. Providing operational support to units in the field.
b. Preventing crime.
c. Enforcement of the law within the community and assistance with the maintenance of discipline.
d. Providing a 24 hour response service of assistance, advice and information.

Operational support includes advising commanders and the staff who produce the operational movement plans. RMP traffic posts are deployed along the main operational movement routes and provide a constant flow of traffic information regarding the progress of front line troops and the logistical resupply. RMP with a vehicle to man ratio of 1:3 are also a valuable force for the security of rear areas. In addition there is a highly trained RMP close protection group that specialises in the protection of high risk VIPs.

The RMP provide the day to day police support for both the army in the UK and dependents and MoD civilians overseas. RMP units are trained and equipped to deal with the most serious crimes. The Special Investigation Branch (SIB) operates in a similar fashion to the civilian CID.

There are two regular RMP regiments and in mid 2004 the strength of the Provost Branch was 2,040.

The Military Provost Staff

AGC(MPS) staff are recruited from within the Army are carefully selected for the leadership, management and training skills necessary to motivate the predominantly young offenders with whom they work. The majority of AGC(MPS) personnel are located in the Military Corrective Training Centre (MCTC) at Colchester where offenders sentenced by military courts are confined.

The Role of the ETS Branch

The AGC(ETS) Branch has the responsibility of improving the efficiency, effectiveness and morale of the Army by providing support to operations and the developmental education, training, support and resettlement services that the Army requires to carry out its task. ETS personnel provide assistance at almost all levels of command but their most visible task is the manning of Army Education Centres wherever the Army is stationed. At these centres officers and soldiers receive the educational support necessary for them to achieve both civilian and military qualifications.

The Role of the ALS Branch

The AGC(ALS) Branch advises on all aspects of service and civilian law that may affect every level of the Army from General to Private soldiers. Members of the branch are usually qualified as solicitors or barristers.

In March 2005 the ALS employed 88 solicitors/barristers.

In addition to the AGC personnel attached to major units throughout the Army the Corps is directly responsible for the following:

Smaller Corps

THE INTELLIGENCE CORPS (Int Corps) – The Int Corps deals with operational intelligence, counter intelligence and security. During early 2005 the personnel strength of the Intelligence Corps was 1,380.

THE ROYAL ARMY VETERINARY CORPS (RAVC) – The RAVC look after the many animals that the Army has on strength. Veterinary tasks in today's army are mainly directed towards guard or search dogs and horses for ceremonial duties.

THE ARMY PHYSICAL TRAINING CORPS (APTC) – Consists mainly of SNCOs who are responsible for unit fitness. The majority of major units have a representative from this corps on their strength.

ROYAL ARMY CHAPLIN'S DEPARTMENT (RAChD) – Provides officers and soldiers with religious and welfare support/advice. The RAChD has approximately 140 chaplains who represent all of the mainstream religions.

THE GENERAL SERVICE CORPS (GSC) – A holding unit for specialists. Personnel from this corps are generally members of the reserve army.

SMALL ARMS SCHOOL CORPS (SASC) – A small corps with the responsibility of training instructors in all aspects of weapon handling.

CHAPTER 11 – UNITS OF THE REGULAR ARMY (during early 2005)

The Cavalry
After the re-organisation following the Options for Change review, the cavalry consists of 11 armoured regiments and one mounted ceremonial regiment as follows:

The Household Cavalry
The Household Cavalry Regiment	HCR
The Household Cavalry Mounted Regiment	HCMRD

The Royal Armoured Corps
1st The Queen's Dragoon Guards	QDG
The Royal Scots Dragoon Guards	SCOTS DG
The Royal Dragoon Guards	RDG
The Queen's Royal Hussars	QRH
9th/12th Royal Lancers	9/12L
The King's Royal Hussars	KRH
The Light Dragoons	LD
The Queen's Royal Lancers	QRL
1st Royal Tank Regiment	1 RTR
2nd Royal Tank Regiment	2 RTR

The Infantry
Divided into 40 general service battalions, plus four battalions of the Royal Irish Regiment (1 × General Service and 3 × Home Service battalions).

The Guards Division
1st Bn Grenadier Guards	1 GREN GDS
1st Bn Coldstream Guards	1 COLM GDS
1st Bn Scots Guards	1 SG
1st Bn Irish Guards	1 IG
1st Bn Welsh Guards	1 WG

There are generally three battalions from the Guards Division on public duties in London at any one time. When a Regiment is stationed in London on public duties it is given an extra company to ensure the additional manpower required for ceremonial events is available.

The Scottish Division
1st Bn The Royal Scots	1 RS
1st Bn The Royal Highland Fusiliers	1 RHF
1st Bn The King's Own Scottish Borderers	1 KOSB
1st Bn The Black Watch	1 BW
1st Bn The Argyll & Sutherland Highlanders	1 A and SH
1st Bn The Highlanders	1 HLDRS

The Queen's Division
1st Bn The Princess of Wales's Royal Regiment (Queen's and Royal Hampshire)	1 PWRR

2nd Bn The Princess of Wales's Royal Regiment (Queen's and Royal Hampshire)	2 PWRR
1st Bn The Royal Regiment of Fusiliers	1 RRF
2nd Bn The Royal Regiment of Fusiliers	2 RRF
1st Bn The Royal Anglian Regiment	1 R ANGLIAN
2nd Bn The Royal Anglian Regiment	2 R ANGLIAN

The King's Division

1st Bn The King's Own Royal Border Regiment	1 KOBR
1st Bn The King's Regiment	1 KINGS
1st Bn The Prince of Wales's Own Regiment of Yorkshire	1 PWO
1st Bn The Green Howards	1 GH
1st Bn The Queen's Lancashire Regiment	1 QLR
1st Bn The Duke of Wellington's Regiment	1 DWR

The Prince of Wales's Division

1st Bn The Devonshire & Dorset Regiment	1 D and D
1st Bn The Cheshire Regiment	1 CHESHIRE
1st Bn The Royal Welch Fusiliers	1 RWF
1st Bn The Royal Regiment of Wales	1 RRW
1st Bn The Royal Gloucestershire, Berkshire and Wiltshire Regiment	1 RGBW
1st Bn The Worcestershire & Sherwood Foresters Regiment	1 WFR
1st Bn The Staffordshire Regiment	1 STAFFORDS

The Light Division

1st Bn The Light Infantry	1 LI
2nd Bn The Light Infantry	2 LI
1st Bn The Royal Green Jackets	1 RGJ
2nd Bn The Royal Green Jackets	2 RGJ

The Brigade of Gurkhas

1st Bn The Royal Gurkha Rifles	1 RGR
2nd Bn The Royal Gurkha Rifles	2 RGR

The Parachute Regiment

1st Bn The Parachute Regiment	1 PARA
2nd Bn The Parachute Regiment	2 PARA
3rd Bn The Parachute Regiment	3 PARA

The Royal Irish Regiment

1st Bn The Royal Irish Regiment (Regular)	1 R IRISH
2nd Bn The Royal Irish Regiment (Home Service)	2 R IRISH
3rd Bn The Royal Irish Regiment (Home Service)	3 R IRISH
4th Bn The Royal Irish Regiment (Home Service)	4 R IRISH

* The 2nd to 4th Bns The Royal Irish Regiment are employed exclusively in Northern Ireland and were formerly battalions of The Ulster Defence Regiment.

From April 2002 there will be four infantry training battalions at the Infantry Training Centre located at Catterick in North Yorkshire.

Under Director Special Forces

The 22nd Special Air Service Regiment	22 SAS
Special Reconnaissance Regiment	SRR

The SAS can be classed as an infantry unit but the members of the regiment are found from all arms and services in the Army after exhaustive selection tests.

The Royal Regiment of Artillery (RA)

1st Regiment Royal Horse Artillery	1 RHA
3rd Regiment Royal Horse Artillery	3 RHA
4th Regiment	4 REGT
5th Regiment	5 REGT
7th Regiment Royal Horse Artillery	7 RHA
12th Regiment	12 REGT
14th Regiment	14 REGT
16th Regiment	16 REGT
19th Regiment	19 REGT
26th Regiment	26 REGT
29th Commando Regiment	29 REGT
32nd Regiment	32 REGT
39th Regiment	39 REGT
40th Regiment	40 REGT
47th Regiment	47 REGT

The Corps of Royal Engineers (RE)

1st RSME Regiment	1 RSME REGT
3rd RSME Regiment	3 RSME REGT
21st Engineer Regiment	21 ENGR REGT
22nd Engineer Regiment	22 ENGR REGT
23rd Engineer Regiment	23 ENGR REGT
25th Engineer Regiment	25 ENGR REGT
28th Engineer Regiment	28 ENGR REGT
32nd Engineer Regiment	32 ENGR REGT
33rd Engineer Regiment	33 ENGR REGT (EOD)
35th Engineer Regiment	35 ENGR REGT
36th Engineer Regiment	36 ENGR REGT
38th Engineer Regiment	38 ENGR REGT
39th Engineer Regiment	39 ENGR REGT
Queen's Gurkha Engineers	QGE

The Royal Corps of Signals (R SIGNALS)

1st (UK) Armd Div HQ and Signal Regiment	1 SIG REGT
2nd Signal Regiment	2 SIG REGT
3rd (UK) Div HQ & Signal Regiment	3 SIG REGT
7th (ARRC) Signal Regiment	7 SIG REGT
10th Signal Regiment	10 SIG REGT
11th Signal Regiment (Trg Regt)	11 SIG REGT
14th Signal Regiment (Electronic Warfare)	14 SIG REGT
15th Signal Regiment	15 SIG REGT
16th Signal Regiment	16 SIG REGT
21st Signal Regiment (Air Support)	21 SIG REGT
30th Signal Regiment	30 SIG REGT
Queen's Gurkha Signals	QGS

The Army Air Corps (AAC)

1st Regiment	1 REGT AAC
2nd Regiment	2 REGT AAC (Training)
3rd Regiment	3 REGT AAC
4th Regiment	4 REGT AAC
5th Regiment	5 REGT AAC
9th Regiment	9 REGT AAC
7th Regiment	AAC is a TA Regiment

THE SERVICES

The Royal Logistic Corps (RLC)

1 General Support Regiment	1 (GS) REGT
2 Close Support Regiment	2 (CS) REGT
3 Close Support Regiment	3 (CS) REGT
4 General Supply Regiment	4 (GS) REGT
5 Territorial Army Training Regiment	5 (TRG) REGT
6 Support Regiment	6 (SP) REGT
7 Transport Regiment	7 (TPT) REGT
8 Artillery Support Regiment	8 (ARTY SP) REGT
9 Supply Regiment	9 (SUP) REGT
10 Transport Regiment	10 (TPT) REGT
11 Explosive Ordnance Disposal Regiment	11 (EOD) REGT
12 Supply Regiment	12 (SUP) REGT
13 Air Assault Regiment	13 (AIR ASSLT) REGT
14 Supply Regiment	14 (SUP) REGT
17 Port and Maritime Regiment	17 (PORT) REGT
21 Logistic Support Regiment	21 (LOG SP) REGT
23 Pioneer Regiment	23 (PNR) REGT
24 Regiment	24 REGT
27 Transport Regiment	27 (TPT) REGT
29 Regiment	29 REGT
89 Postal and Courier Regiment	89 (PC) REGT
Commando Logistic Regiment	CDO LOG REGT
Queens's Own Gurkha Logistic Regiment	QOGLR

ACE Mobile Force (Land) Combat Services Support Battalion
There are Combat Service Support (CSS) Battalions with the Royal Marines 3 Commando
Brigade, 16 Air Assault Brigade and 19 Light Brigade.

Royal Electrical and Mechanical Engineers (REME)

1st Bn REME	1 BN REME
2nd Bn REME	2 BN REME
3rd Bn REME	3 BN REME
4th Bn REME	5 BN REME
5th Bn REME	5 BN REME
6th Bn REME	6 BN REME
7th Bn REME	7 BN REME

Royal Army Medical Corps (RAMC)

1 Close Support Medical Regiment	1 CS MED Regt
4 General Support Medical Regiment	4 GS MED Regt
5 General Support Medical Regiment	5 GS MED Regt
16 Close Support Medical Regiment	16 CS MED Regt

Military Bands

Following the 1993 re-organisation of military bands the Regular Army has 30 bands as
follows:

Household Cavalry	– 70 musicians	– 2 bands
Grenadier Guards	– 49 musicians	– 1 band
Coldstream Guards	– 49 musicians	– 1 band
Scots Guards	– 49 musicians	– 1 band
Welsh Guards	– 49 musicians	– 1 band
Irish Guards	– 49 musicians	– 1 band
Royal Artillery	– 49 musicians	– 1 band
Royal Engineers	– 35 musicians	– 1 band
Royal Signals	– 35 musicians	– 1 band
Royal Logistic Corps	– 35 musicians	– 1 band
REME	– 35 musicians	– 1 band
Adjutant General's Corps	– 35 musicians	– 1 band
Army Air Corps	– 35 musicians	– 1 band
Royal Armoured Corps	– 140 musicians	– 4 bands
Scottish Division	– 70 musicians	– 2 bands
Queens Division	– 70 musicians	– 2 bands
Kings Division	– 70 musicians	– 2 bands
Prince of Wales's Division	– 70 musicians	– 2 bands
Light Division	– 49 musicians	– 1 band
Parachute Regiment	– 35 musicians	– 1 band
Royal Irish Regiment	– 35 musicians	– 1 band
Royal Gurkha Rifles	– 35 musicians	– 1 band

Under the terms of the 2004 Future Army Structure there will be a reduction in the number
of bands including four infantry and two RAC bands. Another limited redundancy
programme will be required and full details will be published later in 2005.

CHAPTER 12 – RECRUITING, SELECTION AND TRAINING

Recruiting can best be described as the steps taken to attract sufficient men and women of the right quality to meet the Army's personnel requirements. Selection is the process that is carried out to ensure that those who are accepted into the Army have the potential to be good soldiers and are capable of being trained to carry out their chosen trade. Training is the process of preparing those men and women for their careers in the Army. Training is progressive and continues all the way through a soldier's career.

Overview of Army Training
Since the end of the Cold War, the British Army has been cut in size by around a third, and there have been significant changes in the organisation and structure of army training – and the process of reform continues in 2005. The Adjutant General (Personnel and Training Command) has overall responsibility for army training, and had a budget of over £1.7bn in 2004. Since 1997, the Army Training and Recruiting Agency (ATRA) has been responsible within the Adjutant General (Personnel and Training Command)HQ for the delivery of army recruiting and training.

In 2001, the Defence Training Review (DTR) conducted by the MoD identified possibilities for the rationalisation of defence training on a joint service basis. As one consequence of the review, the Directorate General Training and Education organisation (DG T&E) was launched in September 2002 to provide a much needed central strategy and policy focus to continue the drive for more effective and better value training. Another result was the Defence Training Review Rationalisation Programme. This programme has led to the creation of joint service Federated Defence Training Establishments (DTE), which has already impacted ATRA provision of Phase 2 and Phase 3 army training, and further changes are expected by the end of 2005.

Army Training and Recruiting Agency
The Army Training and Recruiting Agency (ATRA) is responsible for each stage of an officer cadet's or recruit's progress from the recruiting office, through a Recruit Selection Centre, into recruit training, through specialist courses before they are finally posted to their regiment in the Field Army. The ATRA is headed by the Director General Army Manning and Recruiting (DGAMR), a Major General in The Ministry of Defence, who is responsible for ensuring that the Army is properly manned and that sufficient men and women of the right quality are recruited to meet the needs of the service.

The ATRA Headquarters is based at Upavon, close to many of the training units. Recruiting is carried out from 123 sites in towns and cities throughout the country and individual training is conducted at some 40 schools. With a permanent staff of about 12,000, the Agency is responsible for Ministry of Defence land, buildings and field assets valued at more than one and a quarter billion pounds.

The annual ATRA budget is between £600-700m from which ATRA is required to enlist about 15,000 recruits and to train a total of about 100,000 officers and soldiers. ATRA conducts almost 1,500 different types of courses, with over 6,000 actual courses run each year. There are an average of 12,000 officers and soldiers under training at any time.

Across all training phases, the average annual unit cost of training a soldier or officer was over £16,000 in 2001.

ATRA operations are divided into four inter-related functions: Recruiting, Recruit training (Phase 1), Specialist training (Phase 2), and Career training (Phase 3).

Recruiting

An MoD committee called the Standing Committee Army Manpower Forecasts (SCAMF) calculates the numbers that need to be enlisted to maintain the Army's personnel at the correct level. The Committee needs to take account of changing unit establishments, wastage caused by servicemen and women leaving the service at the end of their engagements, and those who might choose to leave before their engagements come to an end (PVR – Premature Voluntary Retirement). The number required in each trade in the Army is assessed and figures are published at six monthly intervals so that adjustments may be made during the year.

Within ATRA, the Recruiting Group runs all Army Recruiting from the headquarters in Upavon. Recruiting activities take place all over the country, using the network of 123 Careers Offices, 61 Schools Advisers, 26 Army Youth Teams and 93 Regimental Recruiting Teams, as of 2003.

The Director of Army Recruiting (DAR), a Brigadier serving in ATRA under the Ministry of Defence, and his staff located throughout the United Kingdom are responsible for the recruiting and selection to meet the personnel targets.

Potential recruits are attracted into the Army in a number of ways including advertisements on the television, in cinemas and in the press. Permanently established recruiting teams from many Regiments and Corps tour the country and staff from the Army Career Information Offices (ACIO) visit schools, youth clubs and job centres. There is a network of ACIOs that operate throughout the UK. There are also Army Careers Advisers who access schools and universities throughout the country. Young, recently trained soldiers are also sent back to their home towns and schools to talk to their friends about life in the Army and are regularly interviewed by the local press.

Annual Army recruiting figures during the recent past are as follows:

	1990/91	2000/01	2001/02	2002/2003	2003/2004
Officers	1,450	870	820	900	880
Soldiers	16,050	13,900	14,030	15,710	14,310

Outflow figures (personnel leaving the army) in the recent past are:

	1990/91	2000/01	2001/02	2002/2003	2003/2004
Officers	1,860	1,150	1,090	980	950
Soldiers	20,960	14,080	13,290	13,580	13,640

Soldier Selection

Potential recruits are normally aged between 16 years and nine months and 27 years, except when they are applying for a vacancy as an apprentice when the age limits are from

16 years to 18 years and six months. As a trained soldier the minimum length of service will be four years from the age of 18, or from the start of training, if over 18.

Under the selection system, a potential recruit will have a preliminary assessment at the ACIO. Here he or she will take the computer based Army Entrance Test (AET) which is designed to assess ability to assimilate the training required for the candidate's chosen trade. The staff at the ACIO will then conduct a number of interviews to decide on overall suitability for the Army. The ACIO staff will look at references from school or any employers and offer advice on which trade may be available and might suit the candidate. A preliminary medical examination will also be carried out that checks on weight, eyesight and hearing.

If these tests and interviews are successfully passed the candidate will be booked for further tests at the Recruit Selection Centre which is closest to his or her home. Recruit selection centres are at Lichfield, Pirbright, and Ballymena in Northern Ireland.

The candidates will remain at the RSC for an overnight stay and undergo another medical examination, a physical assessment test and an interview with a Personnel Selection Officer. The potential recruit will also see at first hand the type of training that they will undergo, and the sort of life that they will lead in barracks if successful in getting into the Army. Physical fitness is assessed based on a 'best effort' 1.5 mile timed run and some gymnasium exercises. After further interviews the candidate is informed if he or she is successful and if so is offered a vacancy in a particular trade and Regiment or Corps.

The selection process is intended to be demanding, and many applicants fail to be accepted for recruit training. As the table shows, the failure rate at the RSC has reduced, but remained high at around 37% of all entrants in 2002.

Recruit Selection Centres: applicants and enlistments

	Applicants	RSC attendees	RSC passes	Failure rate	Enlistments
1999–2000	42,498	23,464	13,418	42.80%	15,026
2000–01	33,332	23,725	14,009	41.00%	13,391
2001–02	38,929	24,735	15,098	39.00%	13,473
2002–03 to end of July 2002	15,389	6,967	4,393	36.90%	3,521

Phase 1 Basic Training for Recruits

Basic Recruit or Phase 1 training comprises the Combat Infantryman's Course (CIC) for infantry and the Common Military Syllabus Recruit(CMSR)for all other British Army regiments and corps.

Recruit Physical Training Assessments – During Recruit Training personnel are assessed at different stages of training as follows:

Test	Introduction	Interim	Final
Heaves	2	4	6
Sit Up Test	1 Min (20 reps)	2 min (42 reps)	3 min (65 reps)
1.5 Mile Run	11 min 30 sec	11 mins 10 min	30 sec

As part of ATRA, the Initial Training Group (ITG) is responsible for Phase 1 (Basic) Training of the majority of soldier recruits, which is undertaken primarily at the four Army Training Regiments; Bassingbourn, Winchester, Lichfield in Staffordshire and Pirbright. Exceptions to this are the adult Infantry recruits who go direct to the School of Infantry at Catterick.

ITG is also responsible for the Army Foundation College at Harrogate and the Army Technical Foundation College at Arborfield (formerly the Army Apprentices College). The group is also responsible for the Recruit Selection Centres where potential soldier recruits undergo initial selection.

Until mid-2002 the Army training organisation carried out centralised Phase 1 Training at four Army Training Regiments (ATRs). Since then, infantry recruits do all of their training at the Infantry Training Centre (Catterick).

School of Infantry, Catterick

Catterick is the home of all Infantry Training at Phase 1 and Phase 2, except Junior soldiers destined for the Infantry who continue to receive Phase 1 training at Bassingbourn and at the Army Foundation College. Catterick comprises the Headquarters School of Infantry and the Infantry Training Centre, Catterick. Also under its Command are the Infantry Battle School at Brecon and the Infantry Training Centre at Warminster, which both provide Phase 3 training for Infantry officers and soldiers.

Combat Infantryman's Course

The Combat Infantryman's Course (CIC) is the framework upon which all regular infantry recruit training is based. The course equips recruits with infantry special to arms skills needed for a rifle platoon ready to deploy on an operational tour after minimal further appropriate pre-operational training in the Field Army. Successful completion of the CIC marks the end of initial army training.

The majority of recruits joining the infantry choose line infantry regiments; they undertake the standard CIC which lasts for 24 weeks. Recruits joining the Foot Guards, Parachute Regiment and the Gurkhas, carry out additional training to meet the particular needs of these regiments. Similarly, recruits from the Army Foundation College at Harrogate undertake a specially adapted, but shorter CIC.

The Combat Infantryman's Course (Single) is structured around three phases as follows:

Weeks 1–6 Individual skills, drill, weapons training, fitness and fieldcraft.
Weeks 7–21 Team skills, endurance training including long runs, patrolling skills.
Weeks 22–24 Live firing and battle camp at Sennybridge in Wales.

The unit costs of recruiting and training infantry are substantial, as shown in the next table.

Costs of infantry recruiting and training (Phase 1 and Phase 2)

Infantry Group	Length of course (weeks)	Cost per trainee for financial year 2003–04 (£)
Line	24	£22,000
Guards	26	£26,000
Para	28	£37,000

Recruits from Nepal joining the Royal Gurkha Rifles, Queen's Gurkha Engineers, Queen's Gurkha Signals and the Queen's Own Gurkha Transport Regiment are trained at the ITC on a 38 week CIC(G). This combines the normal Common Military Syllabus Recruits (CMS(R)) course taught at the Army Training Regiments with the CIC course and it includes a special English language and British culture package.

Royal Irish Regiment recruits also undertake the CIC at Catterick, excepting Junior Entry soldiers whose Phase 1 training takes place at Ballymena in Northern Ireland before Phase 2 training at Catterick.

Army Training Regiments

Phase 1 training for all regiments and corps except infantry comprises Common Military Syllabus Recruit (CMSR). This includes training in the basic military skills required of all soldiers and incorporates weapon handling and shooting, drill, physical fitness, field tactics, map reading, survival in nuclear chemical and biological warfare and general military knowledge. It is an intensive course and requires the recruit to show considerable determination and courage to succeed.

Since 2002, Phase 1 training for regiments and corps excluding infantry is undertaken by four Army Training Regiments as shown below:

ATR Pirbright – The Household Cavalry, The Royal Logistic Corps, the Royal Electrical and Mechanical Engineers and the Royal Artillery.

ATR Winchester – The Royal Armoured Corps, The Army Air Corps, The Adjutant General's Corps (including the Royal Military Police), The Intelligence Corps, Army Medical services and Musicians.

ATR Lichfield – The Royal Engineers and The Royal Signals.

As of early 2005, ATRA is conducting a study to evaluate the capacity requirements for Phase 1 soldier training, and to determine the most long term economical use of the existing Phase 1 training real estate. The study will identify and develop a range of options including the feasibility of closing one of the ATRs.

Junior Entry recruits

ATR Bassingbourne is the centre for training of Junior Entry recruits, most of whom will be 16 years old. The new courses are called:

a. Army Development Course (ADC) – 20 weeks.
b. Army Development Course (Advanced) or (ADC(A)) – 29 weeks.

Both courses will train the recruits in basic soldiering, but the ADC(A) course has an additional education element – Key Skills in literacy, numbers and communication.

Gurkhas

Gurkha recruits are trained in the UK by the Royal Gurkha Rifles. As many as 30,000 potential Gurkha recruits apply to join the British Army each year and between 150 and 200 are selected.

Phase 2 Special to Arm Recruit Training

Phase 2 training is the 'Special to Arm' training that is required to prepare soldiers who have recently completed their basic Phase 1 training, to enable them to take their place in field force units of their Regiment or Corps. This phase of training has no fixed period and courses vary considerably in length.

The 2001 Defence Training Review triggered a rationalisation of Phase 2 training facilities towards a joint service provision, where appropriate.

As of early 2005, Phase 2 training for the major Arms and Services of the British Army is carried out as follows:

Infantry – Infantry recruits do all of their recruit training (Phase 1 and Phase 2) at the Infantry Training Centre at Catterick.

The Royal Armoured Corps – Training takes place at the Armour Centre at Bovington Camp and Lulworth. Recruits into the Household Cavalry Regiment also undergo equitation training.

The Royal Artillery – Training takes place at the Royal School of Artillery at Larkhill in Wiltshire.

The Royal Engineers – Training takes place at the Combat Engineering School at Minley, the Construction Engineer School in Chatham and Blackwater and the Defence Explosive Ordnance Disposals School.

Royal Signals – Training takes place at the Royal School of Signals at Blandford in Dorset. Since April 2004, the Defence College of CIS (DCCIS), based at Blandford, subsumed the responsibilities of the Royal School of Signals (RSS), and the provision of Royal Navy and Royal Air Force Signals training.

Army Air Corps – Training takes place at the School of Army Aviation in Middle Wallop

The Royal Logistic Corps – Training takes place at the RLC Training Regiment and Depot at Deepcut and the School of Logistics at Marchwood – previously under the joint Defence Logistic Support Training Group (DLSTG),and since April 2004 under Defence College of Logistics (DCL), also based at Deepcut. Under these new arrangements, ATRA is also responsible for Royal Navy and Royal Air Force Logistics training. The Army School of Catering, Aldershot, the Army School of Ammunition at Kineton and the School of Petroleum, West Moors are also ATRA logistics training facilities, as is the Defence School of Transport at Leconfield.

Royal Electrical and Mechanical Engineers – Vehicle Mechanics are trained at Bordon and other trades at Arborfield. Since April 2004, the Electro Mechanical elements of the ATRA REME Training Group transferred to the new Defence College of Electro Mechanical Engineering under the command of the Naval Recruiting and Training Agency (NRTA). The Aeronautical elements of the REME Training Group transferred to the Defence College of Aeronautical Engineering under the command of the RAF Training Group Defence Agency (TGDA). The ATRA REME Training Group ceased to exist in name at the end of 2003.

The Adjutant General's Corps – Pay and Clerks are trained at the AGC Depot at Worthy Down near Winchester and the Royal Military Police at Chichester. The Army School of Training Support is at Upavon, the Defence School of Languages at Beaconsfield and the Defence Animal Centre at Melton Mowbray. From April 2002, the School of Finance and Management, previously part of the Group and located at Worthy Down, became part of the Defence Academy, although it will remain at Worthy Down for the present. From April 2004, the Adjutant General's Corps Training Group (AGCTG) and Royal Military Police (RMP) training school transferred to the command of the RAF Training Group Defence Agency (TGDA) at the new Defence College of Police and Personnel Administration. Also from April 2004, responsibility for the Defence Animal Centre came under the Defence College of Logistics.

Intelligence Corps – Have trained since 1997 at the Defence Intelligence and Security Centre (DISC) in Chicksands in Bedfordshire. The DISC is responsible for training all personnel in intelligence, security and information support. In June 2003, command of the Defence School of Languages transferred to DISC, although the school remained at Beaconsfield.

Army Medical Services (AMS) – made up of the Royal Army Medical Corps (RAMC), Royal Army Dental Corp (RADC), Queen Alexandra's Royal Army Nursing Corps (QARANC), and the Royal Army Vetinary Corps (RAVC). Training is conducted by the joint service Defence Medical Training Organisation at Aldershot and Birmingham, the Defence Dental Agency at Aldershot, and the RAVC training centre at Melton Mowbray respectively.

Rationalisation of Phase 2 training

The MoD expects further rationalisation of Phase 2 specialist training by early 2006. It intends to modernise and improve specialist training by rationalising training delivery and facilities on joint service rather than single service lines, and through the more efficient use of a reduced training estate. A partnering arrangement with industry is envisaged to take this programme forward. Two contractual packages are envisaged, comprising:

◆ Package 1: Aeronautical Engineering, Electro-Mechanical Engineering and Communication and Information Systems.
◆ Package 2: Logistics, Police and Personnel Administration and Security, Languages, Intelligence and Photography.

Length of Service

As a general rule, all recruits enlist on an Open Engagement. This allows a recruit to serve for 22 years from their 18th birthday or date of attestation, whichever is the later, and so qualify for a pension.

A soldier enlisted on this engagement has a statutory right to leave after four years reckoned from the 18th birthday or from three months after attestation, whichever is the later, subject to giving 12 months notice of intention to leave and providing the soldier is not restricted from leaving in any way. Certain employments, particularly those involving a lengthy training, carry a time bar which requires a longer period before soldiers have the statutory right to leave.

For the initial period after joining the Army individuals are able to be "Discharged As Of Right" (DAOR). There is no obligation to stay during this time. The length of the period of DAOR is six months for under 18s and three months for over 18s after turning up at the Army Training Regiment. Individuals after this time are committed to serve for a minimum engagement of four years. There are of course allowances made for medical and exceptional compassionate circumstances.

Officer Commissions

There are five main types of commission in the Army. These are:

a. THE REGULAR COMMISSION (Reg C) which is for those who wish to make the Army their permanent career. Regular Officers can normally expect their career to last up to the age of 55 and for some until their 60th birthday.

All candidates for a Regular Commission should hold at least five GCSEs, or equivalent, (grades A–C, including English and Maths, plus a science subject or foreign language) and 140 UCAS Tariff Points at A/AS Level, or equivalent. Two of the passes should be at 'A' level grades A to E. Some Corps only accept candidates with appropriate degrees or professional qualifications. As a general rule, all civilian candidates should be over 17 years and nine months and under 29 on entry to Sandhurst.

b. THE SHORT SERVICE COMMISSION (SSC) which is for those who remain uncertain about their long-term career plans. The SSC lasts for a minimum of three years (six for the Army Air Corps) but can be extended if mutually agreed to a maximum of eight years.

The requirements for a Short Service Commission are less stringent requiring only five passes at GCSE grades A–C including English Language or Mathematics. Candidates for commissions should be over 17 years and nine months and under 25 years old when they begin officer training.

c. SHORT SERVICE LIMITED COMMISSION – The SSLC is a commission that is aimed at those who have completed their 'A' Levels and have a gap year prior to entering University. The selection procedure at RCB has to be completed after which a four-week course at Sandhurst is attended. Those who successfully complete the course join their chosen Regiment or Corps as 2nd Lieutenants for a minimum of four months and a maximum of 18 months with a front-line unit, but not on active service. The purpose of the SSLC is to create a pool of young men and women who will take a favourable impression of the Army into their careers.

d. UNDERGRADUATE ARMY PLACEMENT (UGAP) – UGAP *is* a new Commission for highly motivated undergraduates studying at UK universities requiring a placement as part of their degree. Up to 20 places are available each year. In September 2002, the first selected candidates started the four-week course at RMAS before joining their sponsor regiments.

e. LATE ENTRY COMMISSIONS – A number of vacancies exist for senior Non Commissioned Officers and Warrant Officers to be granted commissions known as Late Entry Commissions. Officers commissioned from the ranks are initially employed in exactly the same way as those granted direct entry commissions but because of their age, generally do not rise above the rank of Major.

Officer Selection and Sandhurst

Candidates for commissions are normally advised by a Schools or University Liaison Officer of the options open to them and who arranges for interviews and familiarisation visits to an appropriate Regiment or Corps. If the Regiment or Corps is prepared to sponsor a candidate they then guide him or her through the rest of the selection procedure. All candidates are required to attend the Regular Commissions Board (RCB) at Westbury, Wiltshire for a three-day assessment prior to which they should have undergone a medical examination and attended a pre RCB briefing so that they know what to expect.

RCB consists of a series of interviews and tests that assess the personality and the leadership potential in applicants. There is no secret in the selection procedures and details are available for all applicants. In 2003/04,RCB filtered over 3800 candidates down to 1673, of whom 1010 received passes, while Territorial Commissions Board (TCB) passed 221 out of 320 candidates.

All potential officers accepted for training attend the RMAS Common Commissioning Course which lasts for 44 weeks with three entries a year in January, May and September. After successfully completing the Sandhurst course a young officer then completes a further specialist course with his or her chosen Regiment or Corps. Females cannot be accepted in the Household Cavalry, The Royal Armoured Corps or the Infantry.

In 2003–2004, the RMAS commissioned 622 Direct Entry Officers into the British Army and trained 68 Foreign and Commonwealth Officers to the same standards. In addition, a further 175 Late Entry Officers and 92 Professionally Qualified Officers (PQOs) successfully completed Regular Army courses at the RMAS and 197 Territorial Army (TA) Officers and 82 TA PQOs were commissioned.

Welbeck College

Welbeck is the Army's sixth form college which offers two year 'A' Level courses for boys and girls who wish to gain commissions in the technical corps. The Welbeck course is science and engineering based and includes leadership training, Welbexians do not need to attend the Regular Commissions Board, but simply require the recommendation of the Headmaster to gain entry to RMAS.

Army Technical Foundation College

The Army Technical Foundation College (ATFC) at Arborfield delivers Phase 1 (initial military) training to Junior Entry recruits in the Technical Corps: the Royal Engineers, Royal Signals, Royal Logistic Corps and Royal Electrical and Mechanical Engineers. The ATFC Mission is to prepare young soldiers of the technical arms for Phase two training and beyond by providing them with challenging foundation training and the opportunity to develop into potential leaders. It is a 28 week course divided into two terms. The course was adjusted in 2002 to improve the success rates of ATFC graduates during their Phase 2 training. The ATFC course content is as follows:

a. Common Military Syllabus (Recruits) – basic training.
b. Leadership training – military exercises, adventurous training, initiative training.
c. Vocational Education – IT, Maths, Military Technology, Communications.

The military training takes place on training areas around the UK and the adventurous training (canoeing, climbing, hill-walking) takes place in Wales. Expeditions are also undertaken to a variety of countries, such as Spain, Norway, and Germany.

Whilst at the ATFC, all recruits will register for a Foundation Modern Apprenticeship, consisting of Key Skills and an NVQ Level 2 in Information Technology. The qualifications are awarded to successful candidates by City and Guilds. On completion of the 28 week course, the trained soldiers will embark on their trade training at their respective regiments.

Army Foundation College

The Army Foundation College (AFC) at Harrogate delivers Phase 1 (initial military) training to Junior Entry recruits destined for the Royal Armoured Corps, Royal Artillery and Infantry. Recruits make their final capbadge selection after week 21. The aim of the course is to develop the qualities of leadership, character, and team spirit required of a soldier to achieve a full career in the Army. The 42-week course is a progressive and integrated package divided into three 14-week terms. It combines the Common Military Syllabus (Recruits) with Vocational Education and Leadership and Initiative Training. Recruits achieve a Foundation Modern Apprenticeship and up to Key Skills Level 3.

Entrants to the college are aged between 16 and 17 years. They are offered the opportunity to pursue a one year Army Foundation Course. This course provides a supportive environment and the Foundation Course allows students to develop a broad range of skills and qualifications that are equally valuable in both Army and civilian life. There are three main elements to the course:

There are 23 weeks of military training, which include basic or advanced soldiering, progressive physical training, infantry weapons, grenades, military leadership, marksmanship, parade ground drill. There is also a two week final exercise in the field.

There are five weeks of leadership and initiative training which includes hill walking, hiking, caving, rock climbing, abseiling, and all types of leadership and command tasks.

Lastly, there are 14 weeks of vocational education which can result in NVQ or SVQ in Information Technology.

About 1,000 young soldiers attend the college each year.

Phase 3 In-Service Training

An officer or soldier will spend as much as one third of their career attending training courses. Following basic Phase 1 and Phase 2 training soldiers are posted to their units and progressive training is carried out on a continual basis. Training is geared to individual, sub-unit or formation level and units regularly train outside of the UK and Germany. As would be expected there are specialist unit training packages for specific operational commitments such as Northern Ireland, Former Yugoslavia, Afghanistan, and Iraq.

For example the training package for personnel warned off for deployment to the former Yugoslavia consists of a 12 day special-to-mission package. The training is carried out by specialist training advisory teams at the Army's Combined Arms Training Centre at Warminster and for Germany based units at the Sennelager Training Centre.

Phase 3 training facilities are the same as those listed under Phase 2, and also includes the Defence Academy located mainly at Shrivenham. Defence Academy training and education facilities incorporate the Joint Services Command and Staff College at Shrivenham, the Defence Academy College of Management and Technology (previously known as Royal Military College Shrivenham), the Royal College of Defence Studies, the Defence Leadership Centre, and Defence School of Finance and Management. The Joint Doctrine and Concepts Centre is colocated at Shrivenham. A Joint Services Warrant Officer's School is part of the Joint Services Command and Staff College at Shrivenham at Shrivenham.

Overseas Students

During any one year, about 4,000 students from over 90 different countries take part in training in the United Kingdom. The charges for training depend on the length of the course, its syllabus and the number taking part. Receipts from overseas governments for this training are believed to be in the region of £30–40 million.

Training areas outside the UK and Europe

The British Army's main training areas outside of the Europe are:

Canada – Suffield

British Army Training Unit Suffield (BATUS) has the responsibility to train battlegroups in the planning and execution of armoured operations through the medium of live firing and tactical test exercise. There are $6 \times$ 'Medicine Man' battlegroup exercises each year in a training season that lasts from March to November.

Canada – Wainright

The British Army Training Support Unit at Wainwright (BATSU(W)) provides the logistic and administrative support for Infantry units at the Canadian Forces training base in Western Canada. During the winter months the unit moves in its entirety to Fort Lewis in the USA where it carries out a similar function. There are usually three battalion group exercises at Wainright and two at Fort Lewis during the course of each training year.

Kenya

British Army Liaison Staff Kenya (BATLSK) is responsible for supporting Infantry battalion group exercises and approximately 3,000 British troops train in Kenya each year in a harsh unforgiving terrain ranging in altitude from 8,000 feet down to 2,300 feet. BATLSK has been based at its present site in Kahawa Barracks since Kenya's independence in 1963.

Belize

The British Army Training Support unit Belize (BATSUB) was formed on 1 October 1994. Its role is to give training and logistic support to Land Command units training in a tropical jungle environment. In general terms BATSUB costs about £3 million per year.

Jungle Warfare School

The Jungle Warfare Wing (JWW) is located on the island of BORNEO close to the border with Sarawak (Malaysia) and is supported by the British Army's Brunei Garrison. JWW exists to provide a jungle training facility to meet the requirement to train jungle warfare instructors for the Field Army of the United Kingdom's Land Forces.

Basic Fitness Test

All recruits and soldiers of all ranks and ages are required to take a basic fitness test. At the Recruiting Selection Centres, potential recruits undergo a series of tests known as Physical Standards Selection for Recruits (PSSR). These are 'best effort' tests that take place in the gymnasium. Recruits are required to complete the 1.5 mile (2.4 km) run. Adult Entry candidates have to complete the run within 14 minutes or less. All Junior Entrants – Army Foundation College, Army Technical Foundation College or the School Leavers Scheme – are required to complete the run in 14 minutes 30 seconds or less. At the RCB selection board for officers, male candidates are expected to run 1.5m in 10 minutes 30 seconds or less, and female candidates in 11 minutes 30 seconds.

Fitness training for recruits and officer cadets raises these fitness standards and requirements. Recruits in training are given 10 mins and 30 seconds for the 1.5 mile run, while officer cadets are expected to run 3 miles in 22 minutes.

In-service fitness requirements seek to maintain these standards. Tests typically require a 1.5 mile run on level ground and in training shoes, in 10-12 minutes for those under 30, and a three mile run (including a 1.5 m walk and run in squads) in 22 to 30 minutes, depending on service arm. There are gradually rising time limits for older personnel The current standards for women are lower, and female recruits are allowed to do the 1.5 mile run in 12 minutes and 50 seconds.

Standard fitness tests currently applied for infantry personnel include:

◆ BPFA Basic Personal Fitness Assessment. Sit ups, press ups, and a 1.5 m (2.4 km) run, all carried out against the clock. This tests individual fitness generally. The minimum fitness goals are: 54 continuous sit ups (with feet supported) and 2.4 km (1.5 m) run in 11 minutes 45 seconds.
◆ ICFT Infantry Combat Fitness Test. A distance of three miles as a squad carrying 56 pounds of kit each, including personal weapon. Timed to be completed in one hour, individuals must stay with the squad, or be failed.

CHAPTER 13 – RESERVE FORCES

There have been reserve land forces in Britain since medieval times. Over time, the titles and structures of these reserve forces changed, but until World War 2 essentially comprised four separate elements: Volunteers, Militia, and Yeomanry provided the part-time, voluntary territorial forces; while retired Regular Army personnel made up the Army Regular Reserve on a compulsory basis, subject to diminishing obligations with age. Today the Army Reserve is formed from the same components – with the difference that the erstwhile Volunteers, Militia, and Yeomanry are now incorporated into a single volunteer force as the Territorial Army (TA). Some 40% of regular Army recruits are said to come from the TA and Army Cadet Force. The TA costs an estimated sum of around £350 million a year – around 1.3% of the defence budget.

Army Reserve manpower strength
As of April 2004, the total army reserve strength amounted to some 180,000 personnel of all ranks. The Ready Reserve, comprising the Army Reserve and Territorial Army, numbered some 64,000 personnel.

Army Reserve manpower, as of April 2004

Component	Category	Officers	Other ranks	Total
Regular Reserve	Army Reserve	9,220	22,000	31,220
	Individuals liable to recall	110,720		110,720
Volunteer Reserve	Territorial Army	5,840	26,590	32,430
	Non-Regular Permanent Staff	270	840	1,110
	OTC		4,780	4,780
Total Reserve Strength	Regular Reserve + Volunteer Reserve	15,060	159,310	174,370
Ready Reserve (= Army Reserve + TA)	Army Reserve + TA	15,060	48,590	63,650
Mobilised manpower	Army Reserve	20	130	150
	Territorial Army	490	2,410	2,900
	Full-Time Reserve Service (FTRS)			280
Total mobilised manpower		510	2,540	3,330

Note: OTC (Officer Training Corps) personnel numbers assume typical substantive rank of Lcpl

In September 2004, the total TA strength was reported as 35,480 personnel, of which number some 2,200 were mobilised, compared to the mobilisation of some 100 Regular Reserve.

More than 9,000 TA personnel were called up for service in Iraq and Afghanistan in 2003 and 2004. They cannot be used in operations for more than 12 months in any three-year period – making most of those who have already served ineligible for call up for the next two years.

Types of Reservist
Members of the Army Reserve fall into two main components:

- Retired regular reserve
- Volunteer reserve

Retired regular reserve forces
The Regular reserve are comprised of people who have a mobilisation obligation by virtue of their former service in the regular army. For the most part, these reservists constitute a standby rather than ready reserve, and are rarely mobilised except in times of national emergency or incipient war. Some 420 retired regular reservists were called-up for Iraq operations in 2003.

The Regular Reserve consists of Individual Reservists (IR), who have varying obligations in respect of training and mobilisation, depending on factors such as length of regular service, age and sex. Categories of Individual Reservists are as follows:

- Officer Reserve – with a compulsory training obligation of 4-6 years after leaving regular or reserve service
- Regular Reserve – non-commissioned officers and other ranks who have a compulsory training obligation of up to 6 years after leaving regular service
- Long-term Reserve – men (but not women) who have completed their Regular Reserve obligation, who serve in this capacity until the age of 45 and who have no training obligation
- Military pensioners – ex-regular personnel who have completed pensionable service, who have a legal liability for recall up to the age of 60 (55 is the maximum age in general practice), and who have no training obligation

Many ex-regulars join the Volunteer Reserve Forces after leaving regular service – giving them a dual Reserve status.

Volunteer Reserve
The Volunteer reserve consists mainly of people who have joined the Territorial Army directly from the civilian community. These personnel form the main part of the active, ready reserve for the British Army, train regularly, and are paid at the same rates as the regular forces on a pro-rata basis.

Most TA volunteers commit to a minimum of some 40 days training a year, comprising one drill night in a week, one week-end in a month and 14 days annual training. Some reservists exceed these minima.

The Reserve Forces Act 1996 provided for other categories of reservists, such as:

- Full Time Reserve Service (FTRS) – reservists who wish to serve full time with regulars for a predetermined period in a specific posting

◆ Additional Duties Commitment – part-time service for a specified period in a particular post.

The Act also provided two new categories of service, including:

◆ Sponsored Reserves, being contractor staff who have agreed to join the Reserves and have a liability to be called up when required to continue their civilian work on operations alongside the Service personnel who depend upon them. Some 1,500 sponsored reservists have served in Iraq.

Territorial Army units are widely dispersed across the country – much more so than the Regular Forces and in many areas, they are the visible face of the Armed Forces. They help to keep society informed about the Armed Forces, and of the importance of defence to the nation, and have an active role supporting the Cadet organisations. They provide a means by which the community as a whole can contribute to Britain's security.

Role of the Territorial Army

Following the 1998 Strategic Defence Review, an extensive restructuring of the Territorial Army took place with the aim of making it more relevant, more usable and more fully integrated into the regular armed forces. As a result of the restructuring, the establishment strength of the Territorial Army reduced to 41,200, while some 35,480 personnel were on strength in September 2004 compared to an establishment 41,820. The Territorial Army was restructured to:

◆ allow it to meet new operational demands – the sort of demands it is likely to face in the 21st century.
◆ maintain close links with the community and society at large through a broad presence across all regions of the country.
◆ provide a degree of insurance to allow the generation of a larger force if required at some time in the future.

The restructured Territorial Army became less focussed on the traditional role of home defence and placed a greater emphasis on more relevant tasks such as supporting and sustaining deployed regular forces in operational areas like the Balkans. In order to do this, the Territorial Army now concentrated on roles such as artillery, air defence, signallers, logisticians and particularly medical services.

The restructured TA is:

◆ more closely integrated with the regular Army.
◆ more able and responsive in meeting changed operational demands.
◆ trained to operate modern battle-winning equipments including Challenger 2 tanks and AS90 heavy artillery.
◆ more demanding of, but also more rewarding to, those who volunteer – providing wider opportunities for service and recognition of skills and training acquired.

More recent operations like Operation TELIC (Iraq) and VERITAS (Afghanistan) have marked the emergence of the TA as the reserve of first choice to support British land forces on operations. Between 1998 and December 2004, 18,979 statutory notices of compulsory mobilization were issued to TA members, and there have been 14,813 acceptances into mobilised service in support of operations overseas. A small number of personnel have been accepted into mobilized service on more than one occasion during the period.

The Army recognises that, at any time, there are some volunteers who are unable to deploy owing to personal circumstances and others who are still under training and not yet ready for operations. TA units will therefore be established so that they are able to recruit and train additional manpower at their peacetime location.

Territorial Army Order of Battle

Territorial Army Order of Battle, as identified in January 2005

Arm or Corps	Number of regiments or battalions
Infantry	15
Armour	4
Royal Artillery	7
Royal Engineers	5
Special Air Service	2
Signals	11
Equipment Support	4
Logistics	7
Intelligence Corps	1
Aviation	1
Medical	11
Military Police	2
Total	70
Independent units (coy strength)	19

Territorial Army units, as identified in January 2005

Unit	HQ Location	Company/Squadron/Battery location
Infantry		
Tyne Tees Regt	Durham	Scarborough; Middlesborough; Bishop Auckland; Newcastle; Ashington.
King's and Cheshire Regt	Warrington	Liverpool; Warrington; Manchester; Crewe.
51st Highland Regiment	Perth	Dundee; Peterhead; Inverness; Dunbarton; Stirling.
52nd Lowland Regiment	Glasgow	Edinburgh; Ayr; Glasgow; Galashiels.
East and West Riding Regt	Pontefract	Huddersfield; Barnsley; Hull; York; Wakefield.
East of England Regiment	Bury St Edmunds	Norwich; Lincoln; Leicester; Mansfield; Chelmsford.
London Regiment	Battersea	Westminster; Edgeware; Balham; Camberwell; Mayfair; West Ham.
3rd (Volunteer) Battalion, Princess of Wales's Royal Regt	Canterbury	Farnham; Brighton; Canterbury.
Royal Rifle Volunteers	Reading	Oxford; Reading; Portsmouth; Milton Keynes.

Rifle Volunteers	Exeter	Gloucester; Taunton; Dorchester; Truro; Exeter.
West Midlands Regiment	Wolverhampton	Birmingham; Kidderminster; Burton; Stoke; Shrewsbury.
Royal Welsh Regiment	Cardiff	Wrexham; Swansea; Cardiff; Colwyn Bay.
Lancastrian & Cumbrian Volunteers	Preston	Barrow in Furness; Blackburn; Workington; Preston.
Royal Irish Rangers	Portadown	Newtonards; Newtownabbey.
4th (Volunteer) Battalion, The Parachute Regiment	Pudsey	London; Pudsey; Glasgow.

Royal Armoured Corps

Royal Yeomanry	London	Swindon; Leicester; Croydon; Nottingham; London.
Royal Wessex Yeomanry	Bovington	Bovington; Salisbury; Cirencester; Barnstable.
Royal Mercian&Lancastrian Yeomanry	Telford	Dudley; Telford; Chester; Wigan.
Queen's Own Yeomanry	Newcastle	York; Ayr; Belfast; Cupar; Newcastle.

Royal Artillery

Honourable Artillery Company	London	5 all based in the City of London.
100 Regiment	Luton	Luton; Bristol; Nottingham.
101 Regiment	Gateshead	Blyth; Newcastle; South Shields.
103 Regiment	St Helens	Liverpool; Manchester; Bolton.
104 Regiment	Newport	Wolverhampton; Newport; Worcester.
105 Regiment	Edinburgh	Newtownards; Glasgow; Arbroath.
106 Regiment	London	Bury St Edmunds; London; Leeds: Southampton.
Central Volunteers HQ RA	London	

Royal Engineers

Royal Monmouthshire RE (Militia)	Monmouth	Cwmbran; Swansea; Warley.
71 Regiment	Leuchars	Paisley; Newcastle.
73 Regiment	Nottingham	Sheffield; Nottingham; Chesterfield; St Hellier(Jersey).
75 Regiment	Failsworth	Birkenhead; Stoke on Trent; Walsall.
101 Regiment	London	London; Rochester; Tunbridge Wells.
131 Independent Commando Squadron	London	
135 Topographical Squadron	Ewell	
412 Amphibious Engineer Troop	Hameln	
Central Volunteer HQ RE	Camberley	

Royal Signals

31 Signal Regiment	London	Coulsdon; Eastbourne; London.
32 Signal Regiment	Glasgow	Aberdeen; East Kilbride; Edinburgh.
33 Signal Regiment	Huyton	Manchester; Liverpool; Runcorn.
34 Signal Regiment	Middlesborough	Leeds; Darlington; Middlesborough.
35 Signal Regment	Coventry	Birmingham; Newcastle-Under-Lyme; Rugby; Shrewsbury.
36 Signal Regiment	Ilford	Grays; Colchester; Cambridge.
37 Signal Regiment	Redditch	Cardiff; Stratford-Upon-Avon; Manchester; Coventry.
38 Signal Regiment	Sheffield	Derby; Sheffield; Nottingham.
39 Signal Regiment	Bristol	Uxbridge; Banbury; Gloucester.
40 Signal Regiment	Belfast	Belfast; Limavady; Bangor.
71 Signal Regiment	London	Lincolns Inn; Bexleyheath; Chelmsford.
1 Signal Squadron	Bletchley.	
2 Signal Squadron	Dundee.	
5 Communications Company	Chicksands.	
63 Signal Squadron (SAS)		
81 Sig Sqn (V)	London	
97 (BRITFOR) Signal Sqn	Balkans	
98 Sig Sqn (V)	Donington	

Royal Logistic Corps

150 (Northumbria) Transport Regt	Hull	Hull; Tynemouth; Leeds; Doncaster.
151 Logistic Support Regiment	Croydon	Romford; Sutton; Barnet; Southall.
156 Transport Regiment	Liverpool	Liverpool; Birkenhead; Salford; Bootle.
157 Logistic Support Regiment	Cardiff	Cardiff; Telford; Swansea; Carmarthen; West Bromwich.
158 Transport Regiment	Peterborough	Peterborough; Kempston; Ipswich; Loughborough.
Scottish Transport Regiment	Dunfermline	Dunfermline; Glasgow; Edinburgh; Glenrothes; Irvine.
168 Pioneer Regiment	Grantham	Grantham; Cramlington; Coulby Newham.
CVHQ and HR RLC TA	Grantham.	

Royal Electrical & Mechanical Engineers

101 Battalion REME	Queensferry	Prestatyn; Coventry; Clifton; Grangemouth.
102 Battalion REME	Newton Aycliffe	Newton Aycliffe; Rotherham; Scunthorpe; Newcastle upon Tyne.
103 Battalion REME	Crawley	Portsmouth; Redhill; Ashford.
104 Battalion REME	Bordon	Northampton.
HQ REME TA	Bordon	

Army Medical Services

201 Field Hospital	Newcastle	Newton Aycliffe; Stockton-on-Tees; Newcastle upon Tyne.

202 Field Hospital	Birmingham	Birmingham; Stoke on Trent; Oxford; Shrewsbury.
203 Field Hospital	Cardiff	Cardiff; Swansea; Abergavenny.
204 Field Hospital	Belfast	Belfast; Ballymena; Newtownards; Armagh.
205 Field Hospital	Glasgow	Glasgow; Aberdeen; Dundee; Edinburgh.
207 Field Hospital	Manchester	Stockport; Blackburn; Bury.
208 Field Hospital	Liverpool	Liverpool; Ellesmere; Lancaster.
212 Field Hospital	Sheffield	Sheffield; Bradford; Nottingham; Leeds.
243 Field Hospital	Keynsham	Keynsham; Exeter; Plymouth; Portsmouth.
256 Field Hospital	London	Walworth; Hammersmith; Kingston; Bow.
306 Specialist Field Hospital	York	
253 Field Ambulance	Belfast	
254 Field Ambulance	Cambridge	
152 Ambulance Regiment	Belfast	Londonderry; Belfast; Bridgend.
C (144) Parachute Medical Squadron	London	
B (220) Medical Squadron	Maidstone	
B (250) Medical Squadron	Hull	
B (225) Medical Squadron	Dundee	
C (251) Medical Squadron	Sunderland	
C (222) Medical Squadron	Leicester	
HQ Army Medical Service TA	York	

Adjutant General's Corps

4 Regiment, Royal Military Police	Aldershot	West Bromwich; Brixton.
5 Regiment, Royal Military Police	Livingston	Livingston; Stockton-on-Tees.
CVHQ AGC	Worthy Down.	

Intelligence Corps

3 Military Intelligence Bn (V)	London	London; Edinburgh; York; Keynsham; Birmingham.

Special Air Service
21 Regiment SAS
23 Regiment SAS

Army Air Corps

7 Regiment AAC	Netheravon
CVHQ ACC:	Netheravon

Officer Training Corps
Territorial Army: Officer Training Corps Units
Aberdeen University Officer Training Corps
Birmingham University Officer Training Corps
Bristol University Officer Training Corps
Cambridge University Officer Training Corps

East Midlands University Officer Training Corps
City of Edinburgh University Officer Training Corps
Exeter University Officer Training Corps
Glasgow and Strathclyde Universities Officer Training Corps
Leeds University Officer Training Corps
Liverpool University Officer Training Corps
London University Officer Training Corps
Manchester and Salford University Officer Training Corps
Northumbrian University Officer Training Corps
Oxford University Officer Training Corps
Queens University Officer Training Corps
Sheffield University Officer Training Corps
Southampton University Officer Training Corps
Tayforth University Officer Training Corps
University of Wales Officer Training Corps

The Territorial Army in the Future Army Structure

The British Army is working through the force generation issues highlighted by Operation Telic and experience on other recent operations. The outcome of this work will be the Future Army Structure (FAS). As of January 2005, FAS plans will further integrate the Territorial Army (TA) and Regular Reserve with the Regular Army, and include the following elements:

◆ The TA will remain the same size as it is today.
◆ The Army Board has agreed the new indicative structure, which sees the TA remain at its current size of about 42,000 (including Officer Training Corps). Some adjustment and re-roling will be required.
◆ The future TA structure will ensure a "more relevant, capable and usable TA"
◆ The Infantry TA will reduce from 15 to 14 battalions and will integrate into the new infantry structure, "restoring a true sense of identity at TA battalion level." They will complement the new regular infantry structure., drawing them closer together to improve operational and training affiliations, greater integration and readiness".
◆ To date, units have been made up to "War-Fighting Establishment" for deployments by a method of regular-to-regular back-filling. More robust establishments will reduce the need for this practice which has, along with a shortage of key enablers, adversely affected the Army 24-month tour interval guideline and unit cohesion.
◆ In future, a unit will deploy with its Deployable Component (for the more likely routine operations) drawing on its Contingent Component (normally from the TA) for the most demanding operations. A unit will also have an Enabling Component (consisting of an established Rear Party and an Infrastructure Element for security and support).

Under the FAS plan, the order of battle of the TA is being revised to reflect the requirement to augment the regular deployable units (adjusted under FAS) for the most demanding Deliberate Intervention operations, as outlined below. The Army Board has agreed the new indicative structure. Some adjustment and re-roling will be required. HQ LAND is developing a detailed plan for implementation of these structural adjustments which will be announced in the summer of 2005.

Infantry

The Infantry will be organised to support and complement the regular regimental structure, thereby restoring a true sense of identity at TA battalion level. There will be 14 TA infantry battalions. These will provide reinforcement of the regular infantry, and resilience to the infantry structure in meeting enduring commitments when Defence Planning Assumptions are exceeded. Manpower has also been included to force-generate the capability of 7 Defence Troops for Armoured and Formation Reconnaissance Regiments.

The affiliation of TA battalions will be driven by the revised Future Infantry Structure (FIS), assigning one TA battalion to each new two or three battalion regular regiments, and two TA battalions to a large regular regiment. To ensure viability, restructuring will be conducted on the basis of a minimum of 400 soldiers per battalion.

Royal Armoured Corps

The Yeomanry will retain a broadly similar structure, with four regiments covering the national area. As a platform-centric Arm, the RAC has a requirement for the provision of AFV crewmen Individual Reinforcements (IRs), which will be a force driver above the Contingent Component (CC) requirement. In outline:

a. One Yeomanry Regiment of up to five squadrons will be earmarked to provide IRs and formed troops to the Joint NBC Regiment and NBC IRs to formation reconnaissance regiments; the detailed requirement is subject to the VCDS's Jt NBC Regt Study.

b. One Yeomanry Regiment will provide the RHQ and one squadron of the Armoured Replacement Regiment. In addition, this Yeomanry Regiment will provide the CC and IRs to armoured regiments.

c. One Yeomanry Regiment will provide the balance of the CC and IRs to armoured regiments.

d. One Yeomanry Regiment will provide the CC and IRs to formation reconnaissance regiments.

Royal Artillery

The RA will continue to provide seven regiments, although the requirement for formed TA Ground-Based Air Defence (GBAD) regiments will be removed. The RA TA will adjust to provide the following:

a. One Regiment will provide a RHQ, a long range communications capability and up to four patrols batteries; three from the TA, the fourth from the Regular STA Battery (4/73 Bty, 5 Regt RA).

b. Three close support regiments will provide the CC to support the three Regular AS 90 SPA regiments and the two Regular light gun regiments. potentially attributed to LSDI. This represents an addition of one gun regiment.

c. Two general support regiments, one providing support to the Regular regiments and the other support to HQ 1 Arty Bde and the Regular UAV Regiment.

d. One GBAD Regiment, providing support to the Regular RAPIER SAM Regiment and IRs and support to the Regular HVM SAM Regiment.

Royal Engineers

The RE TA will include the current five regiment structure, potentially supplemented by up to two new regiments with additional sub-units. RE TA will be structured to provide sub units for discrete tasks. Where possible this will be achieved through capability pairing mechanisms. In addition to providing the CC at LSDI, RE TA will be designed to provide the following:

a. A formed Air Support Squadron capable of independent operation.
b. A formed Squadron to 33 Engr Regt (EOD).
c. A formed Topographic Squadron to 42 Engr Regt (Geo).
d. A formed Amphibious Troop to 28 Engr Regt.
e. Military Works Force (V), providing specialist infrastructure support to the Force.

Royal Signals

The Royal Signals TA will be structured as follows:

a. Three Ptarmigan regiments based within 11 Sigs Bde, providing a composite Ptarmigan Regiment to the ARRC.
b. Within 2(NC) Sigs Bde, a total of eight signals regiments (including 36 and 40 Sigs Regts) and four sub-units that will provide National Communications units in support of the MACA (Home Defence) role established under SDR(NC), plus other bespoke support to OGDs.
c. 63 Sigs Sqn (SAS) will continue to support the SASDSF.
d. An Air Support Signal Troop will be provided for Joint Helicopter Command, for the enduring SSPK operation assumed to be concurrent with LSDI.
e. In addition, Royal Signals TA will provide individual augmentees to the Regular regiments attributed to LSDI.

Army Aviation

The AAC TA will be structured as follows:

a. 7 Regt AAC (V) will continue to provide aviation support to HQ LAND for UK Mainland tasking only.
b. The remainder of the AAC TA will operate from two TA squadrons, to be embedded in the Regular structure at LSDI. These will provide Light Utility Helicopter (LUH) pilots, additional FARP capability and LUH door gunners.

Royal Logistic Corps

The RLC structure will be based around the provision of TA CCs to second line, third line and theatre enabling units. The exact structure and number of regiments will be dependent upon confirmation of demand, ability to force generate Regular unit pairing. and peacetime Regimental C2 and overheads. Pending the outcome of current studies, current indications suggest a structure that comprises of 15 regiments and the Catering Support Regiment RLC (V).

Army Medical Services (AMS)

The AMS will comprise of two Divisional General Support Medical Regiments and one Medical Evacuation Regiment, together with 11 Field Hospitals and six squadrons. TA AMS will provide:

a. A Divisional General Support Medical Regiment (V) for the Divisional Rear Area.
b. A composite Field Support Hospital of 400 beds and a Biological Warfare (BW) facility of 50 beds.

c. A Field Hospital of 25 beds will be provided for the enduring SSPK operations assumed to be concurrent with LSDI.

d. TA medical sub-units embedded in the close support and general support medical regiments, to provide individual augmentees for LSDI.

e. Other Support requirements are to be to other A&SDs, which will be assessed.validated by HQ LAND during implementation planning.

Royal Mechanical and Electrical Engineers (EME)

The REME TA will consist of four battalions, providing:

a. A formed Battalion to support Theatre Troops and the Lines of Communications (LoC).

b. Formed Role 1 support.

c. Individual augmentees, attributed to Regular REME units and to Role 1 support to other Arms and Services (subject to further scrutiny during implementation).

Royal Military Police

The RMP manpower liability will increase, structured on the current four companies, with the additional Military Provost Staff (MPS) under command of MCTC. The RMP TA will be structured to provide:

a. Formed platoons to augment the RMP companies deploying with the manoeuvre brigades, and the Theatre Troops Company.

b. Formed sub-units to provide enhanced Line of Communication coverage.

c. A dedicated Prisoner of War (PW) handling capability and augmentation to Divisional SIB capability.

Intelligence Corps

The TA Intelligence Corps structure is likely to be based on two TA battalions and will provide individual augmentees to tactical HQs and units, and to operational and strategic HQs. It will also provide formed Field Interrogation Teams.

Territorial Army (TA) command structure and organisation

The basic command structure and organisation of TA units is the same as for Regular units, by way of Regimental or Battalion, Brigade, Divisional and District Headquarters. In addition, the Directors of the various Arms and Services have the same responsibilities for the TA as their Regular units. At the Headquarters of Regional Forces, the Commander is also Inspector General of the TA.

Types of TA Units

The most familiar type of unit is the 'Independent'. This will be found at the local Territorial Army Centre (formerly called Drill Hall). One or more Army units will be accommodated at the centre, varying in size from a platoon or troop (about 30 Volunteers) to a Battalion or Regiment (about 600 Volunteers). These units will have their place in the Order of Battle, and as with Regular Army units, are equipped for their role. Most of the personnel will be part-time. Volunteers parade one evening each week and perhaps one weekend each month in addition to the annual two-week unit training period.

Some staff at each TA Centre will be regular soldiers. Many units have regular Commanding Officers, Regimental Sergeant Majors, Training Majors, Adjutants and Instructors. The Permanent Staff Instructors (PSIs) who are regular Senior Non-Commissioned Officers, are key personnel who help organise the training and administration of the Volunteers.

In the main, TA Infantry Units have a General Purpose structure which will give them flexibility of employment across the spectrum of military operations. All Infantry Battalions, including Parachute Battalions, have a common establishment of three Rifle Companies and a Headquarters Company. Each rifle company has a support platoon with, mortar, anti-tank, reconnaissance, MMG and assault pioneer sections under command.

The other type of unit is the 'Specialist'. These are located centrally, usually at the Headquarters or Training Centre of the Arm or Corps. Their members, spread across the country, are mainly civilians who already have the necessary skills or specialities, and require a minimum of military training.

An example of these can be found in the Army Medical Services Specialist Units whose doctors, surgeons, nurses and technicians from all over the country meet at regular intervals, often in York, or at a training area at home or abroad. They are on the lowest commitment for training, which is the equivalent of just two weekends and a two week camp each year, or it can be even less for some medical categories.

Pay

TA personnel are paid for every hour of training. They also receive an annual bonus, known as a bounty, subject to achieving a minimum time commitment. Travel costs for training are refunded. As of January 2005, daily rates of pay are the same for TA personnel and their Regular Army equivalents, from £29.10 for a Private to £102.51 for a Major. The exact rate also varies according to particular trade and type of commitment.

Hourly income is taxable, but the Annual Bounty is a tax-free lump sum. The value of the bounty depends on the specific unit and individual training requirement but, on a higher commitment, TA soldiers and officers start by receiving £350 in their first year. After five years satisfactory service, this rises to £1,380.

The annual training commitment to qualify for bounty is:

◆ Independent Units: 27 days including 15 days continuous at camp.
◆ Specialist Units: 19 days including 15 days continuous at camp.

In each case, individuals may attend one or more courses aggregated to at least eight days duration in lieu of camp, with the balance of seven days being carried out in extra out-of-camp training.

Recruiting and training

Recruits need to be at least 17 years old in order to join the TA. The upper age limit depends on what an individual has to offer, but it is normally 30 for those joining as an officer and 32 as a soldier. There are exceptions to the upper age limit for those with certain specialist skills or previous military experience.

Unless recruits have previous military experience, when they join the TA they will have to undergo basic recruit training. This consists of a number of training weekends, midweek drill nights and finally a two-week recruits course at one of the Army recruit training centres.

During this stage, recruits will learn basic soldiering skills according to the TA Common Military Syllabus. This covers areas as diverse as how to wear uniform, physical fitness, weapon handling, first aid, fieldcraft, map reading and military terminology.

Officer recruiting and training may take one of two forms. Officers can be recruited from the ranks, and appointed officer cadets by their unit commander, before taking the TA Commissioning Course at the Royal Military Academy, Sandhurst. Alternatively, the new direct entry officer training scheme allows potential officers to enter officer training right from the very start of their time in the TA. Initial Officer Training is designed to produce officers with the generic qualities to lead soldiers both on and off operations and includes three weeks spent on the TA Commissioning Course at the Royal Military Academy, Sandhurst.

Mobilisation

Before reservists can be mobilised and sent on operations, a Call Out Order has to be signed by the Defence Secretary. He has the power to authorise the use of reserves in situations of war or on humanitarian and peacekeeping operations.

Before they are sent to their postings, reservists must undergo a period of induction where they are issued with equipment, given medical examinations and receive any specialist training relevant to their operations. For the TA and the RMR, this takes place at the new Reserves Training and Mobilisation Centre.

Under the Reserve Forces Act 1996, principal call out powers would be brought into effect in a crisis by the issue of a call out order. Members of the Reserve Forces are then liable for service anywhere in the world, unless the terms of service applicable in individual cases restrict liability to service within the UK.

Call out powers are vested in and authorised by Her Majesty the Queen who may make an order authorising call-out:

◆ If it appears to her that national danger is imminent
◆ Or that a great emergency has arisen
◆ Or in the event of an actual or apprehended attack on the United kingdom.

The Secretary of State for Defence may make an order authorising call out:

◆ If it appears to him that warlike preparations are in preparation or progress.
◆ Or it appears to him that it is necessary or desirable to use armed forces on operations outside the UK for the protection of life or property.

♦ And for operations anywhere in the world for the alleviation of distress or the preservation of life or property in time of disaster or apprehended disaster.

Under normal circumstances, the maximum continuous periods of permanent service which individuals can serve under the above powers are respectively three years, 12 months and nine months. In exceptional circumstances the three years may be increased to five and the 12 months to two years but under the third power, no extensions can be ordered beyond the maximum of nine months. Under each power, provisions also limit the maximum aggregated time a reservist can spend in permanent service over given lengths of time.

Reservists and employers may apply for deferral of or exemption from call out. It is recognised that those called out may not find the outcomes of their initial applications to their satisfaction. Therefore a system of arbitration has been set up.

The Reserve Forces Act 1996 (RFA96) introduced two new types of reserve categories: Higher Readiness Reserves and Sponsored Reserves.

♦ **Higher Readiness Reserve (HRR):** these are individuals, serving either as members of the volunteer reserves or as individual reserves, who have taken additional liability for call out at any time. They have skills that are in short supply in both the regular and reserve forces. Typically these might be linguists, intelligence staff, media operations staff and specialist support staff.

To be a HRR, a reservist must sign an agreement to that affect and his civilian employer must agree in writing, to his doing so. An agreement, that may be followed by successive agreements, will be for one year. Whilst the agreement is in force the reservist may be called up to serve for up to nine months continuous service. As for other call-out powers, appeals against call-out by reservists or employers may be heard.

The HRR has largely fallen into abeyance as the terms and conditions of service proved to be unattractive. The MoD has largely been able to attract sufficient numbers of reservists to serve on mobilised service and Full Time Reserve Service(FTRS).

♦ **Sponsored Reserves.** There are a number of support functions that are carried out by civilians but which in war are carried out by service personnel, because servicemen must carry out the function on operations. This new category of reserve will allow some of these tasks to be put out to contract, providing that the contractor employs in his workforce a sufficient number of employees willing to serve as a members of a reserve force in the Sponsored Reserve category. If the task was required to be carried out operationally, these employees could be called out to continue providing the required support as servicemen. Sponsored Reserves will have their own call out power and be subject to no other. This and their conditions of service will are tailored to the commercial aspects of the concept.

There has been a delay in introducing this type of service due to the difficulty of agreeing terms of service. Sponsored Reserves will be introduced with the contract awarded to Brown and Root to provide the Army with its tank transporters. Brown and Root personnel will become sponsored reserves.

RFA 96 enables reimbursement to be made to Employers and Reservists for some of the additional costs of employees being called out. Some reservists will have financial commitments commensurate with their civilian salary and so provisions are in place to minimise financial hardship.

The MoD is also able to offset the indirect costs of employees being called out incurred by an employer, for example, the need to recruit and train temporary replacements. If employers or reservists are dissatisfied with the financial assistance awarded they may appeal to tribunals set up for this.

Full and Part Time Service: One provision of the RFA 96 is that reservists can now undertake periods of full or part time employment with the Armed Forces. This is not a call-out but a voluntary arrangement to make it possible for the Services to make more flexible use of their manpower assets. There are no fixed time limits. If a task needs doing, there is sufficient budget and a suitable volunteer is available for the job, then it can be done.

Pensions: Provision has been made in RFA 96 for the protection of Reservist pension rights in the event of call up. The MoD is permitted to pay the employers contributions to a civilian pension scheme.

Call-Out Procedure (TA)

TA soldiers are called-out using the same procedures as for Individual Reservist (IR)s – ie. they are sent a Call-Out Notice specifying the time, date and place to which they are to report. If TA Units or Sub-Units are called-out, they form up with their vehicles and equipment at their TA Centres or other designated locations. They would then be deployed by land, sea and air to their operational locations in the UK or overseas. However, if TA personnel are called-out as individuals, they would report to a Temporary Mobilisation Centre where they would be processed before posting to reinforce a unit or HQ.

Call-Out Procedure (IR)

IR are required to keep at home an Instruction Booklet (AB 592A), their ID card and a personalised Booklet (AB 592B). The AB 592A provides IR with general instructions on what they have to do if mobilised. It contains a travel warrant and a special cash order. The AB 592A is computer produced and updated quarterly as required to take account of such changes as address, medical category and age. It explains where the reservist is to report on mobilisation and arrangements for pay and allotments, next-of-kin, clothing held etc.

Under present legislation IR may only be mobilised if called-out by Queen's Order. Mobilisation may involve only a few individuals/units or any number up to general mobilisation when all are called out. If mobilisation is authorised Notices of Call-Out are despatched to those IR concerned by Recorded Delivery as the legal notification. Announcements of call-out are also made by the press, radio and television.

Under the proposals for the new Reserve Forces Act 1996, IR are will be liable to call-out under the same new provisions as described above for the TA. In addition, the Act will brings the conditions relating to all three Services in line and will includes officers and pensioners who were previously are currently covered by separate legislation/Royal Warrants.

Two structures have been set up within the Territorial Army in order to improve management of reserves:

- ◆ Reserves Manning and Career Management Division
- ◆ Reserves Training and Mobilisation Centre (RTMC)

The role of the first is to centralise the coordination of all personnel management for the TA, bringing it more into line with the regular Army and also providing a single focus for identifying and notifying individuals for mobilisation, while the second is in charge of administrative preparation, individual training and provision of human resources requirements of individual reservists. The RTMC, which was inaugurated in April 1999, managed a first group of reservists in May 1999 for the British forces stationed in Bosnia and Kosovo.

Some 7,500 volunteers were recruited in 2003. In spite of these efforts, there has been a constant decline in the number of reservists. The drop-out rate among volunteers is as high as 30% in the three first years of their engagement.

Territorial Army and Volunteer Reserve Associations
At local level, administration and support of the major elements of the Reserve Forces are carried out through the TAVRAs, working within the context described in the 1996 Reserve Forces Act. This is a tri-Service role which has been carried out by the TAVRAs and their predecessor organisations for many years. It is an unusual arrangement, but has been found to be a successful one. The TAVRA system ensures that people from the local communities in which the Reserve Forces and cadets are based are involved in the running of Reserve and cadet units. It also provides Reserve Forces and cadets representatives with the right of direct access to Ministers, so that they can make representation about Reserves issues. This provides an important balance and ensures that the case for the Reserves is clearly articulated at a high level.

TAVRAs have a second role as administrators and suppliers of services to the Reserve and cadet forces organisations. To reflect the increasing operational integration of Army Reserve and Regular forces, there have been certain changes in the way in which TAVRAs are organised since 1998. It is important that regional commanders take on full responsibility for the operational standards of Army Reserve units in their area; as a result, TAVRA boundaries were altered and brought more in line with the Army's Regular command structure. The new arrangement also took account of the needs of the other Services' Reserve Forces and all the cadet organisations.

Reserve Forces and Cadets Associations (RFCAs)
Members of the Volunteer Reserve Forces are recruited territorially and remain part of the local community. It is important to maintain very good relations with local authorities, chambers of commerce and other influential groups. Much of the task of monitoring and furthering understanding and co-operation falls to the 12 Reserve Forces and Cadets Associations (RFCAs) located throughout the country.

The construction and maintenance of the buildings and some training facilities, as well as the task of local recruiting, is generally the responsibility of the RFCA for the Volunteer units in their area.

Historically, their origins are in the Territorial Associations of old, and the wide number of tasks includes welfare, recruiting and publicity in addition to facilities management. They also have the task of providing onshore accommodation for the RMR (Royal Marines Reserve) and RNR (Royal Naval Reserve) as needed and, accommodation, welfare, recruiting and publicity requirements for the RauxAF (Royal Auxiliary Air Force). Similar tasks are undertaken for the Army Cadet Force and Air Training Corps. They also play an important part in the Volunteer Reserve Forces Campaign and employer liaison.

RFCAs are able to represent appropriate matters directly to Ministers and the higher levels of command in the Armed Services. By watching over the general well being of the Volunteer Reserves and Cadets, they can solve problems that might not be appropriate for consideration by the normal chain of command.

Linking the 14 separate RFCAs and helping to promote the efficiency and well being of the Volunteer Reserve Forces and Cadets, is the Council of RFCAs, which is currently based at the Duke of York's HQ in London. This Council acts as the link between the RFCAs, the Ministry of Defence and other Government Departments.

Each RFCA is an autonomous statutory body, established by Act of Parliament, with its own constitution. Senior members represent the RFCAs from the Council of RFCAs on the Advisory Committee of the TA, under the chairmanship of the Under Secretary of State for Defence. Membership includes representatives from the CBI and TUC as well as senior officers and officials from the MoD.

Each RFCA has a Lord Lieutenant as President. The membership is taken from a wide cross section of the community such as the local authorities and employer's organisations and trade unions, as well as serving and retired regular and volunteer officers.

The control of the day to day function of each RFCA is in the hands of a small permanent staff, many of whom are experienced regular former officers

SABRE (Supporting Britain's Reservists and Employers)

SABRE has grown out of the National Employers' Liaison Committee (NELC) which was formed in 1986 with a brief to provide independent advice to Ministers on the measures needed to win and maintain the support of employers, in both the public and private sectors, for those of their employees who are in the Volunteer Reserve Forces (VRF). The SABRE committee is made up of prominent businessmen and is supported by the secretariat. provides advice on:

◆ The ways of educating employers on the role of the Reserve Forces in national defence, the vital role employers have to play in giving their support, and the benefits to employers and their employees of Reserve Forces training and experience.
◆ The current problems and attitudes of employers in relation to service by their employees in the Reserve Forces.

- Methods and inducements needed to encourage and retain the support of employers
- Appropriate means of recognising and publicising support given by employers to the Reserve Forces.

The former NELC's key recommendation has been for a major long term and high profile campaign to 'market' the Reserve Forces. The Volunteer Reserve Forces Campaign (VRFC) was launched in 1988 and is still ongoing with the following objectives:

- Raising the status of the Reserve Forces, to achieve support and understanding by the general public, giving a positive social environment within which employers and employees react.
- Enlisting the support of employers, and in particular that of top grade, ambitious young executives through peer group image and the belief in the career advantages of Reserve service.

ARMY CADETS

The Role of the CCF
The Combined Cadet Force (CCF) is a tri-Service military cadet organisation based in schools and college throughout the UK. Although it is administered and funded by the Services it is a part of the national youth movement.

The CCF receives assistance and support for its training programme from the Regular and Reserve Forces, but the bulk of adult support is provided by members of school staffs who are responsible to head teachers for the conduct of cadet activities. CCF officers wear uniform but they are not part of the Armed Forces and carry no liability for service or compulsory training.

There are some 240 CCF contingents with 40,000 cadets, of whom some 25,000 are Army Cadets. The role of the CCF is to help boys and girls to develop powers of leadership through training which promotes qualities of responsibility, self-reliance, resourcefulness, endurance, perseverance and a sense of service to the community. Military training is also designed to demonstrate why defence forces are needed, how they function and to stimulate an interest in a career as an officer in the Services.

The Role of the ACF
The role of the Army Cadet Force (ACF) is to inspire young people to achieve success with a spirit of service to the Queen, country and their local community, and to develop the qualities of good citizenship, responsibility and leadership.

Army Cadet Force, as of April 2004
Officers & Instructors	7,880
Cadets	44,240
Total	52,120

Army cadets are said to make up between 25%-30% of regular army recruits. There are about 1,674 ACF detachments based in communities around the UK with a strength of around 440,000 cadets. The ACF is run by over 87,000 adults drawn from the local community who manage a broad programme of military and adventurous training activities designed to develop character and leadership. The Army Cadets are administered by the MoD. The total budget provided to the Army Cadets is approximately £50 million, which comprises: Salaries (all forms) £32m; Cadets estate programme £14m; Cadet activities £3m; Travel and subsistence £1m.

CHAPTER 14 – MISCELLANEOUS

The Military Hierarchy

Rank	Badge	Appointment Example
General (GEN)	Crown, Star & Crossed Sword with Baton	Chief of the General Staff
Lieutenant General (Lt Gen)	Crown & Sword & Baton	Commander ARRC
Major (Maj Gen)	General Star & Sword & Baton	Divisional Commander
Brigadier (Brig)	Crown & 3 Stars	Brigade
Colonel (Col)	Crown & 2 Stars	Staff or School
Lieutenant Colonel (Lt Col)	Crown & 1 Star	Battle Group/Armoured Regiment/Infantry Bn
Major (Maj)	Crown	Sqn/Coy/Bty
Captain (Capt)	3 Stars	Squadron/Company 2ic
Lieutenant (Lt)	2 Stars	Troop/Pl Commander
2nd Lieutenant	1 Star (2/Lt)	Troop/Pl Commander
Warrant Officer First Class	Royal Coat of Arms on Forearm	Regimental Sergeant Major (WO 1) (RSM)
Warrant Officer Second Class	Crown on forearm	Company Sergeant Major (WO 2) (CSM)
Staff Sergeant (Sgt)	Crown over 3 stripes	Coy/Sqn Stores (or Colour Sergeant)
Sergeant (Sgt)	3 stripes	Platoon Sergeant
Corporal (Cpl)	2 stripes	Section Commander
Lance Corporal	1 Stripe	Section 2ic (Lcpl)

Modes of Address

Where appropriate soldiers are addressed by their generic rank without any qualifications, therefore Generals, Lieutenant Generals and Major Generals are all addressed as 'General'. Colonels and Lieutenant Colonels as 'Colonel', Corporals and Lance Corporals as ' Corporal'. Staff Sergeants and Colour Sergeants are usually addressed as 'Staff' or 'Colour' and CSMs as Sergeant Major. It would almost certainly be prudent to address the RSM as 'Sir'.

Private Soldiers should always be addressed by their title and then their surname. For example: Rifleman Harris, Private Jones, Bugler Bygrave, Gunner Smith, Guardsman Thelwell, Sapper Williams, Trooper White, Kingsman Boddington, Signalman Robinson, Ranger Murphy, Fusilier Ramsbotham , Driver Wheel, Craftsman Grease or Air Trooper Rotor. However, it should be remembered that regiments and corps have different customs and although the above is a reasonable guide it may not always be correct.

Regimental Head-Dress

The normal everyday head-dress of NCOs and Soldiers (and in some regiments of all ranks) is the beret or national equivalent. The norm is the dark blue beret. Exceptions are as follows:

a. Grey Beret	The Royal Scots Dragoon Guards	
	Queen Alexandra's Royal Army Nursing Corps	
b. Brown Beret	The King's Royal Hussars	
	The Royal Wessex Yeomanry	
c. Khaki Beret	All Regiments of Foot Guards	
	The Honourable Artillery Company	
	The Kings Own Royal Border Regiment	
	The Royal Anglian Regiment	
	The Prince of Wales's Own Regiment of Yorkshire	
	The Green Howards	
	The Duke of Wellington's Regiment	
d. Black Beret	The Royal Tank Regiment	
e. Rifle Green Beret	The Light Infantry	
	The Royal Green Jackets	
	The Brigade of Gurkhas	
	Adjutant General's Corps	
f. Maroon Beret	The Parachute Regiment	
g. Beige Beret	The Special Air Service Regiment	
h. Light Blue Beret	The Army Air Corps	
i. Scarlet Beret	Royal Military Police	
j. Cypress Green Beret	The Intelligence Corps	

The majority of Scottish Regiments wear the Tam-0-Shanter (TOS) and the Royal Irish Regiment wear the Corbeen.

Rates of Pay – Officers on a Regular Commission (Including Officers of the Royal Irish Regiment – HSFT)
(all figures are £ per annum)

RANK		1 APRIL 2005	
	OF6	**DAILY**	**ANNUAL**
Brigadier	Level 5	230.16	84,008.40
	Level 4	227.79	83,143.35
	Level 3	225.45	82,289.25
	Level 2	223.10	81,431.50
	Level 1	220.75	80,573.75
	OF5		
Colonel	Level 9	203.41	74,244.65
	Level 8	200.98	73,357.70
	Level 7	198.55	72,470.75
	Level 6	196.14	71,591.10
	Level 5	193.72	70,707.80
	Level 4	191.30	69,824.50
	Level 3	188.88	68,941.20
	Level 2	186.46	68,057.90
	Level 1	184.04	67,174.60

	OF4			
Lieutenant Colonel	Level 9	175.68		64,123.20
	Level 8	173.57		63,353.05
	Level 7	171.47		62,586.55
	Level 6	169.38		61,823.70
	Level 5	167.29		61,060.85
	Level 4	165.20		60,298.00
	Level 3	163.12		59,538.80
	Level 2	161.03		58,775.95
	Level 1	158.92		58,005.80
	OF3			
Major	Level 9	135.61		49,497.65
	Level 8	132.81		48,475.65
	Level 7	130.02		47,457.30
	Level 6	127.22		46,435.30
	Level 5	124.41		45,409.65
	Level 4	121.62		44,391.30
	Level 3	118.81		43,365.65
	Level 2	116.03		42,350.95
	Level 1	113.23		41,328.95
	OF4			
Captain	Level 9	106.90		39,018.50
	Level 8	105.69		38,576.85
	Level 7	104.46		38,127.90
	Level 6	102.04		37,244.60
	Level 5	99.60		36,354.00
	Level 4	97.18		35,470.70
	Level 3	94.74		34,580.10
	Level 2	92.30		33,689.50
	Level 1	89.89		32,809.85
	OF1			
Lieutenant	Level 10	77.53		28,298.45
Lieutenant	Level 9	75.68		27,623.20
Lieutenant	Level 8	73.84		26,951.60
Lieutenant	Level 7	72.00		26,280.00
On Appointment	Level 6	70.15		25,604.75
2/Lieutenant	Level 5	58.36		21,301.40

Rates Of Pay For Ratings And Other Ranks (Including Royal Irish Regiment Other Ranks)(Hspt)

RANK	HIGHER BAND 1 APRIL 2005			LOWER BAND 1 APRIL 2005		
	Range 5	DAILY	ANNUAL	Range 5	DAILY	ANNUAL
Warrant Officer 1	Level 7	110.84	40,456.60	Level 7	104.60	38,179.00
	Level 6	109.17	39,847.05	Level 6	101.73	37,131.45
	Level 5	107.26	39,149.90	Level 5	98.95	36,116.75
	Level 4	105.38	38,463.70	Level 4	97.06	35,426.90
	Level 3	103.48	37,770.20	Level 3	95.17	34,737.05
	Level 2	101.73	37,131.45	Level 2	93.29	34,050.85
	Level 1	99.77	36,416.05	Level 1	91.51	33,401.15
	Range 4			Range 4		
Warrant Officer II	Level 9	102.54	37,427.10	Level 9	93.95	34,291.75
Levels 5–9	Level 8	101.10	36,901.50	Level 8	91.87	33,532.55
Staff Sergeant	Level 7	99.68	36,383.20	Level 7	90.70	33,105.50
Levels 1–7	Level 6	98.26	35,864.90	Level 6	89.33	32,605.45
	Level 5	96.14	35,091.10	Level 5	85.47	31,196.55
	Level 4	94.00	34,310.00	Level 4	84.32	30,776.80
	Level 3	91.87	33,532.55	Level 3	82.39	30,072.35
	Level 2	89.73	32,751.45	Level 2	79.80	29,127.00
	Level 1	87.61	31,977.65	Level 1	78.77	28,751.05
	Range 3			Range 3		
Sergeant	Level 7	87.55	31,955.75	Level 7	80.87	29,517.55
	Level 6	85.94	31,368.10	Level 6	80.26	29,294.90
	Level 5	84.33	30,780.45	Level 5	77.58	28,316.70
	Level 4	82.72	30,192.80	Level 4	75.61	27,597.65
	Level 3	81.69	29,816.85	Level 3	74.85	27,320.25
	Level 2	79.67	29,079.55	Level 2	73.02	26,652.30
	Level 1	77.66	28,345.90	Level 1	71.16	25,973.40
	Range 2			Range 2		
Corporal	Level 7	78.67	28,714.55	Level 7	70.75	25,823.75
	Level 6	76.99	28,101.35	Level 6	70.23	25,633.95
	Level 5	75.43	27,531.95	Level 5	69.68	25,433.20
	Level 4	73.65	26,882.25	Level 4	69.14	25,236.10
	Level 3	71.97	26,269.05	Level 3	68.61	25,042.65
	Level 2	68.61	25,042.65	Level 2	65.42	23,878.30
	Level 1	65.42	23,878.30	Level 1	62.60	22,849.00
	Range 1			Range 1		
Levels 1-7 – Private:	Level 9	68.61	25,042.65	Level 9	57.28	20,907.20
Levels 5-9 Lance	Level 8	65.42	23,878.30	Level 8	55.28	20,177.20
Corporal	Level 7	62.60	22,849.00	Level 7	52.86	19,293.90
	Level 6	59.85	21,845.25	Level 6	50.69	18,501.85
	Level 5	57.08	20,834.20	Level 5	48.65	17,757.25
	Level 4	51.62	18,841.30	Level 4	46.17	16,852.05
	Level 3	48.01	17,523.65	Level 3	42.45	15,494.25
	Level 2	43.49	15,873.85	Level 2	40.22	14,680.30
	Level 1	37.99	13,866.35	Level 1	37.99	13,866.35
New Entrant Rate of Pay					DAILY	ANNUAL
					32.26	11,774.90

The Royal Marines

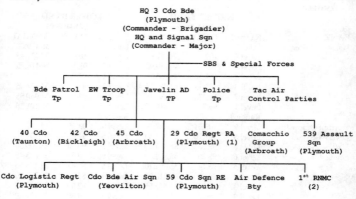

```
                    HQ 3 Cdo Bde
                      (Plymouth)
              (Commander - Brigadier)
              HQ and Signal Sqn
               (Commander - Major)
                                        ──SBS & Special Forces

  Bde Patrol    EW Troop    Javelin AD    Police    Tac Air
     Tp            Tp           TP           Tp    Control Parties


   40 Cdo      42 Cdo      45 Cdo     29 Cdo Regt RA   Comacchio    539 Assault
  (Taunton)  (Bickleigh)  (Arbroath)   (Plymouth) (1)    Group         Sqn
                                                      (Arbroath)    (Plymouth)

Cdo Logistic Regt  Cdo Bde Air Sqn  59 Cdo Sqn RE  Air Defence   1st RNMC
   (Plymouth)         (Yeovilton)     (Plymouth)       Bty          (2)
```

Note:

(1) 29 Cdo Regt RA has one battery stationed at Arbroath with 45 Cdo.

(2) 1st Bn The Royal Netherlands Marine Corps is part of 3 Cdo Bde for NATO assigned tasks.

Although the Royal Marines (RM) are an organisation that is part of the Royal Navy, they are trained and equipped for warfare on land, and it is very likely that they could be involved in operations and exercises with Army units. The Royal Marines number approximately 5,500 officers and men.

The Royal Marines also have detachments on 12 ships at sea and a number of smaller units worldwide with widely differing tasks. However, the bulk of the manpower of the Royal Marines is grouped in battalion sized organisations known as Commando (Cdo). There are three Commando Groups and they are part of a larger formation known as 3 Commando Brigade (3 Cdo Bde).

An RM Cdo equates to an army battalion and would resemble the following:

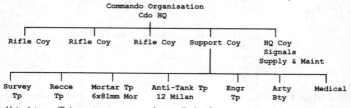

```
                       Commando Organisation
                            Cdo HQ

  Rifle Coy   Rifle Coy   Rifle Coy   Support Coy   HQ Coy
                                                     Signals
                                                  Supply & Maint

 Survey   Recce   Mortar Tp    Anti-Tank Tp   Engr   Arty    Medical
   Tp      Tp    6x81mm Mor    12 Milan       Tp     Bty
```

Note: A troop (Tp) equates to an army platoon. Each rifle company has three troops.

RAF Regiment

Currently the RAF Regiment exists to provide ground and short-range air defence for RAF installations, and to train all the RAF's combatant personnel to enable them to contribute to the defence of their units.

As of early 2002 there were about 2,000 RAF Regiment personnel (including about 250 officers) in units are as follows:

Field Squadrons

No 1 Squadron	St Mawgan	Field Squadron
No 2 Squadron	Honnington	Field /Para Squadron
No 3 Squadron	Aldergrove	Field Squadron
No 34 Squadron	Leeming	Field Squadron
No 51 Squadron	Lossimouth	Field Squadron
No 63 (QCS)	Uxbridge	Ceremonial/Field Squadron

Air Defence

No 15 Squadron	Honnington	6 × Rapier
No 16 Squadron	Honnington	6 × Rapier
No 26 Squadron	Waddington	6 × Rapier
No 37 Squadron	Honnington	6 × Rapier
Rapier OCU	Honnington	2 × Rapier

Other Units

RAF Regiment Depot	Honnington	
No 27 Squadron	Honnington	Joint NBC Regiment
No 1 RAF STO HQ*	RAF Wittering	
No 2 RAF STO HQ	RAF Leming	
No 3 RAF STO HQ	RAF Marham	

* STO – Tactical Survive to Operate HQ

Specialist RAF Regiment training for gunners is given at the RAF Regiment Depot at Honnington. On completion of training at the RAF College Cranwell officers also undergo further specialist training at RAF Honnington and, in some cases, the School of Infantry at Warminster in Wiltshire or the Royal School of Artillery at Larkhill.

The RAF Regiment also mans the Queen's Colour Squadron (QCS) which undertakes all major ceremonial duties for the Royal Air Force. These duties involve mounting the Guard at Buckingham Palace on an occasional basis, and providing Guards of Honour for visiting Heads of State. The Queen's Colour Squadron also has a war role as a field squadron.

There are two basic RAF Regiment squadron organisations – the field squadron organised for ground defence against possible enemy ground action and the rapier squadron organised for defence against lowflying enemy aircraft.

Rapier in service with the RAF Regiment has been upgraded from Field Standard B1(M) to Field Standard C (Rapier 2000). Rapier FSC offers significant enhancements to performance. The towed system launcher mounts eight missiles (able to fire two simultaneously at two separate targets) and is manufactured in two warhead versions. One of these warheads is armour piercing and able to deal with fixed-wing targets, while the other is a fragmentation warhead for the engagement of cruise missiles and RPVs. Rapier 2000 has the Darkfire tracker and a tailor-made 3-dimensional radar system for target acquisition, developed by Plessey.

Rapier has now been sold to the armed forces of at least 14 nations. We believe that sales have amounted to over 26,000 missiles and over 600 launchers.

Codewords and Nicknames

A Codeword is a single word used to provide security cover for reference to a particular classified matter, eg 'Corporate' was the Codeword for the recovery of the Falklands in 1982. In 1990 'Granby' was used to refer to operations in the Gulf in 1990 and 'Op Agricola' was used for operations in support of NATO forces in Kosovo. 'Op Fingle' is the Codeword for land operations in Afghanistan in support of the International Security Assistance Force and 'Op Telic' for current UK operations in Iraq.

A Nickname consists of two words and may be used for reference to an unclassified matter, eg 'Lean Look' referred to an investigation into various military organisations in order to identify savings in manpower.

Dates and Timings

When referring to timings the British Army uses the 24 hour clock. This means that 2015 hours, pronounced twenty fifteen hours, is in fact 8.15pm. Soldiers usually avoid midnight and refer to 2359 or 0001 hours. Time zones present plenty of scope for confusion! Exercise and Operational times are expressed in Greenwich Mean Time (GMT) which may differ from the local time. The suffix Z (Zulu) denotes GMT and A (Alpha) GMT + 1 hour. B (Bravo) means GMT + 2 hours and so on.

The Date Time Group or DTG can be seen on military documents and is a point of further confusion for many. Using the military DTG 1030 GMT on 20 April 2002 is written as 201030Z APR 02. When the Army relates days and hours to operations a simple system is used:

a. D Day is the day an operation begins.
b. H Hour is the hour a specific operation begins.
c. Days and hours can be represented by numbers plus or minus of D Day for planning purposes. Therefore if D Day is 20 April 2002, D-2 is 18 April and D + 2 is 22 April. If H Hour is 0600hrs then H+2 is 0800 hours.

Phonetic Alphabet

To ensure minimum confusion during radio or telephone conversations difficult words or names are spelt out letter by letter using the following NATO standard phonetic alphabet.

ALPHA – BRAVO – CHARLIE – DELTA – ECHO – FOXTROT – GOLF – HOTEL – INDIA – JULIET – KILO – LIMA – MIKE – NOVEMBER – OSCAR – PAPA – QUEBEC – ROMEO – SIERRA – TANGO – UNIFORM – VICTOR – WHISKEY – X RAY – YANKEE – ZULU.

The Mod's Civilian Staff

The three uniformed services are supported by the civilian staff of the MoD. During September 2004 some 108,990 civilian personnel (86,150 in the UK and 22,840 overseas-locally engaged) were employed by the MoD. This figure has fallen from 316,700 civilian personnel in 1980. UK based civilians are employed in the following areas:

MoD Civilian personnel

England	71,370
London	6,420
South East	17,110
East	7,660
South West	23,920
West Midlands	6,430
East Midlands	2,520
Yorkshire and The Humber	3,940
North West	2,870
North East	500
Scotland	7,160
Wales	4,170
Northern Ireland	3,450
Elsewhere (Outside UK and unallocated)	22,840
MoD Total	**108,990**

In a recent clear and unambiguous statement the UK MoD stated that "The Department remains committed to a process of civilianisation. Increasingly, it makes no sense to employ expensively trained and highly professional military personnel in jobs which civilians could do equally well. Civilians are generally cheaper than their military counterparts and as they often remain longer in post, can provide greater continuity. For these reasons, it is our long-standing policy to civilianise posts and so release valuable military resources to the front line whenever it makes operational and economic sense to do so".

The overwhelming majority of the 22,840 deployed 'elsewhere' support the British Forces in Germany.

Military Quotations

Young officers and NCOs may find some of these quotations useful on briefings etc: There are two groups – Military and General.

Military

"It is foolish to hunt the tiger when there are plenty of sheep around."

Al Qaeda Training Manual 2002

"Information is something that you do something with. Data is something that just makes officers feel good! I keep telling them but nobody listens to me."

US Army Intelligence specialist – CENTCOM Qatar 2003

"If you torture data sufficiently it will confess to almost anything".

Fred Menger – Chemistry Professor (1937-)

"If you can keep your head when all about you are losing theirs and blaming it on you – you'll be a man my son".

Rudyard Kipling

"If you can keep your head when all about you are losing theirs – you may have missed something very important".

Royal Marine – Bagram Airfield 2002

"If you claim to understand what is happening in Iraq you haven't been properly briefed".

British Staff Officer at Coalition HQ 2004

Admiral King commanded the US Navy during the Second World War. His daughter wrote – "He was the most even tempered man I ever met – he was always in a rage. In addition, he believed that civilians should be told nothing about a war until it was over and then only who won. Nothing more!"

Mrs Saatchi explained her 12 month silence after her husband started living with Nigela Lawson by quoting Napoleon's dictum

"Never disturb your enemy while he is making a mistake"

"We trained very hard, but it seemed that every time we were beginning to form up in teams, we would be reorganised. I was to learn in later life that we tend to meet any new situation by reorganising, and a wonderful method it can be for creating an illusion of progress, while producing confusion, inefficiency and demoralisation".

Caius Petronius 66 AD

"Having lost sight of our objectives we need to redouble our efforts".

Anon

During the Second World War Air Marshal Sir Arthur (Bomber) Harris was well known for his glorious capacity for rudeness, particulary to bureaucrats. "What are you doing to retard the war effort today" was his standard greeting to senior civil servants.

"The military value of a partisan"s work is not measured by the amount of property destroyed, or the number of men killed or captured, but the number he keeps watching."

John Singleton Mosby 1833–1916
Confederate Cavalry Leader

"Peace – In international affairs, a period of cheating between two periods of fighting."

The Devils Dictionary 1911

"A few honest men are better than numbers."

Oliver Cromwell

"Mr Smith Sir! – As an obvious outsider what is your opinion of the human race?"
Drill Sergeant to a cadet at the Royal Military Academy 1998.

"The beatings will continue until morale improves."
Attributed to the Commander of the Japanese Submarine Force.

"When other Generals make mistakes their armies are beaten; when I get into a hole, my men pull me out of it".
The Duke of Wellington after Waterloo

"Take short views, hope for the best and trust in God. "
Sir Sydney Smith

"There is no beating these troops in spite of their generals. I always thought them bad soldiers, now I am sure of it. I turned their right, pierced their centre, broke them everywhere; the day was mine, and yet they did not know it and would not run".
Marshal Soult – Albuhera 1811

"Confusion in battle is what pain is in childbirth – the natural order of things".
General Maurice Tugwell

"This is right way to waste money"
PJ O'Rourke – Rolling Stone Magazine
(Watching missiles firing during an exercise)

" This is just something to be got round – like a bit of flak on the way to the target".
Group Captain Leonard Cheshire VC –
Speaking of his incurable illness in the week before he died.

"Pale Ebenezer thought it wrong to fight,
But roaring Bill, who killed him, thought it right".
Hillare Belloc

"Everyone wants peace – and they will fight the most terrible war to get it".
Miles Kington – BBC Radio 4th February 1995

"The purpose of war is not to die for your country. The purpose of war is to ensure that the other guy dies for his country".
General Patton.

"War is a competition of incompetence – the least incompetent usually win".
General Tiger -after losing Bangladesh.

"In war the outcome corresponds to expectations less than in any other activity".
Titus Livy 59 BC – 17AD

"Nothing is so good for the morale of the troops as occasionally to see a dead general".
Field Marshal Slim 1891–1970

"It makes no difference which side the general is on".

Unknown British Soldier

At the end of the day it is the individual fighting soldier who carries the battle to the enemy; Sir Andrew Agnew commanding Campbell's Regiment (Royal Scots Fusiliers), giving orders to his infantrymen before the Battle of Dettingen in 1743 shouted; "Do you see yon loons on yon grey hill? Well, if ye dinna kill them, they'll kill you! "

"The only time in his life that he ever put up a fight was when we asked for his resignation."
    A comment from one of his staff officers following French General Joffre's resignation in 1916.

General
Homer Simpson's advice to his son Bart:

Homer to Bart: "These three little sentences will get you through life":

Number 1: "Oh, good idea boss".
Number 2: (whispers) "Cover for me".
Number 3: "It was like that when I got here".

"The primary function of management is to create the chaos that only management can sort out. A secondary function is the expensive redecoration and refurnishing of offices, especially in times of the utmost financial stringency".
    Theodore Dalrymple 'The Spectator' 6 November 1993.

"Success is generally 90% persistence".

Anon

"Anyone sitting on a bus after the age of 30 should consider himself a failure".

Lady Westminster

"It is only worthless men who seek to excuse the deterioration of their character by pleading neglect in their early years".

Plutarch – Life of Coriolanus – Approx AD 80

"They say hard work never hurt anybody, but I figured why take the chance".

Ronald Regan

"To applaud as loudly as that for so stupid a proposal means that you are just trying to fill that gap between your ears".

David Starkey – BBC (4 Feb 95)

"Its always best on these occasions to do what the mob do".
"But suppose that there are two mobs?" suggested Mr Snodgrass.
"Shout with the largest" replied Mr Pickwick.

Pickwick Papers Chapter 13

"Ah, these diplomats! What chatterboxes! There's only one way to shut them up – cut them down with machine guns. Bulganin, go and get me one!"

Joseph Stalin – As reported by De Gaulle during a long meeting.

"Whenever I hear about a wave of public indignation I am filled with a massive calm".

Matthew Parris – The Times 24th October 1994

"It is a general popular error to imagine that the loudest complainers for the public to be the most anxious for its welfare."

Edmund Burke

"He knows nothing and thinks that he knows everything. That points to a political career."

George Bernard Shaw

"The men who really believe in themselves are all in lunatic asylums."

GK Chesterton

"I remain just one thing and one thing only – and that is a clown. It places me on a far higher plane than any politician."

Charlie Chaplin

"What all the wise men promised has not happened and what all the dammed fools said would happen has come has come to pass".

Lord Melbourne

Abbreviations
The following is a selection from the list of standard military abbreviations and should assist users of this handbook.

AWOL	Absent without leave
accn	Accommodation
ACE	Allied Command Europe
Adjt	Adjutant
admin	Administration
admin O	Administrative Order
ac	Aircraft
AD	Air Defence/Air Dispatch/Army Department
ADA	Air Defended Area
ADP	Automatic Data Processing
AFCENT	Allied Forces Central European Theatre
AIFV	Armoured Infantry Fighting Vehicle
Airmob	Airmobile
ATAF	Allied Tactical Air Force
armr	Armour
armd	Armoured
ACV	Armoured Command Vehicle
AFV	Armoured Fighting Vehicle
AMF(L)	Allied Mobile Force (Land Element)

APC	Armoured Personnel Carrier
APDS	Armour Piercing Discarding Sabot
ARV	Armoured Recovery Vehicle
AVLB	Armoured Vehicle Launched Bridge
AP	Armour Piercing/Ammunition Point/Air Publication
APO	Army Post Office
ARRC	Allied Rapid Reaction Corps
ATGW	Anti Tank Guided Weapon
ATWM	Army Transition to War Measure
arty	Artillery
att	Attached
BE	Belgium (Belgian)
BEF	British Expeditionary Force (France – 1914)
BGHQ	Battlegroup Headquarters
BiH	Bosnia and Herzogovina
bn	Battalion
bty	Battery
BK	Battery Captain
BC	Battery Commander
BG	Battle Group
bde	Brigade
BAOR	British Army of the Rhine
BFG	British Forces Germany
BFPO	British Forces Post Office
BMH	British Military Hospital
BRSC	British Rear Support Command
C3I	Command, Control, Communications & Intelligence.
cam	Camouflaged
cas	Casualty
CCP	Casualty Collecting Post
CCS	Casualty Clearing Station
CASEVAC	Casualty Evacuation
cat	Catering
CAD	Central Ammunition Depot
CEP	Circular Error Probable/Central Engineer Park
CEPS	Central European Pipeline System
CET	Combat Engineer Tractor
CGS	Chief of the General Staff
CinC	Commander in Chief
CIMIC	Civil Military Co-operation
COMMS Z	Communications Zone
CVD	Central Vehicle Depot
CW	Chemical Warfare
COS	Chief of Staff
civ	Civilian
CP	Close Protection/Command Post
CAP	Combat Air Patrol
c sups	Combat Supplies

CV	Combat Vehicles
CVR(T) or (W)	Combat Vehicle Reconnaissance Tracked or Wheeled
comd	Command/Commander
CinC	Commander in Chief
CPO	Command Pay Office/Chief Petty Officer
CO	Commanding Officer
coy	Company
CQMS	Company Quartermaster Sergeant
comp rat	Composite Ration (Compo)
COMSEN	Communications Centre
coord	Co-ordinate
CCM	Counter Counter Measure
DAA	Divisional Administrative Area
DTG	Date Time Group
def	Defence
DF	Defensive Fire
DK	Denmark
dml	Demolition
det	Detached
DISTAFF	Directing Staff (DS)
div	Division
DAA	Divisional Administrative Area
DMA	Divisional Maintenance Area
DS	Direct Support/Dressing Station
ech	Echelon
EME	Electrical and Mechanical Engineers
ECCM	Electronic Counter Measure
emb	Embarkation
EDP	Emergency Defence Plan
EMP	Electro Magnetic Pulse
en	Enemy
engr	Engineer
EOD	Explosive Ordnance Disposal
eqpt	Equipment
ETA	Estimated Time of Arrival
EW	Early Warning/Electronic Warfare
ex	Exercise
FRG	Federal Republic of Germany
FGA	Fighter Ground Attack
fol	Follow
fmm	Formation
FUP	Forming Up Point
FAC	Forward Air Controller
FEBA	Forward Edge of the Battle Area
FLET	Forward Location Enemy Troops
FLOT	Forward Location Own Troops
FOO	Forward Observation Officer
FR	France (French)

FRT	Forward Repair Team
FRES	Future Rapid Effects System
FUP	Forming Up Place
FAS	Future Army Structure
GDP	General Defence Plan
GE	German (Germany)
GR	Greece (Greek)
GOC	General Officer Commanding
GPMG	General Purpose Machine Gun
HAC	Honourable Artillery Company
hel	Helicopter
HE	High Explosive
HEAT	High Explosive Anti Tank
HESH	High Explosive Squash Head
HVM	Hyper Velocity Missile
Hy	Heavy
IFF	Identification Friend or Foe
II	Image Intensifier
IGB	Inner German Border
illum	illuminating
IO	Intelligence Officer
INTSUM	Intelligence Summary
IRG	Immediate Replenishment Group
IR	Individual Reservist
IS	Internal Security
ISAF	International Security Assistance Force (Kabul)
ISD	In Service Date
IT	Italy (Italian)
IW	Individual Weapon
JFHQ	Joint Force Headquarters
JHQ	Joint Headquarters
JSSU	Joint Services Signals Unit
KFOR	Kosovo Force (NATO in Kosovo)
LAD	Light Aid Detachment (REME)
L of C	Lines of Communication
LLAD	Low Level Air Defence
LO	Liaison Officer
Loc	Locating
log	Logistic
LRATGW	Long Range Anti Tank Guided Weapon
LSDI	Large Scale Deliberate Intervention
LSW	Light Support Weapon
MAOT	Mobile Air Operations Team
MBT	Main Battle Tank
maint	Maintain
mat	Material
med	Medical
mech	Mechanised

MFC	Mortar Fire Controller
MNAD	Multi National Airmobile Division
NE	Netherlands
MO	Medical Officer
MP	Military Police
MOD	Ministry of Defence
mob	Mobilisation
MovO	Movement Order
msl	missile
MV	Military Vigilance
NAAFI	Navy, Army and Air Force Institutes
NADGE	NATO Air Defence Ground Environment
NATO	North Atlantic Treaty Organisation
NCO	Non Commissioned Officer
nec	Necessary
NL	Netherlands
NO	Norway (Norwegian)
NOK	Next of Kin
ni	Night
NORTHAG	Northern Army Group
NTR	Nothing to Report
NBC	Nuclear and Chemical Warfare
NYK	Not Yet Known
OP	Observation Post
OC	Officer Commanding
OCU	Operational Conversion Unit (RAF)
OIC	Officer in Charge
OOTW	Operations Other Than War
opO	Operation Order
ORBAT	Order of Battle
pax	Passengers
POL	Petrol, Oil and Lubricants
P info	Public Information
PJHQ	Permanent Joint Head Quarters
Pl	Platoon
PO	Portugal (Portuguese)
PSNI	Police Service of Northern Ireland
PUS	Permanent Under Secretary
QGE	Queens Gurkha Engineers
QM	Quartermaster
RAP	Rocket Assisted Projectile/Regimental Aid Post
RJDF	Rapid Joint Deployment Force
RTM	Ready to Move
RCZ	Rear Combat Zone
rec	Recovery
R & D	Research and Development
rebro	Rebroadcast
recce	Reconnaissance

Regt	Regiment
RHQ	Regimental Headquarters
RMA	Rear Maintenance Area/Royal Military Academy
rft	Reinforcement
RSA	Royal School of Artillery
RSME	Royal School of Mechanical Engineering
RTU	Return to Unit
SACUER	Supreme Allied Commander Europe
SATCOM	Satellite Communications
SDR	Strategic Defence Review
SFOR	Stabilisation Force (NATO in Bosnia)
2IC	Second in Command
SH	Support Helicopters
SHAPE	Supreme Headquarters Allied Powers Europe
sit	Situation
SITREP	Situation Report
SIB	Special Investigation Branch
SMG	Sub Machine Gun
SLR	Self Loading Rifle
SMG	Sub Machine Gun
smk	Smoke
SNCO	Senior Non Commissioned Officer
SP	Spain (Spanish)
Sqn	Squadron
SP	Self Propelled/Start Point
SSM	Surface to Surface Missile
SSVC	Services Sound and Vision Corporation
STA	Surveillance and Target Acquisition
STOL	Short Take Off and Landing
tac	Tactical
tk	Tank
tgt	Target
TOT	Time on Target
TCP	Traffic Control Post
tpt	Transport
tp	Troop
TCV	Troop Carrying Vehicle
TLB	Top Level Nudget
TU	Turkish (Turkey)
TUL	Truck Utility Light
TUM	Truck Utility Medium
UK	United Kingdom
UKMF	United Kingdom Mobile Force
UNCLASS	Unclassified
UNPROFOR	United Nations Protection Force
UXB	Unexploded Bomb
US	United States
U/S	Unserviceable

VCDS	Vice Chief of the Defence Staff
veh	Vehicle
VOR	Vehicle off the Road
WE	War Establishment
wh	Wheeled
WIMP	Whinging Incompetent Malingering Person
WMR	War Maintenance Reserve
WO	Warrant Officer
wksp	Workshop
X	Crossing (as in roads or rivers)

This publication was produced by R&F (Defence) Publications
Editorial Office Tel 01743-247038 Fax 01743-241962

E Mail:Editorial@armedforces.co.uk
Website: www.armedforces.co.uk

Managing Editor: Charles Heyman
Deputy Editor: Digby Waller

Other publications in this series are:
The Royal Air Force Pocket Guide 1995
The Armed Forces of the United Kingdom 2004-2005
The Territorial Army – Volume 1 1999

Further copies can be obtained from:
Pen & Sword Books Ltd
47 Church Street
Barnsley S70 2AS

Telephone: 01226 734222   Fax: 01226 734438

9th Edition June 2005

HMSO Core Licence Number CO2W0004896